Lovely, Like Jerusalem

AIDAN NICHOLS, O.P.

Lovely, Like Jerusalem

The Fulfillment of the Old Testament in Christ and the Church

IGNATIUS PRESS   SAN FRANCISCO

Entry of Jesus into Jerusalem
Toros of Taron (13th–14th A.D.)
Vangelo: 1323. MS 6289, f. 121r.
Matenadaran Library, Erevan, Armenia
© Scala/Art Resource, New York

In the portrayal of the Savior entering Jerusalem, the figures on the right are the prophets of Israel; the figures on the left, the apostles of the Church.

Cover design by Roxanne Mei Lum

© 2007 Ignatius Press, San Francisco
All rights reserved
ISBN 978-1-58617-168-1
Library of Congress Control Number 2006924092
Printed in the United States of America ∞

You are beautiful as Tirzah, my love,
lovely, like Jerusalem.

Song of Songs 6:4 (JB)

CONTENTS

PART FIVE
FATHERS AND DOCTORS INTERPRET

PREFACE

Many Catholics complain they cannot see the wood for the trees when they open the Old Testament—or, more likely, when they sample the sumptuous (possibly too sumptuous) offering of Old Testament lections given them in the Roman Mass, as celebrated according to the rite of Paul VI.[1] Ignorance of the Old Testament is a severe disadvantage for understanding of the New. And it makes impossible a grasp of the entire divine plan that stretches between, and over, the two Testaments in their fullness. We cannot read the great theologians of all ages without the Old Testament. The medievals and the writers of the patristic epoch could not open their spiritual riches to us without it. How much, too, of the art of the Church remains opaque to us if the Old Testament is, for us, a closed book.[2] With the help of some biblical students of various Christian communions (notably Evangelicals and Catholic-minded Anglicans), and a sprinkling of the Fathers and Doctors of the Church, I offer in this little book a first glimpse, according to a traditional and

[1] As Evangelicals have pointed out, the present Roman lectionary prescribes "far more public hearing of Scripture than in almost any Protestant denomination." M.A. Noll and C. Nystrom, *Is the Reformation Over? An Evangelical Assessment of Contemporary Roman Catholicism* (Grand Rapids, Mich., 2005), pp. 143–44. From the point of view of real understanding of the Bible, this could be an ambiguous gain.

[2] S. Schrenk, *Typos und Antitypos in der frühchristlichen Kunst* (Münster, 1995).

9

classical kind of perusal. Biblical citations are from the Revised Standard Version, Catholic edition, unless otherwise indicated.

AIDAN NICHOLS, O.P.
Blackfriars, Cambridge
Solemnity of the Incarnation of the Lord, 2005

PART ONE

AN OVERVIEW OF THE OLD TESTAMENT

I

THE TORAH

Introduction

In the opening three chapters of this book, I offer an overview of what the Old Testament is, just by way of re-
minding ourselves of the contents of what the Jews still
call "The Bible", which is by far the longer component
of what the Church regards as the divinely inspired Scriptures. For their part, the Jews call the Bible *Tanakh*, a composite word made out of letters from the names of the
three principal parts of what we call the Old Testament.
And these are (1) *Torah* or "The Instruction", the first five
books of Scripture; (2) *Nebiim* or "The Prophets", which
include not only the four great prophets (Isaiah, Jeremiah,
Ezekiel, and Daniel), and the twelve minor prophets, from
Hosea to Malachi, but also the historical books—Joshua,
Judges, Samuel, Kings—called in ancient times "The Former
Prophets"; and finally (3) what are more loosely described
as "The Writings", *Kethubim*, which cover everything else
found in the Hebrew canon. Of course, Catholics, like the
Orthodox, also recognize an additional collection of books
and passages, the deuterocanonical writings, added to the
Canon by the Greek-speaking Jewish community in Alexandria. If, in and through these four interrelated bodies of literature, the Old Testament can be said to have one theme,

it is surely that the promises of God grow ever greater and greater. Those promises begin on what we might be tempted to call a small scale. They begin in the Torah, the first five books, the "Pentateuch" as Greek-speaking Jews called it, with the promise of the Land.

The Pentateuch

The Torah consists of the five Books of Moses. In the Hebrew Bible, these books are named for the opening words of the Hebrew text, just as are, in medieval and modern Catholicism, papal documents and the constitutions of the ecumenical councils. But in the Latin Bible, they are given titles that tell us what they are about, and we may think this more helpful. Thus the first book is Genesis, the "Book of Beginnings"; the second book is Exodus, the "Book of Emigration"; the third book is Leviticus, the "Book of the Service of the Sanctuary"; the fourth book is Numbers, the "Book of the Numbering of the Host of Israel"; and the fifth book is Deuteronomy, that is, the "Book of the Repetition of the Law". They contain the primitive documents of the revelations, commands, and promises on which God's covenant with the chosen people rests. From a literary point of view, the collection is a composite structure of ancient traditions, the nucleus of which goes back to Moses. It has been suggested that this collection of writings was handed down, and at some points amplified, by the priesthood, since priests were the primary "tradents" or teachers of tradition in ancient Israel. This may well have happened chiefly at two places in particular, both of them at central points in the hill country of Palestine. One was Gilgal/Shechem, where, in the Book of Joshua, Moses' successor held a ceremony of renewing the covenant after the entry into the Land. That was probably the intended sanctuary for the Ark of the Covenant. The other was Shiloh, which we know from the Books of Samuel to have been the chief sanctuary in the period immediately before the monarchy was established. There the Ark of the Lord was kept until the wars with the Philistines when the Ark was captured and the shrine of Shiloh destroyed. After that time, in the age of the kings, the Mosaic tradition took two forms, one in the southern kingdom of Judah, the more important of the southernly tribes, where it was soon associated with the divine promises to David, the first king of Judean stock, the ruler who rescued the Ark and brought it to Jerusalem. The other form in which the tradition was passed on was in the northern kingdom, which took the name that had once belonged to the people as a whole—Israel.

The single most important feature of the modern historical-critical scholarship that entered Catholic biblical studies in the middle decades of the twentieth century has been "source criticism", the aim of which is to establish the internal documentary sources from which any given book had—possibly—been composed. Up until the 1970s there was a well-nigh general consensus among scholars that the Pentateuch had four such sources called in their supposed chronological order: J, E, D, and P. The J or "The Yahwist" source (the initial letter of that word would be J in German, in which language this scheme first emerged), was said to represent the earliest southern Mosaic tradition; E or "The Elohist", slightly later, the northern Mosaic tradition; D or "The Deuteronomist", a much later version from the south, under King Josiah in the seventh century before Christ; and P or "The Priestly Source", the latest of all, written by priests exiled in the Neo-Babylonian Empire. But by the first decade of the twenty-first century this consensus, which was never universal, had largely collapsed. Partly this was due to disagreements as to the nature and dating of these alleged documents. Partly it was owing to arguments that maybe there never was any such preexisting set of texts at all. The main argument for the multiple sources was always the existence of repetitions and the seemingly awkward connections between various passages. But, it is said, while these would indeed seem out of place in a modern book, if they did not appear strange to the editors of the final version of the Pentateuch, why should we today find them so odd as to insist they cannot have existed in the original documents? In fact, repetitions, at least, are commonplace in ancient Near Eastern literature. Ancient people liked them, as do children today.

As one might expect with any revolution in scholarship, there are other arguments too. For example, much was made in the recent past of the two different ways of naming God in the Pentateuch. One such name is *Elohim*, the ancient name for divinity in the Canaanite culture that Abraham entered when, at the divine command, he left Mesopotamia, the country between the rivers, to begin his pilgrimage of faith. That gave its name to the "E" document of Pentateuchal source criticism. The other is the Tetragrammaton, YHWH, not named by the Jews of our Lord's time out of respect and replaced in speech by the title *Adonai*, "the Lord", which is how the divine four-letter word is translated in most English versions of Scripture. This gave its title to the "J" document in historical-critical analysis of the Books of Moses. But now people are asking again: May it not be that the alternation of names was done for stylistic reasons, as in *The*

Iliad, Homer's epic about ancient Greece and Troy, or possibly for theological reasons, to draw attention to God either chiefly as Creator, *Elohim*, or mainly as the redeemer of Israel, whether past or future: YHWH-*Adonai*, "the Lord"?

In any event, there are now scholars who treat the Pentateuch as largely a unitary creation—and these can be either radical scholars who place it late in the history of the ancient Israelites, even after the Exile, or conservative scholars who locate it early and hold that, in all essentials, it was completed by the time of Samuel.[1] The immense antiquity of the source material in Genesis, in particular, is suggested by the large number of Babylonian words in its earlier chapters, the topographical references to settlements that later disappeared, such as Sodom and Gomorrah, and the number of glosses required to bring ancient names up to date. And as for the Pentateuch as a whole, this, so conservative scholars propose, must have existed prior to the political rift between the northern and southern tribes early in the monarchy's history since otherwise there is no way to show how the Samaritan Pentateuch—a northern and ultimately schismatic Pentateuch—can be more or less identical with the Pentateuch of Judah, the Pentateuch of the "Jews".

Where the "guild" of biblical scholars is so divided, there seems little point in building a great deal on hypotheses of analysis and reconstruction in the manner of source criticism. This is not to say that the scholars who have worked with J, E, D, and P—on the "classical" source theory, very much in that chronological order—have wasted their time,

---

[1] There is a helpful survey of the literature by G. J. Wenham, "Pondering the Pentateuch: The Search for a New Paradigm", in D. W. Baker and W. T. Arnold, eds., *The Face of Old Testament Studies: A Survey of Contemporary Approaches* (Grand Rapids, Mich., 1999), pp. 116–44.

even if future students look for guidance elsewhere. Their approach enabled them to identify motifs in this corpus that might have escaped attention otherwise.[2] And certainly I do not wish to follow those who, by selecting the latest possible date for the composition of the Pentateuch, would depreciate its likely historical value even more. So in this little book, which is meant as an exercise in the doctrinal reception of the Bible by way of a markedly *ecclesial* exegesis, I venture to throw in my lot with conservative daters on the ground that this choice is closer to the mind both of the synagogue—the original "faith community" that produced the Scriptures—and of the Church. The present *anomie* may encourage us to look more sympathetically at the scholarship of more traditionally minded twentieth-century critics, who, often, were not less learned but only less fashionable.

Where the Pentateuch is concerned, we can still consistently hold, with much modern scholarship, that, nonetheless, an important figure in fixing the final text, and giving the work as a whole more manifest canonical status was Ezra the scribe—the Ezra who played an important part in reestablishing the Jewish religion in Palestine with the permission and encouragement of the Persian imperial authorities in the fifth century before Christ. It was, we read, by the "Book of the Torah of Moses" (Neh 8:1) that Ezra reestablished the sacred community after the Exile, and one twentieth-century Lutheran theologian described the upshot as follows:

> From his wooden pulpit he read it to the people in the market-place before the water-gate day by day from morning to evening. Pierced to the heart, they broke down; but he

---

[2] I follow this approach in "The Images of Israel", a chapter on the Old Testament background, in my *The Art of God Incarnate: Theology and Image in Christian Tradition* (London, 1980), pp. 13–29.

forbade their weeping. . . . The memory of those days lives
on in the synagogue as "the time of our joy" which reaches
its climax on the day of the "Torah joy" when [in the Has-
sidic tradition] a sevenfold procession with all the rolls of the
Torah . . . makes its way through the house of prayer with
rapturous joy. The people embrace and kiss the adorned and
coronate rolls and dance with them.[3]

What is in these books if we as Christians ought in some
way to follow suit? The answer will not emerge immediately. Part of it will come from looking at what two Doctors
of the Church, one in the patristic period (Saint Augustine),
the other in the medieval period (Saint Thomas) had to say
about the Pentateuch—about Genesis, in Augustine's case,
and about the Mosaic Law in the case of Thomas. But at
least we can make a start.

Genesis

The bulk of the "Book of the Beginnings", Genesis, consists of cycles of material about the patriarchs. These cycles
are introduced by an account of the call of the first patriarch,
Abraham. In order to understand the importance of this call,
Genesis gives us the necessary background and context. That
background and context are, first, a double account of the
creation of heaven and earth, which tells of the wonderful
order with which the Creator originally invested the cosmos
and, within the world, mankind as made in his own image
and likeness. Secondly, that background and context come
in the form of an account of the Fall of man and its consequences, the increasing evils that followed on the unleashing

---

[3] W. Vischer, *The Witness of the Old Testament to Christ* (London, 1949),
p. 36.

of pride, envy, anger, and the other deadly sins. The divine promise that in the future the order of the world will be preserved (the covenant with Noah) is matched and indeed surpassed in advance by a further promise that the human order, on which world breakdown turns, will be restored. That we hear of in the so-called "protoevangelium", or "first Gospel": a divine plan to right the wrong done in the Garden (Gen 3:15). The promise to Eve, in which the Church has found a hint of both the Incarnation and its means in the Immaculate Conception of the Mother of God, alerts the reader of Genesis for the first time to something new. Human life will not proceed in the future simply on the basis set by creation and Fall. There is going to be a bolt from the blue, a divine intervention to initiate a new history of God with man. This intervention has its own beginning in Genesis 12 with the call of Abraham, which is where in the modern Roman Lectionary the continuous reading of the story begins—as it happens, in the twelfth week of the liturgical year. Actually, this is not quite the first we have heard of Abraham in Genesis. In the previous chapter, immediately after the Noah story, we were given his genealogy and heard of how his father had already uprooted his family from their ancestral city of Ur. Ur was probably the richest city of ancient Babylon, but Abraham's father left it to move north and west into a mountainous semi-desert region on the borders of Syria at Haran. There may well be a hint here of a desire to put the family at a distance from a false culture and false religion. Abraham's call will be to go further, to leave his father's house, and to embrace a new personal relation with the God who will make him the father of a people through which all the tribes of the earth shall be blessed.

I interrupt the story here to point out how crucial his-

toricity is for us in the patriarchal sagas. The historical min-
imalism in fashion today in many departments of Old Testament studies is not an adequate basis on which to read
Genesis as Scripture—precisely because the whole point of
the Abraham saga is that this was a new divinely enabled
beginning *in history*, the start of a new history for man. If
the message is a new history, it can hardly be presented via
what historically is fiction! Fortunately, we can find a number of reasons for underwriting the historical value of the
sagas. First, is it true that in the ancient Near East memories
were a matter of oral tradition and only written down after
a very long lapse of time? Or was it the case, rather, that
events regarded by some group as of the highest importance
were recorded at once in inscriptions? Oral transmission, it
would seem, was not so much for the purposes of record as
for the extension of the knowledge involved to wider bodies of people. Secondly, although some of the Near Eastern
customs described or assumed in the patriarchal sagas en-
dured for many centuries and were quite possibly as contemporary to the time of the Exile as they were a thousand
years earlier, it is obvious that the Palestine of the patriarchs
is different from the Palestine of later times. These texts
present the people of the patriarchs living in peace among
the Canaanites with their different religion, something that
is never claimed after the reentry into the Land. Thirdly,
the philological thesis that our texts contain "demonstrably
late words" is no easy one to prove. In Egypt, for example,
a neighboring culture to Israel, some words in inscriptions
on the pyramids fail to recur until two millennia later, in
the Greco-Roman period, but this does not make Egyptol-
ogists claim the pyramids were built by Cleopatra! As one
Old Testament scholar has written of this type of argument
from words:

> Where such critical methods are so obviously inapplicable to
> texts of the Biblical period emerging from the closest neigh-
> bours of Israel, the most serious misgivings about the validity
> of a vast amount of current Old Testament literary criticism
> must be raised; and these are raised on purely literary grounds
> well attested by tangible objective data without any recourse
> to theological predispositions or considerations.[4]

We can note, too, *en passant*, that, to judge by English philo-
logy—not, of course, from a culture close to Israel but
a very well-documented historic language all the same—
words swim in and out of fashion. Numerous examples
are given in the pioneering Victorian philologist Richard
Chevenix Trench's lectures *English Past and Present*. Trench
notes how the dictionary maker Samuel Johnson, for instance, remarked in the mid-eighteenth century of "jeop-
ardy" that it had become a "word not now in use".[5] This
would surprise native English-speakers today!

In the light of the New Testament revelation, the patriarchal sagas contain much that is suggestive. It is said with
reason that the Scriptures show a pattern of promise and
fulfillment, with the Old Testament embodying the call of
Israel and the New Testament the fullness of Israel in the
revelation given in Christ and the Church. We can think, for
instance, of the theophany or divine appearance to Abraham
and the still-childless Sarah at Mamre (Gen 18:1–15), where
the divine encounter is with three men who are addressed
by Abraham as one: here the Fathers and the iconographers

---

[4] R. K. Harrison, *Introduction to the Old Testament* (Peabody, Mass., 2004
[1969]), p. 524.

[5] R. C. Trench, *English Past and Present* 14th ed. (London, 1889), pp. 159–
60.

saw a pre-disclosure of the divine Trinity.[6] Or, still in the Abraham cycle, we can think of the episode of the sacrifice of Isaac, the offspring of Abraham and Sarah, where again the Fathers saw huge significance in the divine intervention to provide a sacrificial victim—the ram caught by its horns in the thicket (22:13) in place of the child of the promise. An exegesis that is merely "social-scientific" and uninformed by the Church's tradition would see in the story of the sacrifice of Isaac only a protest against the practice of human sacrifice. But there is food for thought in the fact that the sacrifice of the son of the promise is *both* asked *and* not asked by the Lord—an intriguing pointer to the eventual world atonement in which the Son of Mary, a child of Abraham and heir of David but also the Divine Word in person, will suffer.

Seen in their original context in the Pentateuch, the sagas of the patriarchs—Abraham, Isaac, Jacob, and finally Joseph —have an overall significance too. The Pentateuch is the epic of Israel's nationhood, the foundation of the people's life. As such, it has two constituent parts: the patriarchal sequence and the Exodus-Sinai sequence. In the former, the Land (Canaan) was promised to Israel's forefathers and to a very limited extent acquired by them. In the latter, the way was opened for their descendants, the land's true inheritors, to return and take formal possession. This obvious connection between the two sequences points to the unity of the Pentateuch, and it brings us to its next book, Exodus, the "Book of Emigration".

---

[6] L. Thunberg, "Early Christian Interpretations of the Three Angels in Genesis 18", *Studia Patristica* 8 (1966): pp. 560–70.

Exodus

The hero of Exodus is of course Moses, who has many roles: prophet, shepherd, legislator, mediator between God and man. It is not difficult to see why, with Elijah, he becomes the representative of the holy nation at the Transfiguration of Jesus, and in the Prologue to Saint John's Gospel represents the Old Testament Torah as a whole. The mediatorial role of Moses, which is founded on his reception of the Sinai revelation, is the basis, in fact, of the Old Testament's Pentateuch ideal. Against all attempts to minimize his significance or even deny his historicity, this literature attests that he played a highly original role in the revelation of the divine nature and will to Israel, as well as in formulating positive law for the people emerging from the experience of the Exodus and the wilderness wanderings.

It is sometimes said that the narratives of Moses' infancy, and especially his acceptance as a foundling by the Pharaoh's daughter, shows his life story to be invention. It can also be argued that finding a credible context for the story is entirely possible. In the so-called New Kingdom period, there were many royal residences in the eastern area of the Nile delta, and in these, women of royal blood lived alongside concubines and others. The "daughter of Pharaoh" who rescued the infant from the river could well be the adolescent offspring of the Pharaoh by a concubine. What of Moses' interviews with Pharaoh? Are they a plausible occurrence? We know of the easy way in which people were able to present petitions to such pharaohs as Rameses II. It is often true in absolute monarchies of a traditional kind—for example at the court of Louis XIV of France. The suggestion that a man of Moses' lowly status would hardly have been literate, in the way the writing of the tablets of the Law requires, is not convincing either. Common workmen on the great tombs of Egypt used a proto-Canaanite alphabet for the purpose of memory aids. And as to the miracles Moses worked to render the Exodus and its outcome possible, only a sceptic should rule out a priori a role for divine agency here.[7]

From the very start of the tradition, as we see from the text of Exodus (the "Book of Emigration"), Numbers (the "Book of the Numbering of the Host of Israel"), and Deuteronomy (the "Book of the Repetition of the Law"), Moses was credited with authoring important portions of the corpus. These include the Decalogue, or Ten Commandments, and the wider "Book of the Covenant", which runs from Exodus 20:22 to Exodus 23:33; the itinerary the people had to follow, by divine command, across the wilderness, as laid out in Numbers 33; the arrangements for the renewal of the covenant in Deuteronomy and the reinforcing of the covenantal law there; as well as the two series of poetic oracles that more or less conclude the book: the "Song of Moses" in Deuteronomy 32 and the "Blessing of Moses" in Deuteronomy 33. In the given context, ascribing both historical records and laws to Moses is not perplexing. Combining history and law was a feature of treaty making in the ancient Near East.[8] Given the fundamental importance of the Sinai revelation for the future, it had to be both

[7] For W.J. Abraham, in his study *Divine Revelation and the Limits of Historical Criticism* (Oxford, 1982), reasonable arguments can be made for belief in occurrences with which the historian has no personal acquaintance. He uses the example of a remote population group becoming convinced through reasonable discussion of claims of man's landing on the moon, even though such an event would be utterly foreign to anything they have known.

[8] The Mosaic origin of some considerable part of the Pentateuchal legislation is argued by J. Coppens, *L'Histoire critique de l'Ancien Testament: Ses origines; Ses orientations nouvelles; Ses perspectives d'avenir* 3rd ed. (Bruges, 1942).

firmly grounded in historical events and expressed in terms of legislation both moral and social.

A great deal of the Exodus-Sinai sequence, then, is concerned with law codes, a fact that takes on even greater prominence when we add to the books already mentioned Leviticus, the "Book of the Service of the Sanctuary". By comparing the codes in the Pentateuch to those we know from nonbiblical sources in other parts of the ancient Near East we can say that, despite the great detail that the biblical codes contain, this is no reason to consider them hopelessly anachronistic. The Law was given to be the supreme guide of conduct and life for the people, and for this reason it had to cover all the aspects of existence they would encounter. Laws concerning agriculture seem out of place in the desert, but the people had been promised a land, and entry into that land was at first promised as imminent. As the Book of Numbers explains, owing to the backslidings of the people, their rebellions against the divine will, they were punished by an "unscripted", enforced sojourn in the wilderness for those forty years. The Israelites had already been pastoralists. For probably around four centuries, they had been farming in the fertile delta of the Nile. Even in the time of the patriarchs, they were not true nomads like the later Bedouin Arabs. They knew they were meant to be farmers again. We must not, however, exaggerate and claim every single detail of the law codes as Mosaic. The vitality of the divine revelation through Moses could allow for the possibility of controlled amplification, by way of adaptation to changing circumstances in Israel's life. Not that we should think of the law codes naturalistically. In day-to-day living, the provisions of the covenant treaty between the Lord and his people were meant to be a profound religious experience, and that is how we see them experienced in the Psalter's psalm in praise of the Torah, Psalm 119:

> In the way of thy testimonies I delight
> as much as in all riches (v. 14).

> I will delight in thy statutes;
> I will not forget thy word (v. 16).

> Thy statutes have been my songs
> in the house of my pilgrimage.
> I remember thy name in the night, O LORD,
> and keep thy law (Ps 119:54-55).

Essentially, the Exodus took place so that Israel could be free to worship the God of the patriarchs in the land that had been promised but—more than that—in the way God desired. The emigration, the emancipation, took place, not so that the Jews could be free to do as *they* wished (which is how we today often misunderstand liberation) but so that they could be free to meet the God of the fathers in the wilderness and there learn to do as *God* wished. The Exodus leads up to Sinai, to the revelation of the meaning of the divine name on Mount Horeb—the mountain of Moses in the wider peninsula of Sinai, the mountain that is also, then, the mountain of God. And it is to the God revealed in *that* name that the cultus laid out in the valley below the mountain, the cultus of Leviticus, is directed.

The revelation of the worshipful name stands at the center of the Sinai tradition. We read in Exodus 6:2-3:

> And God said to Moses, "I am the LORD. I
> appeared to Abraham, to Isaac, and to Jacob, . . .
> but by my name the LORD I did not make
> myself known to them."

In fact, as already mentioned, many texts in the Book of Genesis already use the name "the Lord": this was the starting point of the J document hypothesis in the nineteenth century. Scholars believed the author of J—the "Yahwist" —used the divine name in connection with the patriarchal sequence to make the point that the God revealed at the heart of the Exodus sequence is no different God. But it could be that what is revealed on Sinai is not so much the divine name YHWH itself as *the meaning of the name*. That is the focus, after all, when we look at the account of the disclosure of the name at the burning bush in Exodus 3:13–14. Moses asks to be reassured as to the name of God so that the people can credit his mission. "God said to Moses: 'I AM WHO I AM.' And he said, 'Say this to the people of Israel: I AM has sent me to you.'" God gives Moses an interpretation of the name, to carry back to those who will in some sense know what Moses is talking about. In which case, what was not known previously was the *character displayed in the name*. God did not reveal himself to the fathers in the character the name implies as he is now doing to Moses.

It has been argued that the name YHWH is a shortened form of an ancient Hebrew name for *Elohim*, the Creator God, and originally meant "God who creates the heavenly armies".[9] What is revealed at Sinai is a new divine interpretation of this name as *ehyeh asher ehyeh*: "I AM WHO AM" or "I SHALL BE WHAT I SHALL BE". (By judicious compromise we might render that phrase: "I AM, WHO SHALL BE".) Catholic philosophy—following Philo, the Jewish philosopher of the time of Jesus, and after Philo, the Greek Fathers—has made a great deal of the metaphysical implications of this name: God

---

[9] "El zu yahwi sabaoth": see F. M. Cross, *Canaanite Myth and Hebrew Epic: Essays in the History of the Religion of Israel* (Cambridge, Mass., 1973), pp. 70–71.

is identical with the source of being itself. Hence "I AM". (Naturally, this is as relevant to the future as to the present —or the past.) But equally important are the implications of the name's meaning for salvation history. The God of the fathers is expressing his character as the covenant-keeping God who is already fulfilling the promises once given to the patriarchs. And so "I shall be [with you]".

Leviticus

We move on from Exodus to the remaining books of the Torah. Leviticus, the "Book of the Service of the Sanctuary", is made up of rather technical cultic material that was the special prerogative of the priesthood to use. Arguably, its focal point comes in chapter 16, where the topic at hand is the ritual to be observed on the Day of Atonement. In the first half of the book, chapters 1 to 15, which lead up to this climax, the main subject is the removal of the defilement separating men from God. And then in chapters 16 to the end, the last eleven chapters in other words, the emphasis shifts to the means available for restoring the fellowship between man and God when that fellowship has been disrupted by transgressions.

We can legitimately assume the great antiquity of these cultic arrangements. The practice of scribes in the ancient Near East was to preserve information or procedures of importance to the community at an early stage. This was true not least of liturgies and rituals. There is no reason to think the Israelites were incapable of retaining features from the indigenous religion of their ancestors. Some of these ceremonial provisions, then, could have been pre-Mosaic: after all the patriarchs had a cultus. When the tribal groups in Egypt were united under Moses, the effect may have been to give binding force for all the people to practices once confined de facto to extended families. So the contents of Leviticus may well have been in something very like their present shape in the lifetime of Moses himself. Judging by what we know of the rites of the peoples living around Israel, especially important to contemporaries would have been the prescriptions for the various offerings, the provisions for consecrating priests, the ceremonies of the Day of Atonement, and the rules concerning hygiene—which in the biblical case are notable for their lack of any elements of magic.

We shall look again with Saint Thomas at the significance of the cultus put in place in Leviticus, but we must sketch in its main outlines here. What could be offered were, on the one hand, vegetables and cereals, and, on the other, domesticated birds and animals. The basic idea is that what was produced by human labor, or—in the case of animals and birds —became man's through human enterprise, was man's own property and as such might be offered on his behalf to God. By contrast, it was not permissible to sacrifice wild creatures, since these were regarded as already belonging to God, as we see from Psalm 50:10a: "Every beast of the forest is mine." The system of offerings was not understood as a final and comprehensive way of dealing with sin of all kinds. Much of the atonement procedure was concerned with accidental sins, sins of inadvertence, and sins of omission. No means of forgiveness was envisaged for sins of commission deriving from sheer malice. Sins deriving from contempt or hatred for the divine commands led to excommunication from the covenant community, as the succeeding book of the Torah, Numbers, makes plain in 15:30-31. For such fundamental breaches of the covenant as apostasy or idolatry no sacrifice was of any avail—something that must be borne in mind when in the Prophetic Books we find texts apparently repudiating cultic sacrifice as the divinely provided means of reconciliation. The sacrifices were not intended as reconciliation for sins like those.

Another important feature of the ritual prescriptions in Leviticus is the creation of the tabernacle for the Ark of the Covenant and the associated accouterments of worship. In the period before the entry into the Land, and even to some extent after it, the Ark figured as a "palladium", a mobile shrine that accompanied the people, not least into battle, and once set down for worship purposes was richly "housed" in quite an elaborate way. In its role as palladium, it can be compared to the great icons sometimes sent out processionally with the tsarist armies before the Russian Revolution, which figured as the center of liturgical activities in the field. During the First World War, for example, Nicholas II ordered the "Vladimir" Mother of God to be brought to the army's general headquarters in the field.[10]

Numbers

The Book of Numbers is the "Book of the Numbering the Host of Israel". More widely, it has three themes, each of which occupies roughly a third of the book. They are (1) the preparations for leaving Sinai (1:1–10:10); (2) the journey from Sinai to the plains of Moab (10:11–21:35); (3) and events on the Moabite plain (chapters 22 to the end of the book at chapter 36). In all, the book covers a period of some thirty-eight years, from year 2 of the Exodus to year 40. We can regard it as essentially a product of the desert age. It is a

[10] V. Shevzov, *Russian Orthodoxy on the Eve of Revolution* (New York, 2004), p. 179.

narrative interwoven with legislative matters, which, as we have seen, is characteristic of the Pentateuch, though the way Numbers interweaves cultic, judicial, social, and moral enactments may seem confusing to modern readers.

Numbers opens with the scene that gives it its name, the numbering of the Israelites in the desert. It is generally agreed that the figures given for the Hebrews who escaped from Egypt are much too high. In the census lists, as in the narrative of the Exodus itself, number is used as a symbol of relative importance, power, and triumph. That is characteristic of Scripture's "numerology". But ancient historians have no difficulty in taking as accurate the way the narrator describes the drawing up of the host for the head count. The arrangement of tribes by their standards in the form of a rectangle around the tabernacle mirrors a common deployment of military forces in the period, and the use of such diverse features as ox-drawn wagons and silver trumpets is also attested in nonbiblical sources from the Ancient Near East when describing military arrays.

One high point of the adventures of the people in Numbers—a reprise of a cognate account in Exodus, and Saint Paul will be sufficiently impressed to draw on it—is the episode when Moses struck water from rock for the thirsty people in the wilderness (Num 20:11). Sometimes, owing to lack of information, we read miraculous elements into the text whereas only providential ones were intended. We are reminded of that when we discover that Sinai sandstone has water-retaining properties. That water was found for the people in the desert through striking on rock is not necessarily supernatural except in the sense of a result of divine guidance through special providence—though of course it may be that the water Moses and Aaron gave the people and their animals was miraculously increased in quantity, rather as in Jesus' miracles of the multiplication of the loaves and fishes. Similar arguments may be adduced for the other nourishment-connected "wonder" of the desert wanderings, the gift of the manna. A plant of that region secretes a substance that, when it dries, is edible. How providential! But again, could this have been in the quantities required even when we scale down numbers? So, it was possibly miraculous as well. At any rate, Numbers does not simply catalogue outstanding incidents, but interprets them as demonstrations of the covenantal love of the Lord for his people in their trials—as well as severe judgments called forth by their rebellions.

Deuteronomy

Deuteronomy, sometimes called by the Jews the "Book of Admonitions", is a reiteration of the Law in the form of a collection of addresses by Moses in the plains of Moab, a reminder of the principal points of the Law on the eve of entry into the Land of the promise. It is, as it were, a popular version of what has preceded in the laws found in Exodus, Leviticus, and to some extent Numbers and has been called on this basis "Everyman's Torah". One can view it as basically Mosaic but with supplements entered on the basis of judicial decisions made at the sanctuaries in the period of the settlement. The guiding principle of Deuteronomy is the protection of the people against the idolatrous practices of the Canaanites they would soon encounter by going amongst them whether in war or in peace. If Deuteronomy was the book rediscovered in the archives of the Jerusalem Temple in the reign of King Josiah of Judah in the seventh century, it was probably the incompatibility of the book with tolerance of pagan religious observances that caused the pious king to rend his garments. Deuteronomy looks forward to a national cultic center for all Israel, but this centralization of sacrificial worship was not necessarily intended for Jerusalem. In Deuteronomy 27, Moses orders the building of an altar on Mount Ebal, opposite Shechem, which is where Joshua will celebrate the renewal of the covenant on entry into the Land, and so the likelihood is that the intended cultic center in the first place was there. Jerusalem would fulfill this role, however, when the covenant with David modified the terms of the covenant with Moses.

When Deuteronomy is viewed as a whole, it turns out to have the same overall structure as a typical covenant treaty of the ancient Near East, and this points to its fundamental unity.[11] At all times its focus is on the covenant relation between the Lord and Israel, and it is in the perspective of that relation, and the demands of loyalty—"love"—it sets up, that it considers the events through which the escaping Hebrews have come.[12] A covenant treaty always involves a suzerain saying to a vassal: I have done this and this for you, and I shall do this and this for you, if you remain faithful to me in the ways I here specify. In this respect, Deuteronomy furnishes a clue of singular importance to the rest of the biblical revelation, and indeed to the "structure of biblical authority" itself. "In the treaty documents given by Yahweh at the very origins of the nation Israel, the people of God already possessed the ground stratum of the Old Testament canon."[13]

---

[11] See M. G. Kline, *The Treaty of the Great King: The Covenant Structure of Deuteronomy; Studies and Commentary* (Grand Rapids, Mich., 1963).

[12] See W. L. Moran, "The Ancient Near Eastern Background of the Love of God in Deuteronomy", *Catholic Biblical Quarterly* 25 (1963): pp. 77–87.

[13] M. G. Kline, *The Structure of Biblical Authority* 2nd ed. (Grand Rapids, Mich., 1975), p. 38.

2

THE PROPHETS

The Former Prophets

We turn now to the Former Prophets, the historical books from Joshua to Kings. These are prophetic histories because they judge history in the light of the divine promise to give Israel the Land, but also, and even more strikingly, in the perspective of the Covenant relation, which held out blessing in return for faithfulness, but punishment for infidelity. It is suggested that the final editor of these books fine-tuned his sources so as to echo the message, in this regard, of the Book of Deuteronomy. Hence the name sometimes given to the collection as a whole, "The Deuteronomic History".

Joshua and Judges

Here we are in the thick of "holy war", or so it seems. The first two books, Joshua and Judges, and especially the former, present us with the same issues of disputed historicity attending the patriarchal and Exodus sequences in the Pentateuch. To what extent *was* there a "conquest" of the Land by Israel? Archeology does not necessarily support the case that there was a Hebrew *Blitzkrieg* that utterly changed the Palestinian picture. The truth on the ground seems to be more patchy. Exploration at some sites—such as Bethel, Hebron, Gideon, Hazor—shows clearly that these places were destroyed in the latter part of the Late Bronze Age, which fits with the best date for the Exodus of around 1300 B.C. The situation at Ai, Shechem, and, most controversially, Jericho, is different. To some extent, this is a false problem. The Book of Joshua records a conquest but not a total conquest. Its author has nothing to say about the conquest of central Palestine, an area vital for the rest of Jewish history. The Book of Judges makes it plain that, after Joshua's death, the Canaanite local kings held or resumed territorial control of various city-states, at any rate, temporarily—not to speak of the continuing presence of powerful and dangerous neighbors such as the Philistines.

Still, we can allow that modern historians may be right to suppose that gains made by incomers from Egypt did not add up to *all* the gains made by the devotees of the God of the fathers who had revealed the true meaning of his name to Moses. In the Book of Genesis, not all the descendants of the patriarchs go down to Egypt. The idea is feasible that some of the power-reversals in the "conquest" may have taken the form of insurrections against the petty kings by local people who recognized their affinities with the new arrivals from Egypt. Joshua's resealing the covenant with a united nation at Shechem, a city he is not recorded as having conquered, would be explicable if there was already in existence around Shechem a group of clans who preserved a memory of the patriarchs and made alliance with him. Jericho is a somewhat harder nut to crack, since the Book of Joshua gives a famously dramatic account of its seizure by Israel—a seizure of which modern archeology has uncovered no trace. But it needs to be remembered that "manual" destruction of, for instance, city walls, as distinct from destruction by fire, is notoriously hard to establish from material remains, and that, in ancient times as today, much fighting for the control of cities has taken place in open country where—

unlike in the cities themselves—battle leaves little physical trace. In other respects, the Book of Joshua inspires confidence and gives internal evidence of its closeness in time to the events it describes. It does not, for instance, claim that Israel took Jerusalem—theologically key city though it would be in the future. On the contrary, it records the inability of Israel to expel the Jebusite rulers. Territorial occupation is not of course the same thing as the subjugation of existing inhabitants. The Book of Joshua shows the incoming tribes intent on occupying land and for this purpose destroying some enemy strongholds and bypassing others. The revival of Islamic *jihad* has made readers highly sensitive to the ancient Israelite institution of "holy war". We should note with Hans Urs von Balthasar that the "successive stages of revelation of themselves imply an immanent critique of those that came before them; . . . Old Testament revelation is perfectly well aware of provisional ideologies that must be overcome in profounder, more exact, kinds which belong to the Christ who is to come."[1] Dame Felicitas Corrigan put it more warmly, when she remarked of George Bernard Shaw that he "did not see the God of infinite mercy who, taking an incredibly stupid, obstinate and savage people just as they were—He might have taken the intelligent and highly civilized Greeks or Chinese, but for our everlasting comfort did not—entered into fellowship and loving intercourse with them at different stages according to their several capacities, and patiently prepared them by slow degrees for the full spiritual revelation of the New Testament."[2]

The theology of Joshua is covenantal. The Promised Land

---

[1] H. U. von Balthasar, "Il potere dell'uomo secondo la rivelazione biblica", *Humanitas* 18 (1963): pp. 113–22, here at p. 116.

[2] F. Corrigan, O.S.B., *Friends of a Lifetime: The Nun, the Infidel and the Superman* (London, 1985; 1990), pp. 130–31.

is a gift of God to his Covenant people according to the assurance given to Abraham. In the book that bears his name, the role of Joshua may have been exaggerated for the purposes of epic writing. That would not prevent his playing the major historical part in the final realization of the promise of the Land. Not for nothing is his name—in Hebrew *Jehoshua*, in Aramaic *Jeshua*—the same name the angel will announce to Saint Joseph for the ultimate Child of the promise: "You shall call his name Jesus", he who will save his people—not from temporal enemies as with the first "Jesus", but from spiritual destruction, "from their sins" (Mt 1:21).

What Joshua began, the "judges"—charismatic figures drawn, it is suggested, from the landowning aristocracy—more or less completed. The judges were not only judicial arbitrators, though they were that. They were also men and women raised up to deliver Israel from her enemies through war. The Book of Judges consists of a set of cycles about heroes and heroines, cycles stitched together for the purpose of describing in something like epic form the events of early Hebrew history in the three hundred years or so after Joshua's death. At least three of the cycles appear to be at least partly concurrent, but the authors of Judges were not interested in strict chronology. As John Calvin remarked in a different context, apropos of the Gospels, "I do not wish to be over-precise in matters of chronology, as I have observed how they are disregarded by the Spirit of God", who inspired these texts.[3] We assume that these narratives were composed anonymously in the early years of the monarchy, up to which they lead. Indeed, part of the purpose of the Book of Judges is to show how a centralized hereditary king-

---

[3] Cited in F. Watson, "The Gospels as Narrated History", in *Text and Truth: Redefining Biblical Theology* (Edinburgh, 1997), p. 40.

ship is necessary for the welfare of the Covenant theocracy. More widely, Judges upheld the Torah principle that obedience to God means life, disobedience death (with the multivalent meanings the terms "life" and "death" hold).

Samuel

The Books of Samuel are named for the character who dominates their opening narratives. Samuel is himself a kind of judge as well as seer, but his importance for Israel's future lies in his role, under divine prompting, in choosing and anointing the first kings—Saul and, far more importantly in later perspective, David. The books that take his name for their title are probably more or less contemporary with the events they describe, dating from the tenth century. With Samuel, we get a transition not only to the Davidide monarchy that will be the recipient of the messianic promise of a kingdom that will never end, to be realized in the new Joshua, Jesus the Christ. We find a transition also to an era where prophets are more important than the priesthood, even though the priesthood retains its function in teaching as well as cultic and judicial activity. The books bearing his name present Samuel as the first great religious reformer in Israel since the time of Moses. The corrupt and immoral priestly descendants of Eli at Shiloh, the central sanctuary of the period, bring shame upon their aged father but divine judgment on the house of the Lord. Samuel seems to have reacted with a desire to scale down for the future the spiritual role of the priests and those other main ministers of the sanctuary, the Levites, by employing ecstatic prophets, possibly attached to local shrines.

Like the great prophets of the eighth and seventh centuries before Christ, Samuel emphasizes the primacy of right

motivation in ritual activity, especially the offering of sacrifice. His highlighting of prophets is of great importance.
Prophets—the word appears to mean "one who is called"
—were people who had passed through what would now be
termed a conversion experience, attended, apparently, with
ecstatic outbursts and manifesting itself in a changed emotional and spiritual orientation. But this does not mean that
in the future, as Samuel sees it, such "charism" would replace institution. This is evident from his establishment of a
religiously sanctioned monarchy. The anointing of the early
kings by a theocratic prophet is intended to place them in a
special relation with the God of the Covenant, whose laws
the king is bound not only to keep personally but—more
than this—to bring others to keep by the manner of his
rule. The traditions going into the making of the Books of
Samuel give us a complex figure: an arbitrator between tribes
and clans, leader of the ecstatic prophets, and, as someone
directly called by God, a prophet himself.

Kings

With the Books of the Kings, which take us up to the fall
of the kingdoms—first of Israel to Assyria in 722 and then
of Judah to the Neo-Babylonian Empire in 587, we have
a compilation of different written sources, chronicles and
annals, the titles of which the editor conveniently records
for us in his text. As befits the crowning work of "The
Deuteronomic History", this is history, but history with a
difference. The Books of the Kings, like the Gospels, are
a "narration that is both theologically motivated and genuinely historiographical".[4] One student explains: "Against

---

[4] Watson, "Introduction", in *Text and Truth*, p. 10.

a background of implicit monotheism the compiler(s) endeavoured to show the principles underlying the dealings of God with the theocratic nation, thus demonstrating that the primary concern was not with the problem of secular historiography *per se*."[5] Extracts from Temple records, court memoirs, cycles of stories about the prophets Elijah and Elisha in the north, and, it would seem, even some passages written by the prophet Isaiah:[6] all is grist to the editor's mill and serves his aim of showing how the fall of the dynasties, the Davidide in the south and the various succeeding families who ruled in the north, followed on their infidelity to the covenant as night follows day. The Books of the Kings, like post-Pentateuch Israelite narrative generally, celebrate the benefits the Lord bestowed as faithful Protector of his vassal kingdom and deplore the breaking of the covenant as unleashing on the frequently *un*faithful Israel the evils named in the Mosaic treaties, and notably Deuteronomy.

Naturally enough, given the promises to David and his line, the authors are more hopeful about the ultimate outcome of the monarchy in Judah than in Israel. It has been suggested that in the Elisha cycle the suppression of the name of the Israelite ruler implies that the northern kingdom is already rejected. It is rejected for its failure to implement that supreme demonstration of monotheism by Elijah on Carmel in the miracle of fire when he discomfited the pagan prophets, prophets of the Canaanite god Baal. If so, Elisha may have seen his task, or at any rate the authors of Kings may have seen Elisha's task, as the building up of the righteous remnant divinely promised to Elijah in 1 Kings 19:18—"Yet I will leave seven thousand in Israel, all the

---

[5] Harrison, *Introduction to the Old Testament*, p. 722.
[6] Compare Is 36–39 with 2 Kings 18:1–20:19.

knees that have not bowed to Baal, and every mouth that
has not kissed him.''

Another small hint of how God will redeem the broken
nation in the future comes in the closing verses of 2 Kings
when we hear of how the last king of Judah, Jehoiachin,
who was taken into exile as a teenager after a reign of only
three months is, after thirty seven years of imprisonment,
released and brought with honor to dine at the king of Babylon's table. This seems to be an augury of things to come and
to reflect the way that the writing prophets always include
in their scrolls some reference to "weal"—good, or happi-
ness—that will come about, generally speaking, *through* the
experience of woe.

And Chronicles, Ezra, Nehemiah . . .

Though the collection called "The Former Prophets" ends
at that point, we can add here a reference to *Chronicles*,
which resumes the entire "Deuteronomic History", taking
it slightly further to the conquest of the Neo-Babylonian
Empire by Persia in 523 and the consequent introduction of
a new religious policy allowing Judaism to be reestablished in
the province "Beyond the River", the river Euphrates, what
the Persians called the "Transeuphratic satrapy". That will
be the subject of the books of *Ezra* and *Nehemiah*. Chronicles
is not satisfied, however, with simply regurgitating earlier
material. Indeed, what would be the point? The main doctrinal focus of the authors of Chronicles is on the Jerusalem
Temple. The Temple in Zion fulfills all the previous cultic
institutions God had given to Israel. In 2 Chronicles (3:1),
Zion is identified with Mount Moriah, the hill of Abraham's
sacrifice. Even in the time of Israel's first father, the divine

plan was pointing ahead to the choosing of Jerusalem—and, by implication, of David. This is history told by people who are in love with the liturgy of Israel and for whom the ancient prophets at the cult centers have been transformed into levitical singers, the liturgical musicians of Israel. But we must look now to "The *Latter* Prophets": the great four and the lesser twelve.

The Nature of Prophecy

Though Abraham is called a prophet in Genesis 20:7, the real standard for all later prophetic figures in Israel was Moses. In the Book of Hosea, we read, "By a prophet the LORD brought Israel up from Egypt" (12:13). As Moses himself looks forward to prophets to come in Deuteronomy he says, "The LORD your God will raise up for you a prophet like me from among you, from your brethren—him you shall heed" (18:15). And in the conclusion of Deuteronomy, after Moses' death, an anonymous narrator adds ruefully, "There has not arisen a prophet since in Israel like Moses, whom the LORD knew face to face . . ." (34:10). The prophet is someone called for a special purpose, and yet he—or more seldom she—also has a typical setting, the shrine and sanctuary, or, in later times, the temple and the court of which the temple was from one point of view the chapel. In the ancient Canaanite religion found in Palestine when Abraham first took up his abode there, prophecy was an integral part of the prevailing pagan cultus, as we know from the documents discovered at Ras Shamra in modern Lebanon. It was a common mistake of Protestant scholarship, occasionally emulated by Catholics, to see the prophets as essentially anti-cultic figures. Given the origins of prophecy, this is unlikely, and those passages of the writing prophets that can be read with such a spin are better thought of as repudiations of debased cultic practice, not of the cultus as such. Cultic practice could be debased, even if formally speaking it remained Mosaic—that is, carried out according to the levitical prescriptions. It could be and was debased if the essential ethical elements of right worship were missing. What the prophets wanted was for the various aspects of the moral and ceremonial law to be met at one and the same time. In God's sanctuary-kingdom, cult-like ethics was an expression of the covenant relation. As Meredith Kline observes: "The covenantal nature of Israel's cult gives a peculiar significance to the depositing of Yahweh's treaty at the cultic center, so that the presence of the tables of the covenant in the ark in Israel's sanctuary may be said to epitomize the coalescence of covenant and cult in Israel."[7] And if covenant law was so central, then inevitably covenant morality was also, and such ethics would be at once personal, familial, and for society as a whole.

Key here was the ability of prophetic utterance to present to the prophet's hearers the obligations of covenant relationship, whether there was made an explicit reference to particular laws of the Torah or not. "The distinctiveness of the canonical prophets . . . lay in their particular relationship to, and concern with, the covenant between Yahweh and Israel. . . . [They] actualized the covenant tradition in a situation of crisis, in which the old order has fallen into decay."[8] Sometimes preachers tell us that the prophets did not foretell, they simply told forth. To this the reply must be:

[7] Kline, *Structure of Biblical Authority*, p. 51.

[8] R. E. Clements, *Prophecy and Covenant* (Naperville, Ill., 1965), pp. 127, 123.

they did tell forth, but they also foretold. Permeating their typical utterances was a predictive element, based in part on the prophet's awareness of the future consequences of past and present iniquity, rejection of the covenant ideal. Israel was meant to be a holy nation, whose *mores* would reflect the ardent purity and integrity of her Lord. The prophets could hardly avoid a concern with future time if they spoke, as they surely did, in the name of the Ruler of history: the God who had shown himself that Ruler by the fulfillment of his promise to the patriarchs to draw a people from their loins and give that people the Land.

So far I have described the prophets as "speaking". But it is not at all sure that prophetic oracles were necessarily first given orally. Jeremiah, we know, had secretarial help (Jer 36:4). Though, it is true, one of the secretary's duties was to read out the oracles in public, it may be that the first time some of his public got wind of his utterances was when the literate read them.

The Major Prophets

Isaiah

The first of the major prophets in the canon is Isaiah. Here is a comparable situation to what we found with the source criticism of the Pentateuch. Much criticism argues for three Isaiahs: the original Isaiah of Jerusalem who began to prophesy, as his book tells us, in the year King Uzziah died, 740 B.C., a second Isaiah—Deutero-Isaiah—operating in Babylon during the Exile, and a third—Trito-Isaiah—after that. Of these, the last is less secure than the second (his "book" may only be a loose anthology of oracles), but even the second is not altogether safe. Some modern scholars transfer him back from Babylon to Jerusalem and in so doing suppress the chief reason—a geographical one, then—for separating out the two figures. Unlike the prophet Ezekiel who explicitly says he was in Babylon during the Exile and gives us plenty of local color to support his claim, there is little or nothing in chapters 40 to 55 of the Book of Isaiah to suggest a Babylonian location and a certain amount to suggest otherwise: especially, the appeals to those remaining in Jerusalem and the assumption that, if there is idolatry around, it is Canaanite not Babylonian. For his part, Ezekiel insinuates there is no other prophet in Babylon than himself (Ezek 2:5 and 22:30). Probably, then, if there was a Second Isaiah he, like the First Isaiah, was an "Isaiah of Jerusalem". But *was* there a Second Isaiah? It is not common in literary history for a marvelous writer of poetic prose in any language to disappear so completely, leaving no trace until late nineteenth-century scholars identified his profile. It is sometimes said there is little to connect the writings of the First and Second Isaiah. That is a dangerous argument, for in that case why add his work to that of the original Isaiah in the first place? It seems simpler to hold that, while there may be explanatory glosses by postexilic copyists (that might explain, for instance, the appearance of the name of Cyrus of Persia[9]), what we have in the book is an anthology of pieces from different periods of the long life of a prophet who, as he tells us in the opening verse of his book, lived through four reigns of the kings of Judah. If that be true (we do not positively assert it, but nor do we exclude it: it is good to be reminded that the "settled conclusions" of the

[9] In Is 44:28, 45:1.

dominant scholarship are only hypotheses), then one important thing is indicated: Isaiah is not only a prophet of woe, predominantly but not exclusively in chapters 1 to 39; he is also a prophet of weal, predominantly but not exclusively in chapters 40 to 66.

What we have in chapters 1 to 39 are oracles concerned with the prophet's own contemporaries and their situation (with 36 to 39, however, consisting of historical material which later appeared almost unchanged in the Books of Kings). What we have in chapters 40 to 55 are utterances that presuppose the Exile he saw—or that was—coming. What we have in chapters 56 to 66 are various oracles that parallel concepts used earlier in the book. That prophets could have a message more complex than just woe or simply weal— "everything is going to be ghastly" or "everything is going to be wonderful"—is apparent from Isaiah's contemporary Hosea. Taking seriously *both* transgressions of the will of the Lord *and* the Lord's own faithfulness to his covenant design would naturally lead any prophet to combine elements of woe and weal in his vision. That is why there should be, I believe, an a priori prejudice in favor of all prophets having both messages at once (though, to be sure, some of the minor ones are exceptions that prove the rule). Isaiah's watchword "a remnant shall return" neatly sums this up. It is negative, a woe prophecy: only a remnant will remain. It is also positive, a weal prophecy: this remnant shall indeed return to the land.

Isaiah's call vision, in chapter 6 of his book, is of the holiness of God, and in his prophesying he attempts to apply the idea of the divine holiness to the political affairs of the sacred people. By discouraging the last kings of Judah from placing their trust in foreign alliances, he sought to prevent the nation from succumbing to the taint of paganism. The

woe prophecies make sense because Isaiah saw little chance
of making much impression on an obdurate nation. The
weal prophecies make sense because the Holy One of Israel
—this is the favored title for God in passages of the anthology ascribed both to the First and to the Second Isaiahs—is
also the Lord of history, and he keeps a place for his people
even though this entails the drastic discipline of exile and
the rebirth of spirituality in an alien land. The prophet's
vision involves a concept of salvation in which a faithful
remnant will be forgiven and restored to a recreated Zion.
The oracles in the last chapters, those sometimes ascribed
to a Trito-Isaiah, deal with the ethical prerequisites of the
redemption of Israel and the glories to come when Zion is
regenerated.

As is well known, some of the most beautiful of the oracles in the middle of the book are the "Songs of the Servant"
to which reference is made at crucial points in the Gospels,
not least at the institution of the Holy Eucharist. Who it
was Isaiah understood the Suffering Servant to be has been
a subject of intense scholarly debate: almost everyone from
an ideal Israel to such individuals as the last king of Judah
or the prophet Jeremiah have been suggested. But possibly
the simplest proposal is that in the first instance Isaiah had
himself in mind, given the opprobrium his message must
have attracted: a message that Israel must be punished while
other nations are invited to share her blessings. The mind
of the New Testament Church is that this, however, was
not the whole story. Isaiah's vision left a space open for a
realization of the role of the Suffering Servant far beyond
this, indeed on the cosmic scale of a God who as man dies
for the entire world.

Jeremiah (with Lamentations and Baruch)

Jeremiah's message is cognate with Isaiah's in that it invites people to place their trust in the Lord. That is so even though its political thrust looks very different. The situation had moved on by the time Jeremiah was writing, in literally the last days of an independent Judean state. His original message is not to fear becoming a vassal of Babylon—the Neo-Babylonian Empire—so as to be spared the horrors of invasion and destruction. To hostile observers, Jeremiah was an appeaser and a potential collaborator, and indeed when disaster came for Judah, the Neo-Babylonian ruler Nebuchadnezzar treated Jeremiah with great respect.

His book has some kind of plan, albeit not a very tidy one. Chapters 1 to 25 comprise his oracles to Judah; chapter 26 to 45 describe his personal life and trials and tribulations; chapters 46 to 51 consist of prophecies against foreign nations, showing he was hardly aiming to undermine the specificity of the holy people. Jeremiah's aim is spiritual regeneration. He elevates the moral law over the ceremonial, as Jesus himself will do in his own teaching.

We should add a reference to the separate little prophetic book called the Lamentations of Jeremiah. It is prominent in the Paschal Triduum in the old Roman Liturgy. The message of this book—clearly the work of an eyewitness of the events of 587—is that, whereas Jerusalem deserved her fate, the God who allowed this destruction to come upon her is still her covenant Lord. The two sides of his activity, negative and positive, are intimately interrelated because God requires the unswerving loyalty of his people as the necessary prerequisite of his blessings. The book is structured according to the letters of the Hebrew alphabet, the name of each letter introducing a verse: a device originally thought up to teach Egyptian children their letters. In Lamentations, this pattern gives us a sense of the comprehensiveness of a lament expressing the full range of human sufferings but does so with a grief that is controlled, restrained, and on that account the more affecting.

Jeremiah's secretary, Baruch, also left us a composition of his own, a kind of mosaic of verses not only from Jeremiah but also from Isaiah, Daniel, and Job. The Book of Baruch is addressed from the situation of exile to deportees in Babylon and is concerned with Israel's sin, punishment, and forgiveness. Baruch speaks of the Torah in glowing terms:

> She is the book of the commandments of God,
>   and the law that endures for ever.
> All who hold her fast will live,
>   and those who forsake her will die.
> Turn, O Jacob, and take her;
>   walk toward the shining of her light.
>
>   (Bar 4:1-2)

The book ends with the "Letter of Jeremiah"—a kind of pamphlet written to attest the powerlessness of idols and the futility of their worship.

Ezekiel

Ezekiel, coming from a priestly family and possibly a priest himself at the Jerusalem Temple in the last days of Judah, was deported to Babylon in 597 along with a group of Judean nobles. The first twenty-four chapters of the Book of Ezekiel give his call vision and original prophecy, recorded (we are told) by a scribe as Ezekiel spoke. Chapter 25 consists of oracles against those nations that took advantage of the fall of Judah to hurt her the more. That might make us think

Ezekiel will be essentially a prophet of vengeance, but chapters 26 to 39, while quite varied, can all be brought under the more positive rubric of attempts to build the remnant the Lord will restore, an attempted realization of Isaiah's earlier hope. Then in chapters 40 to 48 we have the amazing vision of the ideal Temple, committed to writing after some kind of ecstatic experience. Here the prophet contemplates the future of the theocratic city, in which divine holiness will be the regulatory feature. Ezekiel's overall message is plain, and R. K. Harrison puts it neatly: "Earlier prophets had proclaimed that the very concept of the divine holiness demanded the rejection of rebellious Israel, if only for a short period. Ezekiel, however, argued conversely that this same holiness rendered the ultimate restoration of the national inevitable, since divine honour was bound up with the destiny of Israel."[10] The restoration needed and offered is radical. Ezekiel pictures it as dry bones of the dead being clothed again with living flesh. The promise of the resurrection was itself an act of divine grace, meant to lead to repentance by at least a faithful minority among the exiles.

Daniel and Companion Pieces

The last of the major prophets is Daniel. Daniel's message fits far better with the other major prophets than is often said. When his book is called "apocalyptic", the revelation of heavenly mysteries, rather than "prophecy", this is largely a distinction without a difference. The entire Old Testament is eschatological in that, as I remarked in introducing this "overview", it looks to the fulfillment of greater and greater promises. Eschatological prophecy typically refuses to lose

[10] Harrison, *Introduction to the Old Testament*, p. 853.

hope in God in the face of his judgments and instead projects that hope to the ultimate boundaries of existence. Apocalyptic, as represented by Daniel, is not doing anything so very different from such prophecy. In apocalyptic prophecy, it is emphasized that the whole cosmos must be interpreted in the light of the truth learned from God's revelation in the history of Israel. Already for the postexilic prophets in particular, salvation extends beyond history, reflecting a God who, though revealed in the cosmos, also transcends it. In certain respects, Daniel's theological outlook is especially close to that of Ezekiel. (There is the same emphasis on divine transcendence, and the doctrine of angels is prominent in both.) But the vision of the angelic defender of Israel, "like a son of man", coming from the divine throne to save her is unique to Daniel, and it is of unique importance to our Lord's presentation of his own identity to his contemporaries as one sent from the Father for the purposes of saving struggle with the powers of evil and falsehood.

Where we can draw a contrast with the other major prophets is in the *manner* of the hero-author's inspiration. Daniel's type of inspiration does not seem not classically prophetic, but harks back to more ancient times. For Daniel, like Joseph in the Book of Genesis, is a statesman at a pagan court, and, again like Joseph, he has received psychic powers enabling him to interpret dreams and visions, mostly the dreams and visions of others. It became common in modern scholarship to date the Book of Daniel much later than it itself asserts (the sixth century) and to situate it not where it claims to be situated, in the years when the Neo-Babylonian Empire was about to succumb to Persia, but in the Hellenistic period when the Jews were in trouble with the Greek-speaking empires that came into being after the amazing Eastern conquests, right to the Indus Valley

—modern Pakistan—of Alexander of Macedonia. This late dating is not self-evident. The arguments for it are generally twofold: the book's language, which is not Hebrew but Aramaic, deemed to be a *parvenu* language, and the alleged fact that the author gets so much basic Babylonian and Persian history wrong, something more or less inconceivable were he a contemporary of the events he describes. As to the Aramaic, *which* type is significant, and some students recognize the type of Aramaic the author uses as the so-called official Aramaic employed as a lingua franca in diplomatic circles in the Near East from as early as 1100 B.C. and right down to the age of Persian hegemony. The seeming confusions as to basic political facts can also be sorted out with some degree of plausibility—though not to the satisfaction of all. Alone among ancient writers, Daniel claims that Nebuchadnezzar, the conqueror of Jerusalem, became incapacitated by a disease that led him to behave like a beast, going on all fours and eating grass. There *is* a recognized psychiatric malady of this kind, boanthropy, which, like other forms of monomania leaves the other abilities of the person intact. Again, the book holds the last ruler of the Neo-Babylonian Empire to be Belshazzar when actually it was his father, Nabonidus. But Belshazzar is known to have been co-ruler for much of his father's reign. Furthermore, in the scene at Belshazzar's feast, that "Darius the Mede" into whose hands Belshazzar's kingdom was given, after Daniel interpreted aright the writing produced by an invisible hand on the wall, is unknown to history—but not so if he was the figure mentioned in the Nabonidus Chronicle as "governor of Babylon and the region beyond the river".

The Septuagint, followed by the Catholic and Orthodox churches, has expanded the book by three interesting, additional small sections: first, the "Song of the Three Young

Men in the Furnace", the *Benedicite*, a wonderful hymn of
praise from the cosmos and Israel on behalf of mankind,
much used in the Roman Liturgy, chiefly at Morning Prayer
on feast days; secondly, the tale of Susanna, an encouragement and a warning about the practice of justice, integrity,
and chastity; and thirdly, a parody on the Neo-Babylonian
religion, Bel and the Dragon.

The Minor Prophets

What of the twelve minor prophets? We must deal with
them more expeditiously.

Hosea may be minor, but he is great in his passion for the
purity of Israel's relation with the Lord and the beauty of
his imagery. He felt himself called to take a wife who, he
knew, would probably betray him—to take her, that is, as a
prophetic sign. He knew the waywardness of his wife from
the very start of their marriage, just as God knew Israel's infidelity from the time of the wilderness wanderings. That the
very religious festivals had become times of license shows
how low Israel had sunk, since these should have been above
all times for remaking her vows. For Hosea, restoration is
still possible for her, but only on the basis of contrition, and
unfortunately, Israel is conspicuously deficient in just those
moral and spiritual qualities that would ensure her return to
a God full of *chesedh*: loving kindness or mercy.

Joel, next in our modern Bibles, seems to be a Jerusalem
prophet and probably one attached to the Temple. A dev-
astation caused by locusts becomes at his hands a symbol

of the crisis in which God will preside as Judge over the nations. Joel reflects the particularism by which Israel concentrated on her own special status as the beneficiary of divine favor—perhaps a view more common in priestly than in prophetic circles and one with which the infant Church would have to deal in the circumcision crisis described in Acts and the Pauline Letters. It is more than usually difficult to date this little book, but it looks as if Joel's appeal to the people for repentance meets with immediate positive response—which is why he goes on to predict a time not only of material sufficiency but also, more importantly, of the spiritual blessings to follow. Famously, his prophecy of an outpouring of the Holy Spirit on Israel will be taken up in Saint Peter's sermons in Acts.

Amos, by contrast, has an agricultural background. He stresses his humble background and his lack of religious training in the prophetic guilds that dated, perhaps, from the time of Samuel. A Judean, he evokes the most brilliant period in the culture of the neighboring northern kingdom: the long and prosperous reign of Jeroboam II, and he excoriates it for the corruption of its plutocracy and its revival of erotic Baalism. The message of Amos is that a holy and just God can only be properly served by a nation that itself reflects those qualities in its way of life. For Israel, he warns, the Day of the Lord, looked forward to in her liturgy, the day when the triumph of Israel's God shall be complete, will be a day not of celebration but of lamentation. Unlike Hosea, who emphasizes the divine *chesedh*, loving mercy, Amos stresses the complementary quality of *tsedeq*, righteousness. He presents God as Creator, as Master of the destinies of the nations and as Judge. He is the Maker of the Covenant but precisely as such gives Israel not only privileges but also responsibilities.

Obadiah is likely to be a Judean likewise, and the background of his highly defensive oracles is the traditional enmity between the Hebrews and the Edomites, which broke out anew when Edom capitalized on the plight of Judah after the devastating invasion of 587. Writing a hundred years or so later, Obadiah points out that Edom should beware: the Arabs are pressing her from the other side. This is a judgment on Edom, in fact a perfect exemplar of divine judgment, for her lack of humanity toward Judah was a crime calling to heaven for retribution.

Jonah is a more attractive—or at any rate a more unconsciously amusing—prophet than is Obadiah. He appears to be the Jonah who puts in a cameo appearance in 2 Kings as a prophet from Gath-hepher near Nazareth, operating like Amos under Jeroboam II. This encourages some interpreters to see the Book of Jonah as historical, rather than an allegory. How about the whale? Well, large marine species are capable of swallowing sizeable objects, though not of regurgitating living ones without miraculous assistance. Could Nineveh, the Babylonian city, really have been converted to monotheism of any kind? Even without invoking direct divine intervention, the author may have been aware that toward the end of the ninth century there was an effort in Babylonia to concentrate the cultus around the god Nebo —just one example of monotheizing movements in the paganism of Mesopotamia and Egypt at various times. What about the castor oil plant that springs up overnight? Again, there is an answer. In tropical locations such plants can indeed grow by a foot a day. But the allegorical take on Jonah is also possible. In Hebrew, *Jonah* means "dove", which, as the Psalms show us, was long a symbol of Israel. The "fish" would be, then, the Babylonian Empire, which swallowed the Hebrew people during the Exile and disgorged them during the restoration period. Allegorically, the message of the book would be the failure of Israel in her mission to be the true people of God. Like Jonah himself, she has neither the charity nor the zeal God desires. It is a book that leaves us with a question mark in more than one sense.

Micah, like probably all the six remaining minor prophets, comes from the south, and is working in the 730s. As with Amos, who hailed from a place only twenty miles away, he is critical of social injustices, and it may be under Amos' influence that he turned first to attack the capital of the northern kingdom, at Samaria, before giving his attention to Judah. He is the great champion of the small farmers, and for this reason was much admired by the twentieth-century Distributivist movement, which took its inspiration from the social encyclicals of Pope Leo XIII. Indeed, these—the movement and the encyclicals—have some claim to a basis in Hebrew prophetism.

Nahum is preaching a century later, in the turbulent context of the disintegration of the Assyrian Empire, which, having overwhelmed the northern kingdom of Israel in 722, found itself breaking up almost exactly a hundred years later, with the death of King Ashurbanipal in 627. Nahum predicts the fall of Nineveh to Babylon, so he is a good example of a prophet who foretells. But he also tells forth, because his book is a classic critique of militarism. Those who live by the sword shall die by the sword.

Habakkuk seems to be a cultic prophet living in Judah around the year 600. The Neo-Babylonian Empire, which he refers to as "the Chaldeans", is looming in the distance, but it is not quite yet the menace it will become just a few years later. The problematic identified by Habakkuk is the seeming divine injustice that allows a wicked nation to punish a people more righteous than itself. The answer is given in Habakkuk 2:4. Human arrogance carries within it the seeds of its own ruin, whereas the person of faith is assured of divine favor. The wonderful poem in chapter 3 has sometimes been said to have no obvious connection with the rest of the book, but it can be interpreted as a theophany in which God comes in majesty to judge the pagans and bring joy and salvation to the chosen people. The message, in other words, is not just a consolation. It is a prediction of divine intervention to come, to be identified by the Christian reader with the Parousia and its anticipation and instrument, the paschal mystery.

Zephaniah is an example of a court prophet par excellence, since he was of royal blood, the great-grandson of King Hezekiah. The minor prophets are not laid out in strict chronological order in the Bible, but this is another seventh-century prophet, if a little earlier than Nahum and Habakkuk. Zephaniah is preoccupied with the possibility of invasion from the far north, in the shape of the warlike Scythians, but he recognizes that Assyria is a graver threat in the long term. His oracles predict Assyria's eventual downfall and final salvation for a remnant of the people. He is a good example of a prophet who combines weal and woe, the elimination of the theocracy and its regeneration.

The last three prophets—*Haggai, Zechariah, Malachi*—are near contemporaries in the period of the Return to Palestine. In 537, when Haggai and Zechariah were most likely still children, the foundation stone of the second Temple was laid. Huge hopes were aroused, but the growing boys would have witnessed the deterioration of morale that followed and that can be read between the lines in the historical books of Ezra and Nehemiah. In his oracles, Haggai summons the governor Zerubbabel and the high priest Joshua to get a move on with rebuilding the Temple fully. Zechariah belonged to a returning priestly family and should probably be classed as a cultic prophet. He has a comprehensive message: the necessity for repentance and purification, the exaltation of Jerusalem as the nation re-forms, the subjection and conversion of Israel's enemies. Finally, Malachi, whose name is likely to be a *nom de plume*, as it simply means "My messenger", an appropriate pseudonym for a prophet, wrote around 450. He is very much an eschatological prophet, as befits the last prophet before John the Baptist, to whom he prophetically refers in the opening of chapter 3 of his book: "Behold, I send my messenger to prepare the way before me, and the Lord whom you seek will suddenly come to his temple" (Mal 3:1).

3

THE WRITINGS

The Wisdom Literature

The Wisdom Books of the canon follow next: Job, Proverbs, and the Psalms, or as the Jews call them "the Praises", and then two sharply contrasting texts, The Song of Solomon and Ecclesiastes, with, lastly, in the Catholic and Orthodox canon, Ecclesiasticus and Wisdom. Israel's Wisdom literature is sometimes regarded as her natural theology, and there is an element of truth in this. Yet one very striking thing about Israel's Wisdom literature generally is that the quality it prescribes as really foundational for the acquiring of worthwhile wisdom is the fear of the Lord.[1] There is something more authoritative about the voice of the Wisdom literature than the phrase "natural theology" might suggest. Israel's sages claim inspiration, as in Proverbs 2:6, where we read, "For the LORD gives wisdom; from his mouth come knowledge and understanding." The counsel of her sages is not just simple advice that one can take or leave. Rather, it is presented more as a decree, and the reason is, surely, that natural experience for the sages of Israel is seen through

Note: like the rabbis, I am using this compendious category as a receptacle in which to place all the books as yet unaccounted for—which means in my case the books of the (longer) canon of Greek-speaking Jewry and the Church.

[1] Prov 1:7; 9:18; Job 28:28; Eccles 12:13–14.

the lens of covenant faith. Or at any rate, where seeing it that way is suspended for a time—as with the author of Ecclesiastes, who found wickedness in place of justice (3:16), or the author of Job, who discerned no moral order in the world (9:22)—things never end on that note. Before a book is finished, the lens is put back in position.

The starting point, then, may be natural experience— with Ecclesiastes, it is the cycles of creation; with Job, it is his personal misery. But in both cases a supernatural perspective is eventually available. The Wisdom Books testify to the fact that there is a divine order in the world. God has implanted wisdom in creation as a kind of primordial revelation of his own divine wisdom.[2] It may not be possible always to discern that immanent wisdom merely by inspecting the way the world goes. That is why the author of Proverbs calls on his readers for a childlike faith in the Lord as the One who upholds righteous order.

Job

Job is the Wisdom Book printed first in our modern Bibles. The name of the hero is bemusing. Is he intended as an historical figure or does his name mean "Everyman"? Apparently the name "Job" was a common designation for western Semites in the second millennium before Christ. There is some reason to think the location of the story may be Edom—so, on the margin of Israel, perhaps significantly. But other scholars think the setting is left purposely vague, which would fit well with the Everyman idea. Job is depicted as a semi-nomad who lived in a walled city during the wintertime and migrated with his flocks for the rest of

[2] Thus G. von Rad, *Wisdom in Israel* (Nashville and London, 1972), p. 191.

the year. A case can be made for the book's extreme antiquity, making it pre-Mosaic. The background seems to resemble that of the patriarchal sagas. Neither priesthood nor central sanctuary is mentioned. The human enemies around the place are marauding nomads. But it is the psychology of the central figure, not his sociological or political setting, that is the center of interest in the Book of Job.

As the book opens, we have a Job who is the very picture of serene moral innocence. As the book proceeds, we have a character who is by turns rebellious and querulous or at the least questioning. But then there is an explanation for the change. The book opens with a deeply religious figure in harmony with his surroundings and at peace with God and man. Subsequently, however, his cherished beliefs and ideals, precisely the inner factors that enable him to live serenely, are rudely, not to say traumatically, shaken. They are shaken by the realization that God has not acted in the fashion that conventional accounts of divine behavior would suggest.

Job is a fascinating character because of his inner division: at one level he feels that his friends, who tell him it must be that he is being punished justly for some hidden misdemeanor, are surely correct. At another level, he knows they are nothing of the sort. The final theophany closing the book reveals that there is indeed chaos in the world, but it is divinely bounded chaos, which is contained within an ultimate order that may not be discoverable at any given time. The important speech of the young man Elihu throws further light on this. Correcting his elders—an astonishing phenomenon in ancient society—Elihu maintains that suffering may have a providential value. It does not have to be punitive. It may be disciplinary, a matter of divine teaching, for, as we often forget, the English word "discipline" comes from the Latin word *disciplina*, whose original sense is better expressed nowadays when we think of the "disciplines" taught at a university. In the inscrutable ways of God, affliction may be a means of growth in understanding—not so much academic understanding as existential—and indeed, through the transforming of existence, a way to personal deliverance from evil. In a Christian retrospect, this can be considered a discreet pointer to the Passion of Christ. In the words of one commentator: "Job does not set out to answer the problem of suffering, but instead shows that even a righteous man can utilize such an experience as that through which the hero passed to attain to new heights of emotional and spiritual maturity."[3] As we shall see, this is pertinent to how one of the Latin doctors, Saint Gregory the Great, approached this text in his book *Morals on Job*.

The Psalms

In the Latin Bible, the Psalms—which in the Hebrew Bible are placed first in the third collection of the canon, the *Kethubim* or "Writings"—come next. The Psalter is a wonderful topic for a Christian religious such as myself, since every day we reacquaint ourselves with its contents through the various Offices of the Liturgy of the Hours with all the changes they ring in different seasons, on different feasts. When Yves Congar visited Oxford for the seventh centenary of the death of Saint Thomas in 1974, he remarked on his failure to understand the younger Dominicans of that period in the Province of France, who were in revolt against regular observance, saying that, for himself, he could no more live without the recitation of the Psalter than a fish can live out of water.

The Psalms are highly varied, which is how their Chris-

[3] Harrison, *Introduction to the Old Testament*, p. 1046.

tian apologists (like Saint Athanasius of Alexandria)[4] have been able to describe them as comprising the entire gamut of human emotion and experience. Their variety is what struck many modern scholars too, when they pronounced the judgment that the Psalter is a marvelously motley medley, the "hymn book" of the Jerusalem Temple. But more recently, the emphasis in scholarship has come to lie on the unity of the Psalter and a search for the principles of its internal organization.[5] Certainly there are some features of the Book of Psalms that might make us wonder whether it had more design to it than meets the eye.

Thus for instance, the first psalm is a psalm about how to meditate on the divine instructions, the Torah. And the last psalms are the psalms of praise that give the whole collection its Hebrew title. So perhaps we could say on the strength of its beginning and end that the Psalter is about how to live life thoughtfully while praising the Lord. The Psalter has sometimes been divided into five books, and the first four each end with a psalm that closes with a short doxology, "Blessed be the Lord", in one case, and in the remaining three, "Blessed be the Lord, the God of Israel." Perhaps that is meant to underline this initial impression from the first psalm and the last. As to particular themes of the Psalter, Psalm 2—which is, then, the first psalm after the introduction to the whole collection and so might be thought to occupy a special place—announces what are perhaps the most important of these: the sovereignty of the God of Israel and derivatively that of his anointed, the king, who is his vice-regent on earth. The idea of earthly kingship exercised by the Lord's adopted son, the Davidic king, serves as a basis

---

[4] A translation of Athanasius' wonderful *Letter to Marcellinus on the Interpretation of the Psalms* is available in R. C. Gregg, ed., *Athanasius. The Life of Anthony and the Letter to Marcellinus* (Mahwah, N.J., 1980), pp. 101–29.

[5] See Baker and Arnold, *Face of Old Testament Studies*, pp. 332–44.

here for fostering the messianic hope. The psalmists proved their value as agents for spreading and perpetuating this great spiritual expectation. To summarize, we might say that the Psalter is a book of true wisdom, containing the Lord's instruction for the faithful and emphasizing his kingship. This approach based on the unity of the Psalter stresses the way it could be used by individual readers.

But the Psalter is also of course part and parcel of Israel's liturgy. The person praying enters into Israel's liturgy by means of prayer for the deliverance of Israel, and at the same time he exalts the sovereignty of God over Israel and the world. The Psalms teach one how to carry out those basic acts of prayer implied by the Torah's covenant relation with God—petition, thanksgiving, contrition, adoration. They assure the covenant community that the course of history is under God's control, and they proclaim as the greatest blessing of life covenant fellowship with God, both in Temple worship on the feasts of Israel and in the worship of everyday existence. The Psalms treat the Divine Presence as overshadowing all our ordinary affairs, which is why they recur time and again in Christian mysticism.

Seventy-three psalms are ascribed to King David, and, given what "The Former Prophets" say about David's musical talents and his concern for worship in connection with both the Ark and the Temple it was left for his son Solomon to build, we can assume that the nucleus of the Psalter is indebted to David's inspiration and example. There are also ascriptions that point to an origin for other psalms in levitical circles, beginning no doubt under the monarchy and continuing into the period after the Exile. The Psalms considered most ancient are generally royal psalms but also psalms mentioning the northern kingdom, which disappeared in 722. Scholars claim to detect signs of great antiquity in psalms that draw on certain images used, albeit in a different fashion, in Canaanite religious texts.

If we are concerned with dating or the growth of the Psalter, it seems reasonable to think that psalms of corporate lamentation and psalms dealing with the betrayal of Judah by those who wished her ill, like the Edomites, might come from the time of the Babylonian Exile. Finally, psalms dealing with the problem of the righteous sufferer, à la Job, or with the way the Torah should be observed or with the nature and significance of wisdom might come from any period, including, or perhaps especially, the age after the Exile, when the lesson taught by such prophets as Jeremiah and Ezekiel that each Israelite must take responsibility for his own personal attitude to the covenant God had begun to sink in.

Proverbs

The Book of Proverbs is the first of three books ascribed to King Solomon. Solomon's reputation for wisdom, which drew the queen of Sheba to his court, is extolled in the Books of Kings, and if Proverbs has a Solomonic nucleus, that would explain its dedication. Some people think Proverbs began as a textbook in a royal school or a school for scribes. (Indeed, a portion of it, 22:17—23:11, appears to have drawn on work used in Egypt for the training of civil servants, *The Instruction of Amenemope*). But by and large it is perhaps better suited to home-schooling: the more practical, down-to-earth education needed for the children of small farmers. At various points the Book of Proverbs seems to imply that parents will do the teaching. Thus we read in the opening chapter:

> Hear, my son, your father's instruction,
>   and reject not your mother's teaching.
>
>   (Prov 1:8)

And later on, by way of report on experience:

> When I was a son with my father,
>   tender, the only one in the sight of my mother,
> he taught me, and said to me,
> "Let your heart hold fast my words;
>   keep my commandments, and live;
> do not forget, and do not turn away from the words
>   of my mouth.
>   Get wisdom; get insight.
> Do not forsake her, and she will keep you;
>   love her, and she will guard you."
>
>   (Prov 4:3–6)

So Solomon seeks to transmit his wisdom to Israel through the home, just as in Deuteronomy Moses planned to disseminate the Torah through the parents of Israel's children: "And these words which I command you this day shall be upon your heart, and you shall teach them diligently to your children, and shall talk of them when you sit in your house, and when you walk by the way, and when you lie down, and when you rise" (Deut 6:6–7).

The material contained in the Book of Proverbs is sometimes regarded as simplistic. It is held to be rather commonplace or naïve advice about what constitutes successful living. What is often overlooked is that in this book the word *life* does not just mean any kind of decent human existence but specifically life through relation with God. Proverbs is not just this-worldly know-how.

The Book of Ecclesiastes is one of the strangest books in the canon because for most of its course it challenges the normal beliefs of Judaism. True, there is a change of mind-set at the end when the writer concludes, in the spirit of the rest of the Wisdom literature of Israel: "Fear God, and keep his commandments; for this is the whole duty of man. For God will bring every deed into judgment, with every secret thing, whether good or evil" (12:13). But in all other respects Ecclesiastes is in the Bible so as to show the depth of the questions divine revelation must face and answer. In this book—whose title means "The Gatherer" (whether of people or of sayings is left unexplained)—the first chapters ask: What is good? while the last six chapters ask: How is human knowing possible? In other words, Ecclesiastes raises in a sceptical and agnostic tone of voice the questions of fundamental ethics and epistemology. It seems to say: Don't expect much certainty from the wisdom of man on these matters, as it won't be forthcoming.

Perhaps the best clue to the significance of Ecclesiastes' rather bleak and negative message is furnished by the French Catholic writer Georges Bernanos when he writes: "To be prepared to hope in what does not deceive we must first lose hope in everything that *does* deceive."[6] In a nutshell: life is devoid of final meaning if it is without God. The American philosopher of religion Peter Kreeft remarks, insightfully, that Ecclesiastes "is divine revelation precisely in being the absence of divine revelation. It is like the silhouette of the rest of the Bible . . . , revelation by darkness rather than by light. In this book God reveals to us exactly what life is when

---

[6] Cited in J. Ellul, *Reason for Being: A Meditation on Ecclesiastes* (Grand Rapids, Mich., 1990), p. 47.

God does not reveal to us what life is. Ecclesiastes frames the Bible as death frames life."[7] And again, "There is nothing more meaningless than an answer without its question. That is why we need Ecclesiastes."[8]

The Song of Songs

A rabbinic tradition has it that Proverbs belongs to Solomon's mature years and Ecclesiastes to his old age. The same tradition, not surprisingly, ascribes the Song of Solomon to his young manhood. At any rate, it may belong, like the other books, to the period of his reign. The Song is a collection of love songs, but not a mere collection, or it could not have provoked such profound spiritual interpretation. It is, we can say, an extended *double entendre* for in it the theme of human love is interpenetrated by a concept of mystical love of a very deep order. The Aramaic paraphrase of the Song of Solomon was not far off the mark in interpreting it, accordingly, as a celebration of the gracious love of the Lord for his people. The Hebrew name for the Song of Solomon is "The Song of Songs", and that is a Hebraism for *the* Song, the greatest song ever sung.

Wisdom and Sirach

Wisdom is a marvelous book, which Protestantism is unfortunate not to have in its Bible. What was its author's purpose? It may have been to write an apologia for the faith

[7] P. Kreeft, *Three Philosophies of Life: Ecclesiastes: Life as Vanity; Job: Life as Suffering; Song of Songs: Life as Love* (San Francisco: Ignatius Press, 1989), p. 23.
[8] Ibid., p. 19.

of Israel to Gentiles, and in so doing to answer in more than the cursory way of the last two verses of Ecclesiastes the challenge to a philosophically confident religious world view that Ecclesiastes had mounted. It is usually thought to have been written in the third or the second century B.C., either in Palestine or in Alexandria. The author sees the Divine Wisdom at work not only in creation but also in Israel's history and thus prepares the way for the Book of Sirach or Ecclesiasticus, which goes on to identify Wisdom with the Torah. Wisdom here is the explication of the covenant of Sinai. That brings us full circle, to the start of this overview of the Jewish Bible.

The Remainder

Ruth, Esther, Judith

Having looked at the Wisdom literature, taken as including the Psalter, that leaves us still to consider a small number of works from "The Writings" not as yet touched on—and some still left over from the longer canon recognized by the Church.

Ruth is a beautiful little book that achieves several aims with great economy of means: to trace the ancestry of David, to inculcate in its readers a sense of the importance in life of unselfish devotion, and to make the controversial point that a pious foreigner, if he really trusts in the providence of God is worthy to be included among the chosen people. It probably dates from the early days of the monarchy since the opening historical chapter correctly portrays a friendly relation between the Jews and their neighbors, the Moabites, which unfortunately did not survive that period.

Esther, also a book with a heroine, concerns the epoch of Persian dominance and shows a knowledge of Persian customs and the geography of the Persian capital, Susa, as well as including many Persian names and loanwords. Its historical value has been slighted since no Persian queen of this name, or indeed any Persian queen of Jewish faith, has left any mark on documents or inscriptions. Nor is the Nazi-style "final solution" of a threat to exterminate the Jews in the Persian Empire evidenced elsewhere. As often in ancient literature, hyperbole has been operative here. However, as one scholar has written: "There is no difficulty in supposing that . . . one who occupied the position of a secondary wife [to the Persian ruler] was made the means of averting some calamity that threatened at least some of her compatriots and that the extant narrative of the book was formed upon this foundation."[9] Esther's key concept is the way divine providence can override human malice. In its Hebrew form, the Book of Esther has the peculiarity that it never actually mentions the name of God, and probably this is the reason why in the longer canon of the Greek-speaking synagogue the book was amplified by the addition of explicit expressions of Esther's faith and prayer.

Judith, which completes the trilogy of books centered on women, is a rather bloody tale of female fortitude that is almost certainly allegorical in character. The name "Judith" simply means "the Jewess", and the enemies of Israel in the book are a hybrid creation—a conflation of the Assyrian, the

[9] Harrison, *Introduction to the Old Testament*, p. 1098.

Neo-Babylonian, and the Persian Empires. Thus Nebuchadnezzar is Babylonian, his capital Assyrian, and his hench-
men Persian. Judith's triumph over the "Assyrian" general
Holofernes is the reward of prayer and exact observance of
all the prescriptions of the Torah.

Tobit

This trilogy—Ruth, Esther, Judith—dealing either with affairs of state or at any rate, in the case of Ruth, with the
bloodline of kings, stands in contrast to the Book of Tobit,
which is an entirely domestic story. It concerns a righteous
captive of the northern Diaspora, and its author claims to
have been one of the prisoners taken to Nineveh by Shal-
maneser V at the time of the fall of the northern kingdom in
722. This may be a literary device, but the main themes of
the book are perennial aspects of the faith of Israel: trust in
the providence of God, faithfulness to the Torah, and such
virtues as humility and justice.

What seems to some readers an anticipation of the Judaism
of our Lord's time and later is the emphasis on almsgiving
and fasting as well as prayer. In this regard, Tobit had quite
an influence on the development of Christian asceticism.

Maccabees

That leaves us in conclusion with the Books of Maccabees.
Their subject is the wars that pitted zealous supporters of
the Torah against a culturally imperialistic pagan Greek-
speaking empire in the second century B.C., the period when
the religious parties of which we hear in the Gospels—
Pharisees, Sadducees, Zealots—were forming. Contrary to

what one might think from comparison with the two Books of Samuel, the two Books of Kings and the two Books of Chronicles, the two Books of the Maccabees do not describe consecutive slices of history. The second book revisits part of the period covered in the first in order to treat it in the spirit of a preacher rather than a chronicler or historian.

Not of course that the author of 1 Maccabees is altogether uninterested in religious questions. For him, Israel is the holy congregation of God, and he shows an unswerving trust in the ability of God to bring salvation out of apparent defeat. In 2 Maccabees, the writer expands these themes considerably. The lesson he draws from recent history is that divine chastening, though painful, is far preferable to the more drastic form of punishment provided for the pagan nations, for this consists in something far worse—being left alone by God. Like the author of Tobit, the author of 2 Maccabees sees agents from the unseen world functioning in man's affairs. He enunciates a clear doctrine of the resurrection of the body, which influenced the Pharisees of the time of Jesus and prepared the way for the disciples' eventual understanding of the Resurrection of the Lord. Famously, he also affirms the value of prayer for the departed, something that did not commend his book to the Reformers of the sixteenth century A.D. Perhaps his single most important contribution, however, to the biblical corpus is his theology of martyrdom. The sufferings of the martyrs are due to the sins of the nation. But they are efficacious in expiating God's righteous anger against his holy people. This too was vital in preparing the ground for Jesus' contemporaries to get a first inkling of what his death might mean—a death that saves.

PART TWO

THE PATTERN OF REVELATION

4

THE PATTERN OF REVELATION:
A CONTENTIOUS ISSUE

We need now to stand back from the materials we have
surveyed and ask about the pattern of revelation they show
—always in relation to our more familiar New Testament,
since the Church's Bible is a unity of two collections representing the two Covenants, Old and New. These two
Covenants, like the two collections of books that are their
witnesses, are not just two disparate bodies of literature that
happen to lie side by side. They are, so to speak, made for
each other: the Old Testament is constituted in its very
identity as "old" by the New Testament, and the same is
true of their relation when seen the other way round: the
New Testament is what it is only because of the Old.

Neo-Marcionism

This is a doctrinal truth rarely recognized in academy departments for the study of religion where most professional
study of the Old Testament goes on. But I know from hearing of the experiences of students in Cambridge, which can
hardly be wholly untypical in this respect, that they have
great difficulty as a consequence in making theological use

of the Old Testament and, if they are ordinands, getting any idea of how it might be used in preaching or in the catechetical activity of the Church. And that is so even though it is only through the Church that this literature becomes specifically the "Old" Testament in the first place. The academic desire to free the foundational literature of Judaism from the Church (which is not in order to return it to Judaism since generally people in academic faculties are as little interested in rabbinic Judaism as they are in Christian orthodoxy) fuses with an attitude of disdain toward the Old Testament in the liberal Protestantism that is the chief background of university theology in the English-speaking, as in the German-speaking, world—if not only there.

In the nineteenth and twentieth centuries, there took place in the professional theological faculties of Protestant Europe and eventually North America a resurgence of the heresy of Marcion, the second-century admirer of Saint Paul who wished to abandon the Old Testament entirely as incompatible in its spirit with the Gospel proclaimed by the Church. Following the depiction by English Old Testament scholar Francis Watson, it can be said to have had three main figures: the systematic theologian Friedrich Schleiermacher, often called the father of modern (Protestant) theology, who lived from 1768 to 1834; the historian of theology Adolf von Harnack, who lived from 1851 to 1930, and the exegete Rudolf Bultmann, who lived from 1884 to 1976. I furnish below the essentials of Watson's account.

Schleiermacher

For Schleiermacher, Jesus and the apostles only appealed to the Old Testament owing to their historical situation. In the future, he thinks, the Old Testament might well be printed simply as an appendix to the Bible—that is, to the New Testament. The only things Schleiermacher values in the Old Testament literature are such prophetic oracles as can be held to express the striving of human nature at large toward the divine or the infinite—and of course one can find such texts outside the Old Testament, or indeed outside any sort of sacred writings for that matter.

Saint Paul, after all, told his spiritual children not to cling to the letter of the Law (Rom 7:6; 2 Cor 3:6). Schleiermacher thinks the same advice can be given about everything to do with the Old Testament—and much in the New Testament as well, especially when it is dependent on the Old. He complains of Christian teachers who try to defend the historicity and spiritual value of the Old Testament as "theologians of the letter" who seek to restore "the fallen walls of their Jewish Zion and its Gothic pillars"[1]—to no purpose.

Harnack

For Harnack too Christianity is a completely new beginning that depends on the unique psychology of Jesus, from which flows Jesus' teaching about universal benevolence founded on the love of God and a love of neighbor that recognizes the irreplaceable value of each human soul. The Old Testament contains much that is irrelevant to this teaching, or even antithetical to it. Accordingly, argues Harnack, to see

[1] F. D. E. Schleiermacher, *Über die Religion: Reden an die Gebildeten unter ihren Verächtern* 29, no. 17 and 4, no. 3, cited in Watson, "Erasing the Text: Readings in Neo-Marcionism", in *Text and Truth* 127–76, here at p. 131. That is because for Schleiermacher, real religion consists in a state of consciousness focused on the Infinite, which makes Christianity the perfect religion not for any reason to do with texts but because the Holy Spirit makes possible Christ's perfect consciousness of God.

the two Testaments together, the Law and the Gospel, is to destroy the essence of the second and only worthwhile member of this pair—the Gospel.

The key for Harnack is to be found in the words of Jesus in Matthew 11:27: "No one knows the Son except the Father, and no one knows the Father except the Son and any one to whom the Son chooses to reveal him." This saying was already cited by Marcion in its almost exactly identical form in Saint Luke's Gospel (10:22), and his use of it was challenged in his lifetime by the early ecclesiastical writer Tertullian. Tertullian points out that in its context in Saint Luke's Gospel we are assured that this revelation of the Father through the Son does not take place without vital Old Testament preparation. Just before it we have the Transfiguration episode where, it is true, the divine voice tells the disciples to listen to Jesus, not to Moses or Elijah. But how strange it is, comments Tertullian, that if Jesus came to destroy the Law and the prophets and not to fulfill them that he associates at this climactic moment with the representatives of that Law and those prophets! And Tertullian makes the beautiful reply to Marcion, "This is how he destroys them [i.e., how Christ 'destroys' the Law and the Prophets]: he irradiates them with his own glory."[2] It is fitting for the Creator, the God of the Old Testament, to manifest his Christ, says Tertullian: "In the company of those who announced his coming, to let him be seen with those to whom he had revealed himself, to let him speak with those who had spoken of him, to share his glory with those by whom he used to be called the Lord of Glory."[3]

[2] Tertullian, *Adversus Marcionem*, 4.22, cited in Watson, *Text and Truth*, p. 148.

[3] Ibid. Hans Urs von Balthasar remarks that any talk of Jews and Christians as heirs to a twofold covenant will "always hark back to the conversation held

Now Harnack does not regard the Transfiguration episode as authentic, but he does accept the historicity of the remark of Jesus to the disciples that follows the key saying in Saint Luke about only the Son knowing the Father. This "remark" is Jesus' exclamation to the disciples: "Blessed are the eyes which see what you see! For I tell you that many prophets and kings desired to see what you see, and did not see it, and to hear what you hear, and did not hear it" (Lk 10:23–24). As the contemporary exegete who coined the term "Neo-Marcionism", Francis Watson, has put it: "This can only mean that the knowledge of the Father through the Son is the fulfillment of what was proclaimed in the Old Testament, and not its replacement by a reality whose links with the Old Testament are purely accidental. . . . Marcion and Harnack are too hasty in their assumption that, whatever the prophets may have accepted, it bore no relation to what actually takes place in Jesus Christ."[4]

But how are we to respond to Harnack's allegation that much in the Old Testament concerns a tribal god, such that what is said there is unworthy of Jesus and his Father? For Tertullian, much that is in the Old Testament, and in the New Testament for that matter, can be described as (in his words) a "self-abasement unworthy of God". But this self-abasement unworthy of God is altogether necessary for man, and therefore "for this very reason [it is] worthy of God, because nothing is so worthy of God as the salvation of man".[5]

---

on the Mountain of the Transfiguration, when the Son of Man conversed with Moses and Elijah" since the "range" of that conversation "must . . . be such as to reckon with heaven and earth". *Martin Buber and Christianity: A Dialogue between Israel and the Church* (London, 1960), p. 7.

[4] Watson, *Text and Truth*, p. 149.

[5] Tertullian, *Adversus Marcionem*, 2.27, cited in Watson, *Text and Truth*, p. 151.

If the Divine Son accepted the humiliation of the Incarnation and Passion, why should he not condescend to commune with patriarchs and prophets and so prepare for the human existence that would one day be his? When refined people read the Old Testament, they think what distresses them is human crudity. But perhaps they are also disturbed by the "saving divine condescension finally disclosed in the incarnation of the Word".[6] Harnack knew Tertullian's treatise, but he disregarded its arguments. For him Protestantism should finish what Luther started. Luther freed the Church from the dead weight of tradition. His successors should now free it from the burden of the Old Testament, which should be deprived of its canonical status and declared simply a set of books that can sometimes be religiously helpful to read—which is what the Reformers said about the deuterocanonical books—Wisdom, Tobit, and the like—when they removed them from their official Bibles.

Bultmann

The third and last Neo-Marcionite to be mentioned is Bultmann. Bultmann's attitude toward the Old Testament follows from his belief that divine grace strikes men only as individuals, not as members of empirical historical communities such as the people of Israel. Of course the Church is also a community, although not an ethnic one, but for Bultmann she is simply that community where the message that divine grace strikes people as individuals is proclaimed —an empty space, so to speak, for the proclamation of this "word".

[6] Ibid.

Contrast Saint Paul's perspective in the Letter to the Romans, Hans Urs von Balthasar explains it:

> The spiritual children [Christians] are grafted into the root that they may share in the living sap of the holy olive tree, but not in such a manner as to bypass the bodily Israel since "God hath not cast away his people, whom he foreknew" (11:2), and because "the gifts and the calling of God are without repentance" (11:29), but so as to become part of that indivisible and living whole which grows naturally, *kata physin* (11:24), starting from the patriarchal root and leading into the Israel of the New Testament. The Gentile Christians are admonished to be humble, for by comparison with that natural development they have been engrafted "against nature", *para physin.*[7]

And as if answering Bultmann, von Balthasar continues: "Although the word of God never coincides with human history, nevertheless it reveals its sovereignty—its judgment and its grace—in the depths of that history. It is never an abstract word addressed to man, but the articulation of the covenanted union between God and man."[8]

Bultmann considers appeals to the fulfillment of prophecy or the continuity of saving history in Israel and the Church to be not only irrelevant but misleading and therefore dangerous. They distract attention from the individual's need to place himself before the divine word, which judges and saves. The only point Bultmann can see to the Old Testament is that it can bring people to realize they are entangled in sin, caught up in self-assertion and pride. In that sense —and that sense alone—it prepares them for the Gospel. But to Bultmann's mind the same service can be performed

---

[7] Von Balthasar, *Martin Buber and Christianity*, pp. 18–19.

[8] Ibid., p. 21.

equally well if not better by, say, Greek tragedy or modern existentialist philosophy.[9] The Old Testament, so Bultmann thinks, ends badly as well. So far as history is concerned, it finishes up in the unattractive priestly theocracy described in the books of Ezra and Nehemiah. (Of course, as a Protestant, Bultmann does not include the Books of Maccabees in the canon.) Bultmann calls this last stage of the sacred people a "miscarriage of history" and feels it should serve as a suitable warning to all those who try to identify divine revelation with any empirical reality such as a holy people or sacred institution. But to this an answer can be made. The Old Testament's account of *Heilsgeschichte*, saving history, ends with a priestly theocracy which is only, in Bultmann's words, "absurd" and "grotesque" because in the words of the prophet Malachi the priests "have corrupted the covenant of Levi" (Mal 2:8). So far as prophetic judgments on history are concerned, the Old Testament

> ends where the New Testament begins, with the promise that, before the great and terrible day of the Lord, Elijah will come to turn the hearts of fathers to their children and the hearts of children to their fathers—the closing two verses of Malachi, 4:5 and 6, taken up in all three Synoptic Gospels.
>
> From a Christian perspective, the function of Old Testament *Heilsgeschichte* is . . . to prepare the way of the Lord. This history could only be said to have "miscarried" if it had failed to provide the matrix within which Jesus was nurtured and out of which he came forth to preach peace to those who were far off and those who were near, so that Gentile and Jew together should gain access in one Spirit to the Father (Eph 2:17–18).[10]

[9] Watson, *Text and Truth*, pp. 161–62.
[10] Ibid., p. 165.

But the Old Testament did *not* fail to provide this matrix, as succeeding events in the New Testament prove.

A Better Way

As the great Old Testament scholar Gerhard von Rad shows —and he is an encouraging example of how it is possible, even in Protestant faculties of divinity, to escape the snares of Neo-Marcionism—the structure of the two Testaments is essentially one of promise and fulfillment.[11] So when Saint Peter preaches his first sermon at the first Pentecost, a sermon reproduced in the second chapter of Acts, he rightly takes it for granted that the life, death, and Resurrection of Jesus must be understood in the light of the Old Testament, just as in turn the true scope and bearings of the Old Testament now, with the events of the Incarnation and the paschal mystery, come to light for the first time. As Francis Watson, again, writes: "The risen Jesus sends his apostles to proclaim to all nations the history of his own life, death and resurrection in its unity as God's definitive act for the salvation of humankind. Yet that history is neither self-contained nor self-explanatory; it is to be understood in the light of those sacred writings that it retrospectively reconstitutes as Old Testament."[12]

[11] G. von Rad, *Old Testament Theology*, vol. 2 (Edinburgh and London, 1965); also two essays: "Grundprobleme einer biblischen Theologie des Alten Testaments", *Theologische Literatur Zeitschrift* 68 (1943): pp. 225–34, and "Typologische Auslegung des Alten Testaments", *Evangelische Theologie* 12 (1952): 17–33, of which an English translation appears in C. Westermann, ed., *Essays on Old Testament Hermeneutics* (Richmond, 1963), pp. 17–39. We shall return to von Rad's work when looking at the significance of typology.

[12] Watson, "Old Testament Theology as a Christian Theological Enterprise", in *Text and Truth*, p. 183.

So the New Testament needs the Old: one can only make sense of the fulfillment in the light of the promise. But reciprocally, on the promise-fulfillment schema, the Old Testament needs the New: one can only make sense of the promise in the light of the fulfillment. Cardinal Joseph Ratzinger (now Pope Benedict XVI) remarks:

> For the Christian, the Old Testament represents, in its total-ity, an advance towards Christ; only when it attains to him does its real meaning, which was gradually hinted at, become clear. Thus every individual part derives its meaning from the whole, and the whole derives its meaning from its end —from Christ. Hence we only interpret an individual text correctly (as the fathers of the Church recognized and as the faith of the Church in every age has recognized) when we see it as a way that is leading us ever forward, when we see in the text where this way is tending and what its inner direc-tion is.[13]

Evidently, tracing what I call the "pattern of revelation" is going to be very important.

[13] J. Ratzinger, *In the Beginning: A Catholic Understanding of the Story of Cre-ation and the Fall* (Huntington, Ind., 1990; 1995), pp. 9–10.

5

THE PATTERN OF REVELATION DISPLAYED: THE MESSIANIC HOPE, BROADLY CONCEIVED

Introduction

If we can find the theme giving the two Testaments their unity, then that theme can be called, surely, the central theme of the Bible. And in fact it is not far to seek. It is *the messianic hope*, not taken *narrowly*, as is often the case, but when seen in its broadest perspective, its full diversity of manifestations.[1] That is not the only Old Testament theme of concern to New Testament Christians, not the only feature of the Old Testament revelation that has entered into the doctrine of the Church. In later presentations, we shall be looking at a couple more such themes that seem especially important to my case—indeed, so important they can be called presuppositions of the pattern we shall find. But if there is a pattern to revelation, then in all likelihood that pattern has a central, recurring motif, around which other

[1] A. G. Hebert, *The Throne of David: A Study of the Fulfilment of the Old Testament in Jesus Christ and His Church* (London, 1941), p. 39. For the life and work of Gabriel Hebert (1886–1963), see C. Irvine, *Worship, Church and Society: An Exposition of the Work of Arthur Gabriel Hebert* (to mark the Centenary of the Society of the Sacred Mission [Kelham] of which he was a member) (Norwich, 1993), pp. 3–21. Curiously, the account of Hebert's death is postponed till the chapter entitled "Ecumenism and Worship", pp. 83–84.

motifs can be arranged—as is the way with patterns. And that claim entered, the suggestion is that "messianic hope" —as I say, broadly defined—is it.

I proposed at the outset of this book that the Old Testament—indeed, we could say the Bible as a whole—is the revelation of the greater and greater promises of God. It is also concerned with the realization of those promises, giving them cash value. In the words of the Catholic-minded, Anglican biblical theologian Gabriel Hebert, whose work I shall be using in this chapter and the next: "Old Israel, believing in Yahweh and confessing that He has chosen her to be His People, looks forward to a time when He will have completed the Purpose which He has taken in hand; this will be the accomplishment of what He intended when He created man. The Christian Gospel is the announcement that the time is fulfilled and the promised Reign of God has arrived."[2]

Study of the messianic hope in the Old Testament should not be restricted to those passages that speak particularly of a personal Messiah, the Son of David. Certainly those are important and will be mentioned first. But the messianic hope includes a great number of subthemes as well. We can list them: not just the Son of David but also the gift of a New Spirit, Paradise restored, homecoming to Mount Zion, the remnant, the Bride of the Lord, the New Covenant, the restored sanctuary, the Servant of the Lord. All of these contribute to the messianic idea as we find that fully embodied, and realized, in Christ and the Church. When considered within the terms of the Old Testament taken by itself, these subthemes are rather like pieces of a jigsaw puzzle that

[2] Hebert, *Throne of David*, p. 39.

doesn't quite add up because something is missing. If we approach the Old Testament in abstraction from the New, they do not form a unity. What the prophets see is a variety of partial visions, "as men straining their eyes to discern the outlines of God's future reign and the completion of His gracious purpose".[3] "Israel in fact remains expecting an indefinite future, and, while its whole structure is messianic, it is not the Messiah. That is the great mystery which, because it is unfathomable, confers upon the existence of Israel a strange and awe-inspiring character."[4]

That incompleteness or lack of total convergence is readily recognized by Saint Peter in his first Letter, where we read:

> With the hope of this coming salvation the prophets wrestled, peering into the future to discern the outlines of that which has come to you as the Gospel-message, and endeavouring to understand the time and manner of the fulfillment of the mysterious things which the Spirit of the Messiah, when that spoke in them, was pointing to when it spoke of the future sufferings of the Messiah and the glory that should be won thereby.
>
> They knew that they would not see these hopes realized in their life-time, but that they were for a future generation— for you, who have heard of the fulfillment of them on the lips of those who brought to you the Gospel, with divinely-given wisdom to interpret its meaning (1:10–12).[5]

---

[3] Ibid., p. 40.

[4] Von Balthasar, *Martin Buber and Christianity*, p. 27. Von Balthasar comments later in this study, "Israel's innermost nature implies a Christology", ibid., p. 78.

[5] I cite 1 Peter here in Hebert's own translation.

The Son of David

The easiest place to begin an account of this central theme of
the Testament is with the expectation of a Davidic king who
will realize on a scale hitherto unconceived the hopes once
vested in David himself—in the covenant with David, which
was, in the minds of many people in the southern kingdom,
the instrument whereby the more ancient and comprehensive covenant with Abraham was to be effected.

What we are dealing with is a person who sums up in himself the characteristics of God's messianic reign. The original promise to David is given in 2 Samuel: "When your
days are fulfilled and you lie down with your fathers, I will
raise up your offspring after you, who shall come forth from
your body, and I will establish his kingdom. He shall build
a house for my name, and I will establish the throne of his
kingdom for ever" (7:12–13).

The establishment of a covenant with David is reflected
in a fully messianic sense in some of the psalms ascribed to
him, notably Psalm 89, where we read of the Davidic king:

> He shall cry to me, "Thou art my Father,
>   my God, and the Rock of my salvation."
> And I will make him the first-born,
>   the highest of the kings of the earth. . . .
> Once for all I have sworn by my holiness;
>   I will not lie to David.
> His line shall endure for ever,
>   his throne as long as the sun before me.
>
> (Psalm 89:26–27, 35–36)

And linking up with these promises, Psalm 132 finds a special place in the messianic hope for the city of Zion, Jerusalem, the place of the throne of David and the sanctuary where the name of God was sent to dwell, and which as a consequence his glory overshadowed.

> For the LORD has chosen Zion;
>   he has desired it for his habitation:
> "This is my resting place for ever;
>   here will I dwell, for I have desired it.
> I will abundantly bless her provisions;
>   I will satisfy her poor with bread.
> Her priests I will clothe with salvation
>   and her saints will shout for joy."
>
> (Ps 132:13–16)

Bewilderment followed the failure of the original reign of David to sustain the expectations attached to it when the kingdom split into two after Solomon, traditional enemies like Moab and Edom regained their independence (2 Kings 3 and 8:20), Assyrian aggression brought disaster on the north, and a similar fate hung over the south. Psalm 80 testifies to this stupefaction. If ruin and destruction lie ahead, then what was the point of the Exodus in the first place?

> Thou didst bring a vine out of Egypt;
>   thou didst drive out the nations and plant it.
> Thou didst clear the ground for it;
>   it took deep root and filled the land.
> The mountains were covered with its shade,
>   the mighty cedars with its branches;
> it sent out its branches to the sea,
>   and its shoots to the River.
> Why then hast thou broken down its walls,
>   so that all who pass along the way pluck its fruit?
>
> (Ps 80:8–12)

The answer given by the eighth-century prophets to this question is clear. The people are being punished for their sins: sins of the paganizing of worship by turning to the gods of Canaan, Baal, and Astarte, of darker superstitions like child sacrifice too, and sins of the oppression of the poor, especially since the rise of a money economy put small farmers in the power of the landowners.

In these unpropitious conditions Isaiah declares that God's promises to David will indeed, despite all appearances, be fulfilled. After a terrible chastisement of which only a remnant will survive, God purposes to send a Davidic king who will rule in righteousness. What is at stake is a new governance, which restores the God-directed rule of the people under Moses' leadership in the desert, but this time it will be centered on Jerusalem, as the opening chapter of the Isaian anthology tells us:

> And I will restore your judges as at the first,
>   and your counselors as at the beginning.
> Afterward you shall be called the city of righteousness,
>   the faithful city (Is 1:26).

It is only later in the book, at 7:14, that we hear of the birth of a prince, and in chapter 9 that we have a full encomium on him:

> For to us a child is born,
>   to us a son is given;
> and the government will be upon his shoulder,
>   and his name will be called
> "Wonderful Counsellor, Mighty God,
>   Everlasting Father, Prince of Peace."
> Of the increase of his government and of peace,
>   there will be no end,

> upon the throne of David, and over his kingdom,
>   to establish it, and to uphold it
> with justice and with righteousness
>   from this time forth and for evermore.
> The zeal of the LORD of hosts will do this.

(Is 9:6–7)

It is important to guard against a merely political construal of this oracle. The oracles found in chapter 11 of the book of Isaiah serve this purpose. They adumbrate two further subthemes: the gift of a New Spirit and the restoration of Paradise.

The Gift of a New Spirit

First, then, the Spirit of the Lord will be poured out with a lavishness hitherto unheard of on the messianic King. Isaiah returns to his subject, the Son of David, and then amplifies it by reference to that Spirit:

> There shall come forth a shoot
>   from the stump of Jesse,
>   and a branch shall grow out of his roots.
> And the Spirit of the LORD shall rest upon him,
>   the spirit of wisdom and understanding,
>   the spirit of counsel and might,
>   the spirit of knowledge and the fear of the LORD,
> And his delight shall be in the fear of the LORD.

(Is 11:1–2)

That fear, we recall, is the guiding motivation of Old Testament wisdom.

In Isaiah, the messianic hope for a new heart and a new spirit through an outpouring of the Spirit of the Lord is effectively confined to the king. It is on the royal Child that the seven gifts of the Holy Spirit are to be outpoured. So far as the people are concerned, Isaiah thinks rather of a process of purging unworthy citizens, getting rid of the dross and leaving the gold of what he calls those have "been recorded for life in Jerusalem" (4:3b). But with Jeremiah an inward change of the whole people is the essence of the New Covenant the Lord will make in place of the Old. Chapter 31 of his book makes that plain:

> This is the covenant which I will make with the house of Israel after those days, says the LORD: I will put my law within them, and I will write it upon their hearts; and I will be their God, and they shall be my people. And no longer shall each man teach his neighbor and each his brother, saying, "Know the Lord," for they shall all know me, from the least of them to the greatest, says the LORD; for I will forgive their iniquity, and I will remember their sin no more (Jer 31:33–34).

The prophet Ezekiel goes deeper still, to the inner cleansing that belongs to the heart of the New Testament concept of repentance, and the gift of a new heart and a new spirit to the people as a whole.

> For I will take you from the nations, and gather you from all the countries, and bring you into your own land. I will sprinkle clean water upon you, and you shall be clean from all your uncleannesses, and from all your idols I will cleanse you. A new heart I will give you, and a new spirit I will put within you; and I will take out of your flesh the heart of stone and give you a heart of flesh. And I will put my spirit within you, and cause you to walk in my statutes and be careful to observe my ordinances. You shall dwell in the land which I gave to your fathers; and you shall be my people, and I will be your God (Ezek 36:24–28).

In the vision of the dry bones, which follows this chapter of Ezekiel, when the prophet sees the Lord cover with flesh the bones of the scattered and hopeless house of Israel, and animate them by his Spirit, the consequences expected are not only political—a return to the Land and the reunion of the broken halves of the people, Israel and Judah. Those consequences are also spiritual—a renewed faithfulness to the Lord, to walk in his statutes, the covenant provisions of the Torah, and to practice them from the heart.

A similar outpouring of the Spirit on the whole people is predicted by Joel, but in his case the fruits of the Spirit are more in the intellectual order than the moral. They are expansion of insight—both qualitatively and quantitatively.

> And it shall come to pass afterward,
>> that I will pour out my spirit on all flesh;
> your sons and your daughters shall prophesy,
>> your old men shall dream dreams,
>> and your young men shall see visions.
> Even upon the menservants and maidservants
>> in those days I will pour out my spirit.
>
> (Joel 2:28–29)

So this is a hope for a renewed and enhanced outpouring of the Spirit of God as in the Pentateuch that Spirit had fallen upon Moses and Aaron and the elders at Sinai, and then, in "The Former Prophets", after the entry into the Land, had also affected the "judges" in the book of that name.

But we can notice how in the book of the principal prophet of the new spirit, Ezekiel, this expectation of a new coming of the Spirit does not render superfluous the simultaneous coming of a Son of David who will govern the people in the name of God the Good Shepherd. In Ezekiel 34, when the shepherds of Israel are condemned for neglecting the pastoral care of the people, we find a prophecy both that in the future the Lord himself will be their Shepherd, and that he will appoint an under-shepherd to be as it were his human instrument. And who will this under-shepherd be if not the perfect Davidide king? "And I will set up over them one shepherd, my servant David, and he shall feed them: he shall feed them and be their shepherd. And I, the LORD, will be their God, and my servant David shall be prince among them; I, the LORD, have spoken" (34:23–24).

Paradise Restored

To return to the oracles of Isaiah that first prophesy the coming of a Savior-King: I said that what saves them from any merely naturalistic coloring is partly the prediction that the Lord's Spirit will be given to the messianic Child with unheard-of fullness (that we have now looked at) and partly also the connection Isaiah makes between the future king and the restoration of Paradise. For the expectation of a restoration of Paradise is another of the subthemes expressing the messianic hope, the chief common theme of the two Testaments, Old and New. It is another piece in the jigsaw puzzle to which the realities of the New Testament will add what are missing pieces and enable us to see the whole picture.

Isaiah combines the promise of a redeemed politics with imagery from a much older source. Certainly the Son of David will rule justly:

> With righteousness he shall judge the poor,
>   and decide with equity for the meek of the earth;
> and he shall smite the earth with the rod of his mouth,
>   and with the breath of his lips he shall slay the wicked.

Righteousness shall be the girdle of his waist,
    and faithfulness the girdle of his loins.

(Is 11:4-5)

But without a break, the prophet turns to the context and consequence of the advent of the wondrous Child, and this is, in imagery borrowed not so much directly from Genesis 2 as from the ancient Near Eastern folklore that underlies the Garden of Eden story, the return of Paradise to the world.

The wolf shall dwell with the lamb,
    and the leopard lie down with the kid,
and the calf and the lion and the fatling together,
    and a little child shall lead them. . . .
They shall not hurt or destroy
    in all my holy mountain;
for the earth shall be full of the knowledge of
      the LORD
    as the waters cover the sea.

(Is 11:6, 9)

This ruler, though he may need to smite in order to save, is actually the Prince of Peace. For the prophet Zechariah, he will come to Jerusalem not riding on horse or chariot, regarded as the proper vehicles of kings from Solomon's time onward, but riding rather on an ass.

Rejoice greatly, O daughter of Zion!
    Shout aloud, O daughter of Jerusalem!
Lo, your king comes to you;
    triumphant and victorious is he,
humble and riding on an ass,
    on a colt the foal of an ass.
I will cut off the chariot from Ephraim
    and the war horse from Jerusalem;
and the battle bow shall be cut off,
    and he shall command peace to the nations;

> his dominion shall be from sea to sea,
>> and from the River to the ends of the earth.
>>> (Zech 9:9–10)

Cosmic peace, supernatural healing, and previously unheard-of fruitfulness for the earth are the main features, indeed, of the restored Paradise expected in the prophetic tradition. And to look ahead to the New Testament fulfillment:

> The idea of Paradise Restored fills an important place in the New Testament and in the Christian scheme. There is an obvious rightness in the thought that the Restoration of all things through the Saviour of mankind should bring with it the accomplishment of the original plan of man's creation. Thus the New Testament speaks of the Messiah as the Second Adam; of redeemed humanity as the Second Eve, the Church his Bride; of man's deliverance from sin as the recovery of a childlike innocence; and of a new heaven and a new earth different from the present order of things much as the blessedness of Eden was different from man's condition after the Fall. Later theology has loved to dwell on the thought that part of the work of Grace is to restore man's life to the condition that is truly natural to it, even in this world; while at the same time it is only in a future paradisal world that man's full beatitude can be attained.[6]

In Psalm 95, the people are warned not to harden their hearts as the Israelites did of old in the desert when they provoked God's wrath; therefore, we read, "I swore in my anger, that they should not enter my rest" (v. 11). But the writer to the Hebrews points out that as the recipients of this psalm were already in the Promised Land, the "rest" in question cannot be simply the Land of Palestine. The psalmist must be thinking of the Sabbath rest of the messianic king-

---

[6] Hebert, *Throne of David*, pp. 47–48.

dom. As Hebrews puts it: "For if Joshua had given them rest, God would not speak later of another day. ["O that today, you would hearken to his voice! Harden not your hearts", Ps 95:7-8]. So then, there remains a sabbath rest for the people of God; for whoever enters God's rest also ceases from his labors as God did from his" (4:8-10). Entering into God's rest *is* a restoration of Paradise. This will be a major preoccupation of our Lord in his public ministry, in his reinterpretation of the Sabbath.

Homecoming to Mount Zion

The Isaiah oracle with which we began our examination of the messianic hope in the larger sense as hope for a restored creation included the words "They shall not hurt or destroy in all my holy mountain", and this brings us to another piece of the puzzle, the role of Mount Zion in the promises to Israel. As has been said, there is a sense in which the whole Bible, both Old and New Testaments, is an account of how the word "Jerusalem" came to have its mystical meaning. The seat of David's throne and the place of the sanctuary, Jerusalem was in both respects the center of Israel's unity.

> Psalmists and prophets assigned to it a central place in their delineations of the Messianic Hope: it was to them the centre of the national unity of Israel, and also the place to which the Gentiles would come, seeking Israel's God. When the Messiah came, it was the place toward which the action of His Ministry moved, as all the gospels testify; there it was that He died and rose from the dead, and there His Church was founded. Ever since, it has stood in the Church's liturgy and in her thought partly for the Church on earth as the New Israel, but more for the Church eternal in the heavens, and the Church made perfect in the World-to-come: the Jerusalem

which is above and is free, the heavenly Jerusalem, the Bride, the Lamb's Wife, the City which hath foundations.[7]

Isaiah has an extraordinary notion, which could be considered a first intuition, in symbolic language, of this marvelous future. In an oracle in chapter 2 of his book, he holds that the Gentiles will stream up to a Mount Zion that has now been placed on the roof of the world.

> It shall come to pass in the latter days
>   that the mountain of the house of the LORD
> shall be established as the highest of the mountains,
>   and shall be raised above the hills;
> and all the nations shall flow to it (Is 2:2).

Psalm 48 has the same idea, expressed in the language of a fabulous geography: a mountain in the uttermost north that can in principle be seen from all over the world.

> Great is the LORD and greatly to be praised
>   in the city of our God!
> His holy mountain, beautiful in elevation,
>   is the joy of all the earth,
> Mount Zion, in the far north,
>   the city of the great King (Ps 48:1–2).

In the Book of Zechariah, the future recognition of the transcendence of Jerusalem is expressed in terms of miraculous geological changes. In Zechariah 14:10–11, we find the curious notion that the mountainous country of Judea, from a point six miles north of the city to somewhere around thirty-five miles southwest, is to sink to the level of the Dead Sea, which, with Jerusalem retaining its normal elevation, would give the city a height of nearly four thousand feet above the surrounding countryside. From this elevated

[7] Ibid., p. 38.

navel of the earth, living waters will then flow out to the east and to the west, a symbol of universal grace.

The presupposition of these prophecies is, of course, that Zion is indeed the place of the throne of David and also, and even more importantly, the central sanctuary of Israel. As we have seen, the Mosaic Torah prescribes such a central sanctuary, originally probably meant to be on Mount Ebal, which overshadows the sites of both Shechem and Gilgal, and then, in the age of Samuel, at Shiloh. But from the time of King Josiah in the early seventh century, there was in Judah the only really strenuous attempt to realize the principle of the single sanctuary, this time located at Jerusalem with, in its holiest place, the Ark, the desert palladium where the Lord's glory dwelt above the figures of the cherubim. In the Books of Kings, the Deuteronomic Historian rejects the policy of the northern kingdom of establishing its own shrines at Bethel and Dan, not only because of anxiety over the kind of sacred images used in those places but also because their very creation was implicitly schismatic. These alternative centers were undermining the worshipping unity of the holy people. Already in Solomon's times, regular pilgrimages to Jerusalem were being mounted from all over the country. "And she remained the centre; longed for in her desolation during the period of the captivity, 'by the waters of Babylon', she became more and more after the Return the centre and the gathering-point, calling forth the love and longing to which the Gradual Psalms [or "Psalms of Ascent"] testify."[8] A good example is found in Psalm 122.

> I was glad when they said to me,
> "Let us go to the house of the Lord!"

[8] Ibid., p. 52.

> Our feet have been standing
>   within your gates, O Jerusalem!
> Jerusalem, built as a city
>   which is bound firmly together,
> to which the tribes go up,
>   the tribes of the LORD,
> as was decreed for Israel,
>   to give thanks to the name of the LORD.
>
>   (Ps 122:1–4)

Israel's missionary vocation takes form as the plan of gathering together first Israelites and then Gentiles to the place that will be acknowledged as the spiritual center of mankind. In Zechariah 8 we read:

> Many peoples and strong nations shall come to seek the LORD of hosts in Jerusalem, and to entreat the favor of the LORD. Thus says the LORD of hosts: In those days ten men from the nations of every tongue shall take hold of the robe of a Jew, saying, "Let us go with you, for we have heard that God is with you" (Zech 8:22–23).

In the messianic fulfillment, the concept of a spiritual center to which all human beings will be drawn is retained, albeit also transformed.

The Bride

If Zion can be spoken of in nuptial imagery—and she can, as we read in an oracle in chapter 62 of the book of Isaiah: "as the bridegroom rejoices over the bride, / so shall your God rejoice over you" (v. 5b)—this is because Israel herself is seen as the Bride or Wife of the Lord. And this is the next piece in the puzzle. It is Hosea who sees Israel as the faithless Bride whom the Lord will "allure" again into the wilderness, there to "speak tenderly to her" so that "she shall answer in the days of her youth, / as at the time when she came out of the land of Egypt" (2:14, 15b). That is fitting for the prophet of the divine mercy, but Jeremiah, who uses the same image and also proclaims that God will "not be angry for ever" (3:12b), knows of the "new heart and new spirit" (Ezek 36:26) required for any abiding covenant relationship between the people and its Lord.

> You have played the harlot with many lovers;
>   and would you return to me? says the LORD.
>
> (Jer 3:1b)

Ezekiel has the most elaborate deployment of the nuptial theology, which occupies the whole of chapter 16. But he is also the most severe: all the House of Israel's covenant blessings will be taken away until the people repent and return again. The Bride theme only fully becomes a subtheme of the messianic hope, accordingly, in the last chapters of the Book of Isaiah, where the prophet foresees a new adorning of a bridal Israel who then proceeds to become the spiritual mother of many nations, the Church.

> I will greatly rejoice in the LORD,
>   my soul shall exult in my God;
> for he has clothed me with the garments of salvation,
>   he has covered me with the robe of righteousness,
> as a bridegroom decks himself with a garland,
>   and as a bride adorns herself with her jewels. . . .
> The nations shall see your vindication,
>   and all the kings your glory;
> and you shall be called by a new name
>   which the mouth of the Lord will give.
>
> (Is 61:10; 62:2)

The Remnant

It is, however, a recurring feature of the "anthology" we call the Book of Isaiah that these prophecies concern only a remnant of the people. The eighth-century prophets are convinced that the purging of the people by and for the day of the Lord—the fulfillment of Israel—will be exceedingly severe. Amos says:

> Woe to you who desire the day of the LORD!
>   Why would you have the day of the LORD?
> It is darkness and not light (Amos 5:18).

He compares what will be left of Israel to two legs of a sheep, or even worse, just a piece of an ear, which the shepherd rescues from a marauding lion. The remnant theme matters so much to Isaiah that he calls his son after it (7:3; 10:20–22), and the purging is to be radical, "like a terebinth or an oak, whose stump remains standing when it is felled" (6:13). Jeremiah sees it as his mission to watch over the remnant in the hour of its passion, and Ezekiel declares that when the city falls the remnant will be saved. In his vision, a man with an inkhorn goes through the city and puts a mark on the foreheads of all who sigh for the abominations done in it. When the slaughter begins, none of them is touched (9:2–6). The Psalter presents the remnant as "the poor of the Lord", forming as it were a little church within the wider assembly of Israel, a larger entity regarded as worldly and indifferent, indeed at times paganizing and persecuting. Probably, in the Son of Man prophecy in the Book of Daniel, "the saints of the Most High", with whom the transcendent yet human figure of the Son of Man is identified, are also a reflection of the remnant doctrine. The remnant persevere, struggle, and are ultimately, by the grace of God, victorious. So when the

Messiah finally comes, it is a remnant who believe in him, as Saint Paul attests in the Letter to the Romans, where he compares the situation of the infant Church with the seven thousand righteous men in the time of Elijah who did not bow the knee to Baal. As Paul writes in Romans: "So too at the present time there is a remnant, chosen by grace" (11:5). The Messiah comes as Savior and Judge, and both his salvation and his judgment are continuously operative within the Church: "I am the true vine, and my Father is the vinedresser. Every branch of mine that bears no fruit, he takes away, and every branch that does bear fruit he prunes, that it may bear more fruit" (Jn 15:1–2).

The Servant of the Lord

The most sublime expression of the remnant doctrine is found in the prophecies of the Servant of Yahweh found in chapters 42 and 49 to 52 of the Book of Isaiah.

> Behold my servant, whom I uphold,
>   my chosen, in whom my soul delights;
> I have put my Spirit upon him,
>   he will bring forth judgment to the Gentiles.
>
>   (Is 42:1, translation slightly altered)

The Servant is the pattern of what God means Israel to be. He is shown as the sufferer and martyr, "bruised for our iniquities" (53:5) say the people, his life a sacrifice, but his martyrdom leading through to triumph and peace. Now, as has been said: "These poems were not reckoned by the Jews as Messianic. No one dared to think of the Messiah as suffering and dying, till He Himself [Jesus] did so. It is

He who broadens out the Messianic Idea, till it is seen to gather up in itself all Old Testament theology."[9]

Bringing the Pieces Together

We can think of this process as including the testimony of all the individual witnesses in whom in the Parable of the Vineyard in Saint Mark's Gospel Jesus sees that "principle of victory-through-suffering which finds its supreme exemplification in His own passion",[10]—in other words as including all righteous prophets and kings. We can think of it as including too the experience of Israel, from the Exile onward, as the "martyr-nation", not least in the time of the Maccabees. And we can think, once again, of the cult of Israel down the centuries, the offering of the levitical sacrifices, which, with their ritual of blood-shedding and death, pointed the same way—to the redemptive meaning of suffering. All these things are, in the broadest sense, messianic. And yet, in Hebert's words:

> their Messianic significance could not come to light till it was interpreted by the creative wisdom of Him who in "fulfilling" it, gathered it all into one, at the central point in the history of the world. The Biblical prophecies of the Messiah and His Kingdom gain immensely in importance and interest after the Messiah has come, because they are visions of the theological meaning of His Coming, and of the Divine Reign, and of the completion of the Divine Purpose for Israel. It is in the light of the prophecies that He and His Office are to be understood; they mark out beforehand the place He is to fill.[11]

[9] Ibid., p. 69.
[10] Ibid.
[11] Ibid., pp. 70, 72.

In the *Confessions*, when Augustine writes to Saint Ambrose in Milan telling him of his desire to receive baptism as a Catholic Christian, what does Ambrose do? He tells him to go away and read the prophet Isaiah.[12] In Frank Sheed's translation: "In a letter I told Your bishop, the holy Ambrose, of my past errors and my present purpose, that he might advise me which of Your Scriptures I should especially read to prepare me and make me more fit to receive so great a grace. He told me to read Isaias the prophet, I imagine because he more clearly foretells the gospel and the calling of the gentiles than the other Old Testament writers."[13] "More clearly"—well, each prophet's vision was imperfect and incomplete. As the writer to the Hebrews says, "In many and various ways God spoke of old to our fathers through the prophets" (1:1). Yet despite this fragmentariness, as Hebert movingly declares: "The imperfections are all corrected in Him, and the incompletenesses do not matter when the texts are used of Him; all the broken lights have their place in the radiance of the Light of the World."[14] Or, as Hebert puts it elsewhere, slightly more soberly: "How it was all to work out in detail could not be known till He came who alone could fit the various elements together, being Himself the Wisdom of God."[15] (That is very much the view Hans Urs von Balthasar takes of the relation between the two Testaments likewise.)

In the next section, we must look at the other point the Book of Isaiah raised in the mind of Saint Augustine: how that book foretold not only the Gospel but also "the calling of the Gentiles".

[12] Augustine, *Confessions*, 9.5.

[13] F. J. Sheed, trans., *The Confessions of St Augustine* (London, 1944), pp. 150–51.

[14] Hebert, *Throne of David*, p. 72.

[15] A. G. Hebert, *The Authority of the Old Testament* (London, 1947), p. 69.

The other aspect of the pattern is Israel's universal mission and her simultaneous glory in it and failure at it. A consideration of this will form, for reasons that should become clear as we proceed, the immediate preamble to the coming of the Messiah as Jesus Christ and the fulfillment of the promises. "If the Messianic Idea is rightly defined as the completion of the Purpose which God took in hand when He chose Israel to be His People, then the extension of the faith of Israel to all the nations of the world is part of the Messianic Hope."[16]

But *that* part of the hope—the extension of the faith of Israel to all the nations of the world—is more than somewhat problematic. Throughout the Old Testament, albeit with very varying degrees of clearness, it is recognized that Israel has been given a universal mission. And yet, so things turn out, she is "unable to make more than a faint movement toward fulfilling it till the Messiah comes".[17] Saint Paul gives us a very clear statement of how Israel knew her significance to be universal when he writes in the Letter to the Galatians: "The scripture, foreseeing that God would justify the Gentiles by faith, preached the Gospel beforehand to Abraham, saying, 'In you shall all the nations be blessed'" (Gal 3:8).

It has been pointed out that Israel's sense of her universal vocation was closely bound up with her consciousness of her own exclusiveness. Exclusiveness and universality were coexistent principles in Israel, just as they would be later (and for the same reasons) for the Catholic Church. To link

[16] Hebert, *Throne of David*, p. 73.
[17] Ibid.

exclusivity and universality seems paradoxical, but really it is not so. It is because Israel was aware that her God was different in kind from all the other deities people worship that she was compelled to guard her faith and religious practice from contamination by extraneous pagan influence. And by the very same token she came to understand that such a faith in the true Maker of all mankind must finally be available for all men. The two dimensions—exclusivity/universality—belong together.

The conflict of Israel with paganizing tendencies runs throughout the whole of the preexilic history. In the Deuteronomic version of the Torah, it is emphasized that, upon arrival in the Land, the Israelites must guard their separateness for fear that their religion should become paganized (cf. Deut 4:33–38). Some of the, to later sensibility, most distressing aspects of the Mosaic legislation, such as the need to show no mercy in battle with the inhabitants of Canaan, have their setting in life here. The contrast of this with Deuteronomy's emphasis on the merciful goodness of the Lord and the humane dealings that merciful goodness painfully requires of each of the people with his neighbor is very marked. But it must be remembered that, first, the depravity of some at least of the pagan religious practices—which could include child sacrifice—was very great, and secondly, and more widely, that the entire divine plan for realizing the fulfillment of the Creator's intention for mankind turned on Israel's fidelity to her original call. When Hosea complains the Land has forsaken the Lord and gone after the Baalim, the gods of Canaan (Hos 2:2–13), or Solomon admits polytheism into Jerusalem itself by building shrines for the gods of his foreign wives (1 Kings 11:1–8), or Elijah campaigns against the prophets of the Tyrian Baal encouraged by queen Jezebel, in the struggle that reaches its climax in the sacrifice on Mount

Carmel (1 Kings 18), it is, not just humanly speaking but in the providence of God, the entire divine design that is at stake. The Exile brings its own temptations to syncretism or apostasy, as Jeremiah reminds his readers in the context of idol-worship, "Learn not the way of the nations . . . for the customs of the peoples are false" (10:2).

Now it is out of this exclusiveness of Israel that her missionary vocation arises. At least some representatives of foreign peoples sense that Israel's religion has a reality others have not. In the Second Book of Kings, Naaman the Syrian, healed of leprosy by Elisha, promises in future to sacrifice to the Lord alone (5:17); an oracle in Isaiah seems to speak of ambassadors with a religious quest from Ethiopia, "a people tall and smooth, . . . whose land the rivers divide" (18:7); and centuries later, in our Lord's day, according to Luke's Gospel a Roman centurion builds the Jews a synagogue (7:5), while in the second part of Saint Luke's work, the Acts of the Apostles, we hear of another centurion, Cornelius, who liberally gives alms to needy Jews and prays constantly to God (10:2). These are examples, presumably, of what the prophet Zechariah had in mind in chapter 8 of his book: "Thus says the LORD of hosts: Peoples shall yet come, even the inhabitants of many cities; the inhabitants of one city shall go to another, saying, 'Let us go at once to entreat the favor of the LORD, and to seek the LORD of hosts; I am going'" (Zech 8:20).

This is predictable. First, the knowledge of the Lord must from the inner necessity of the case become universal, since he *is* the Lord, the Maker of heaven and earth. This is the conviction of the author of, for example, Psalm 96:

> For all the gods of the peoples are idols;
> but the LORD made the heavens. . . .

> [So] ascribe to the LORD, O families of peoples,
>   ascribe to the LORD glory and strength!
> Ascribe to the LORD the glory due his name;
>   bring an offering and come into his courts!
> Worship the LORD in holy array;
>   tremble before him, all the earth!
> Say among the nations, "The LORD reigns!"
>
> (Ps 96:5, 7–10a)

But then secondly, there is something more: the power of God is at work to help true faith in the real Lord prevail. It just *is* the truth, and great is the truth and must prevail. As the examples of Naaman, the ambassadors, and the centurions in the Gospel might suggest: "The attraction which the faith of Israel visibly exercises on the pagans is a sign that a mighty reality is present, causing the attraction: it is the Will of God, drawing all nations to come and seek him."[17]

An oracle in the Isaian anthology declares:

> Turn to me and be saved,
>   all the ends of the earth!
>   For I am God, there is no other.
> By myself I have sworn,
>   from my mouth has gone forth in righteousness
>   a word that shall not return:
> "To me every knee shall bow,
>   every tongue shall swear."
>
> (Is 45:22–23)

This text is an important one for the New Testament owing to the way it is taken up in Saint Paul's Letter to the Philippians. When in the Christological hymn embedded in Philippians 2, Paul declares that "God has highly exalted him and bestowed on him the name which is above every

[17] Ibid., p. 79.

name, that at the name of Jesus every knee should bow, in heaven and on earth and under the earth, and every tongue confess that Jesus Christ is Lord, to the glory of God the Father" (vv. 9–11), this indicates that the Isaian prophecy has now found its fulfillment.

Examining a Spectrum

If we look at those oracles that tell of the Gentiles coming to the Holy Land, and above all to the center of Israel's unity, the holy city, in the service of Israel's God, we find something of a spectrum of texts. At one end, are passages that speak rather minimalistically of the Gentiles helping to bring the Israelite exiles home and ministering to them. Isaiah 49 includes an example:

> Thus says the Lord GOD:
> "Behold, I will lift up my hand to the nations,
>   and raise my signal to the peoples;
> and they shall bring your sons in their bosom,
>   and your daughters shall be carried on their shoulders."
>
> (Is 49:22)

That is one way, but rather a restricted one, in which to acknowledge the Holy One of Israel—the Gentiles acting rather like the stretcher-bearers at Lourdes, bringing the enfeebled and the weary to the sanctuary. Again, in Psalm 72, it seems to suffice for the nations merely to pay tribute to the Davidide king who is the Lord's vice-regent on earth:

> May all kings fall down before him,
>   all nations serve him!
>
> (Ps 72:11)

Here there can only be at best an indirect acknowledgment of Israel's God. Isaiah 60 is rather more generous. There the Gentiles are portrayed coming gladly to Zion and admiring the glory of the Lord. It is the text the liturgies have seen as a prophecy of the Epiphany of the Lord in Saint Matthew's Gospel.

> They shall bring gold and frankincense,
>   and shall proclaim the praise of the LORD.
>
> (Is 60:6)

An oracle in the final chapter of the Isaiah collection goes further and says that when the Gentiles are converted to the God of Israel, the Lord will take priests and Levites from among their number (66:21)—a native clergy, so to speak.

We move closer to the other end of the spectrum of Old Testament positions on the matter—the maximalist end as we might call it—with an early entry in the Book of Isaiah, a famous passage from chapter 2 that also occurs, curiously, in the Book of Micah.

> Many peoples shall come, and say:
> "Come, let us go up to the mountain of the LORD,
>   to the house of the God of Jacob;
> that he may teach us his ways
>   and that we may walk in his paths."
> For out of Zion shall go forth the law [the Torah],
>   and the word of the LORD from Jerusalem.
>
> (Is 2:3; cf. Mic 4:2)

There it is clearly a case of the conversion of the pagan nations to the revelation given to Israel, of which they become full recipients. But above all it is the Suffering Servant who is to teach the Gentiles the true religion. He is to give them *torah*, instruction in God's Law, and what Isaiah calls *mishpat*, a term which can be translated "judgment" and therefore "justice", but also "spiritual wisdom", or "true religion". Those are the words behind the last two parallel propositions in Isaiah 42:4:

> He will not fail or be discouraged
>> till he has established justice [*mishpat*] in the earth,
>> and the coastlands wait for his law [*torah*].

In Isaiah 49, we hear how this is absolutely integral to the Servant's mission when the Lord says:

> It is too light a thing that you should be my servant
>> to raise up the tribes of Jacob
>> and to restore the preserved of Israel;
> I will give you as a light to the nations,
>> that my salvation may reach to the end of the earth.
>
>> (Is 49:6)

The Isaianic corpus is not out on a limb here. A number of the Psalms affirm the universal scope of Israel's religion, most memorably Psalm 67 with its refrain:

> Let the peoples praise thee, O God,
>> let all the peoples praise thee!

Psalm 87 is the most concrete and graphic: in the Jerusalem Bible translation the "glorious predictions" the Lord has for his city are spelled out by saying in his name:

> "I will add Egypt and Babylon
>> to the nations that acknowledge me.
> Of Philistia, Tyre, Ethiopia,
>> 'Here so and so was born' men say.
> But all call Zion 'Mother',
>> since all were born in her."
>
>> (Ps 87:4–5)

And the psalmist adds his own comment:

> It is he who makes her what she is,
>   he, the Most High, Yahweh;
> and as he registers the peoples,
> "It was here," he writes "that so and so was
>   born."
> And there will be princes dancing there.
>   All find their home in you.
>
> (Ps 87:6–7)

However, this is not the whole story. It is clear that ancient Israel never sent out missionaries—whatever may have been the practice of the Pharisees in our Lord's day (see Mt 23:15). Though its unity was that of a covenant people more profoundly than that of an ethnicity, de facto the laws gave only rather grudging consent to the admission of proselytes. Deuteronomy requires a period of probation of three generations for an Egyptian or an Edomite before he could enter the assembly of Israel, and for an Ammonite or Moabite the period is extended to as many as ten generations. That is a long period of inculturation indeed. The Old Testament contains attempts to mitigate the force of this legislation, notably in the Book of Ruth, which shows a Moabitess being admitted into the commonwealth of Israel in only one generation and going on to become the great-grandmother of King David. Also, the words used by our Lord at the cleansing of the Jerusalem Temple, "My house shall be called a house of prayer for all the nations" (Mk 11:17), are taken from an oracle of Isaiah about a far more generous reception of Israelites than the Mosaic provisions envisage.

> And the foreigners who join themselves to the LORD,
>   to minister to him, to love the name of the LORD,
>   and to be his servants . . .

> these I will bring to my holy mountain,
> and make them joyful in my house of prayer.

> (Is 56:6a, 7a)

Other texts, by contrast, are even more negative than the Law itself. For the enemy nations Ezekiel can only prophesy complete disaster (cf. 29:9–12 and chap. 35). Joel not only takes the same view but even seems to rule out individual proselytes or potential proselytes from the restored Zion:

> And Jerusalem shall be holy
> and strangers shall never again pass through it.

> (Joel 3:17b)

Obadiah too appears to have no hope of the conversion of the pagans. The message of the Book of Jonah is that Israel lacks compassion for the pagans. But there is in Jonah no suggestion of a missionary program toward them, only the merciful act of going to warn them of their impending judgment.

Mysterium Judaicum

So what is going on? Are we simply to say that in some of the Scriptures the hagiographers, the inspired writers, failed to receive the truth of Israel's universal call to which others of the Scriptures bear witness? Could the grace of inspiration be so incompetent? It is better to say that the truth is found in both the negative and the positive texts surveyed. For negatively, Israel as she actually existed was impotent to carry out the mission to the Gentiles, whereas positively that universal issue of her own call was nonetheless God's purpose for her. The Holy Spirit had to "get across" a twofold truth that can be described as *both* God's purpose for Israel and *also* the fact that this high calling lay beyond her power to fulfill. It is very significant that Israel both had high insight into the truth of God and was yet unable firmly to hold onto it. As Gabriel Hebert puts it:

> The . . . Church, which believes that Yahweh the God of Israel is the true God, the maker of heaven and earth, thereby confesses that the Eternal, willing to make his Name known to men, condescended to take upon Him the form of a tribal God according to the Semitic notion, as in the Incarnation He accepted the limitations of human nature. Thus Israel, as the people of Yahweh, was a nation among the nations, and yet unique, having in her the potentiality of the Universal Church. But she was unable to realize that potentiality till God's Hour had come.[19]

That combination of preparedness and impotence is especially clear when we consider the nature of the Law, where —as Saint Paul saw, looking back from the vantage point of the Incarnation and the atonement—Israel was powerless to give full effect to her own insights. The coming of the Messiah will bring this to light. Thus for example, while a number of prophetic passages and psalm texts show an awareness that ritual uncleanness is above all a metaphor for the defilement of the soul that is sin, not till the Messiah comes can the law of ritual uncleanness be abrogated. Israel had first to grasp in an outward form the notion of a guilt that separates from God and from the holy assembly before she could understand its spiritual application. But in premessianic days the Jew was under the Law and must keep it, with the danger of falling into the error that certain natural things and states were *inherently* unclean, a false position incompatible with the doctrine of creation.

[19] Ibid., p. 96.

Again, on the topic of sacrifice we are presented with a similar antinomy or near contradiction. The prophets frequently condemn the profanation of the cultus and, along with the psalmists, express delight in its celebration, but they are also aware of its drawbacks and deficiencies. The author of Psalm 51 goes so far as to say:

> Thou hast no delight in sacrifice;
>> were I to give a burnt offering, thou wouldst not be pleased.
> The sacrifice acceptable to God is a broken spirit;
>> a broken and contrite heart, O God, thou wilt not despise (Ps 51:16–17).

In comparison with that costly repentance, the offering of a goat in sacrifice is just outward show, and yet the ritual carried out with the animal victim is still the only appropriate symbol the Israelite can find of the interior process of reconciliation to God. It has been put very judiciously thus:

> Dumbly [the sacrifices] testify that Yahweh is the God of the whole earth and is the holy God, and that He will call man at last to come to Him, and to adore Him worthily, and be forgiven all his sins, and be at peace with Him and his fellow-man (for the ritual plainly indicates that this is the end for which sacrifice exists); and further, that this end is somehow to be attained through the offering to God by man of that which is infinitely costly, and through blood-shedding and death. At times the worshipper will have seen a glimpse of this. But it was only too clear that the sacrifices, as they stood, did not solve the problem and meet the need.[20]

Only in the figure of the Suffering Servant, who is both victim and priest, offering his life in intercession for sin, are we on the level of the New Testament concept of sacrifice

[20] Ibid., pp. 113–14.

transformed or sacrifice fulfilled. That shows the heights to which, under the impact of the charism of inspiration, Israel could attain. But in the "working system" of the Israelite cultus, the spiritual was too often dragged down by the carnal, by obsession with mere ritual performance. In his essay "Mysterium judaicum", Hans Urs von Balthasar writes: "The entire Old Testament has for content the struggle of God with his people over the recognition of grace."[21] Standing back, and looking, then, at the whole scenario, there is only one possible conclusion, and it is for our purposes an interesting one. The Old Testament cannot bring about its own fulfillment. Hans Urs von Balthasar wrote: "It is precisely here that our considerations require completing by a theology of the New Testament: only the entire biblical revelation mediates in a total form what God wanted to communicate to us of his glory."[22]

[21] H. U. von Balthasar, "Mysterium judaicum", *Schweizerische Rundschau* 43 (1943): pp. 211-21, here at p. 213.
[22] H. U. von Balthasar, *The Glory of the Lord: A Theological Aesthetics*, vol. 6, *Theology: The Old Covenant* (San Francisco: Ignatius Press, 1991), p. 416.

6

THE PATTERN OF
REVELATION DISPLAYED:
THE FULFILLMENT

On, then, to the New Testament fulfillment. It is not difficult to see how the apostles were interpreting the Old Testament in (roughly) the two decades after Pentecost. The
speeches furnished in the Acts of the Apostles give us an
excellent idea of the original "apostolic preaching".[1] The
outstanding speeches are those made by Peter at Pentecost
in Acts 1 and 2, his speech at the Beautiful Gate in Acts 3
and its sequel, after his interrogation by the Sanhedrin in
Acts 4; Philip's address to the Ethiopian eunuch in Acts 8;
Peter's speech at Caesarea in Acts 10; and Paul's at Antioch
of Pisidia in Acts 13. By examining them, we can get very
close to how the original preaching of the Church saw the
Old Testament fulfilled in Jesus. Gabriel Hebert found that
the various points made in these speeches can be strung together in a logical order as follows:

1. The God of Abraham, Isaac, and Jacob, the God of our
   fathers (cf. Ex 3:6), who made the heaven and the earth and
   the sea and all that is in them is (cf. Ex 20:11), who of old
   led our fathers forth out of Egypt with a mighty arm (cf. Ex
   6:6), suffered their ill behavior in the wilderness, and when

[1] See C. H. Dodd, *The Apostolic Preaching and Its Developments* (London,
1940).

he had destroyed seven nations in the land of Canaan gave them their land for an inheritance (cf. Deut 1:31 and 7:1).

2. This God has fulfilled the promises made to our fathers (cf. Ps 2:7), by sending a word of salvation (cf. Ps 107:24), preaching good tidings of peace (cf. Is 52:7), for you and all that are afar off, even as many as he shall call (cf. Is 57:19), that so in Abraham's seed all the families of the earth might be blessed (cf. Gen 22:18), through his Church, which he has set for a light for the Gentiles (cf. Is 49:6), for God is no respecter of persons (cf. Deut 10:17).

3. This God has done through Jesus, born of the seed of David, that man after God's own heart (cf. 1 Samuel 13:14), to whom holy and sure blessings were promised (Is 55:3), to whom God swore that he would set one of the fruit of his loins upon his throne (cf. 2 Sam 7:12 and Ps 132:11).

4. This Jesus is the Lord's Messiah (cf. Ps 2:2), anointed with the Holy Spirit (cf. Is 61:1), the prophet like unto Moses, to whom the people were solemnly warned to hearken (cf. Deut 18:15), the Servant of the Lord (cf. Is 42 and the other Isaian "Songs of the Servant").

5. He was led to the slaughter, dumb as a lamb before its shearers (cf. Is 53:7), for against him the Gentiles raged, and the rulers were gathered together (cf. Ps 2:1–2) and pronounced him accursed, hanging him upon a tree (cf. Deut 21:22).

6. But God did not suffer his Holy One to see corruption (cf. Ps 16:8–11), but called him "my Son" (cf. Ps 2:7) and made the stone set at naught by the builders to be the head of the corner (cf. Ps 118:22).

7. God has made this Jesus sit at his right hand (cf. Ps 110:1).

8. And so the messianic gift of the Spirit is poured out on all flesh (cf. Joel 2:28–32).

9. Beware, then, lest you despise the Gospel message and perish, for this is the work of God (cf. Hab 1:5).

Notice how the Church's earliest preachers think of the messianic hope in all—or nearly all—its dimensions, with the various aspects we looked at in Old Testament expectation. This enables them to give a pretty complete interpretation of the life and mission of Jesus as the fulfillment of the Old Testament promises of a Day of Deliverance by the Lord. And they see his death and Resurrection—the paschal mystery—as the crucial events in the working out of that deliverance. Jesus is the Christ, the promised King who is to reign on David's throne, but that does not stop him from being also the prophet like unto Moses to whom the people were to listen and—above all—the Suffering yet vindicated Servant of the Lord, pressing into service what we shall learn to call Old Testament "types".

The Titles of the Lord

As is well known, our Lord tended to avoid the title "Christ" because of the inappropriately political or even military overtones it had acquired, not least in the intertestamental period through such texts as the pseudonymous Psalms of Solomon, written perhaps not more than forty years before Jesus' birth. On two occasions in the Gospels when others call him the Christ, he accepts the title because to deny it would be more erroneous than to affirm it, but in each of these two occasions—the first to Simon Peter at Caesarea Philippi, and the second at his trial before Caiaphas—he corrects any false implications by going on immediately to speak of himself as the Son of Man. This is a term that is not used in the Gospels by anyone other than Jesus himself, with the single exception of Saint Stephen, who dares to use it as a title of Jesus in the moment of his martyrdom in Acts 7:56: "Behold, I see the heavens opened and the Son of man standing at the right hand of God." The extreme reverence paid to this name by the apostles is evidenced by its absence in their preaching.

This enigmatic term has a double background. It derives in part from the vision of God and the glorious angel defender of Israel in Daniel 7. But it is also found as the humble name given to Ezekiel when the Word of the Lord comes to him about the desolation yet consolation of Israel. It is a title that has caused gallons of ink to flow in modern scholarly discussion. We can say that it embraces both heavenly glory and earthly humiliation. "The glory is concealed, till under the conditions of the Resurrection and Ascension and [the Parousia] it is manifested; and yet the glory is here, operating under the conditions of earthly humiliation, and showing itself as redeeming love, able to save that which was lost."[2] To say Jesus is the Son of Man is to make a theological affirmation of the highest rank. In effect, it is to affirm the union of the divine and human natures in the mystery of the saving Incarnation. At the same time, however, to a careless listener the title would give nothing away, since "son of man" can also mean in colloquial Aramaic quite simply a "man", "oneself".

The Gospel of the Kingdom

In the Gospels, which are the apostolic preaching in its written form, we see more. First, in the fulfillment of the hope of Israel, the King cannot be separated from the Kingdom. As the tenth chapter of Saint Mark's Gospel shows, the formula "to follow me" is synonymous with the formula "to enter the Kingdom of God". To put it in later Christian terms,

[2] Ibid., p. 135.

we cannot have the personal Savior without his Mystical Body, the New Israel that is the Church. But secondly, to follow him and enter the Kingdom is, in the same chapter of Mark, also "to inherit eternal life" and "to have treasure in heaven". In the messianic hope as we find it in the Old Testament, an expectation of a renewed earthly blessing tends to be one thing, an expectation of heavenly blessing another. Eschatology can locate its goal either in a continuation of historical time or in a meta-historical time, beyond the conditions of created existence as we know it. But in the Gospel fulfillment, these two—the meta-historical and the inner-historical—are brought together, because the Kingdom by its nature reflects the being of the Son of Man who is both "from heaven" as God and therefore otherworldly, and yet "earthly" as human and therefore this-worldly. The parables of the Kingdom told by Jesus in the Gospels express this.

> [The Kingdom] is from heaven; there, with God, its fullness and perfection is. This our Lord pictures as the Harvest, the full-grown Tree in whose branches the birds of the heaven lodge, the catch of fish gathered in, the complete Flock of a hundred sheep, the Wedding-Feast full of guests, the Marriage of the Bridegroom with the Bride. But the Kingdom of God is not purely "other-worldly"; for as the heavenly Son of Man is present among men on earth, so is the Kingdom of God present on earth, like the Wheat growing in the field, the Fish being caught, the Lost Sheep being found, the guests already beginning to eat of the Wedding-feast, waiting for the King to come in and see them.[3]

The Kingdom is both future and present, just as the Church is both the Bride of Christ, without spot or wrinkle or any

[3] Hebert, *Throne of David*, p. 140.

such thing, as Saint Paul says in Ephesians (5:27), the holy Church we profess in the Creed, and yet her members— the members of Christ's body—are still groaning in their struggle with sin. In the day-to-day life of the Church, by

> daily contact with the Messiah by means of His Word, His Sacraments, and the members of His mystical Body, human nature is purged and transformed, becoming conformed to the image of the Son. Here is the means, provided by God, whereby the renewal of heart and spirit which Jeremiah and Ezekiel foretold can at last take place. They saw that it must be; they did not know how. They could not see beforehand, as we can see after it has happened, that it could only be through a Divine Intervention, through God coming in person to fight His own battle, and taking on Him the form of The Servant.[4]

Two signs of the New Testament fulfillment of the Old Testament hope are especially striking. They are the beginning of the peace of God, the final Sabbath rest—and we can look at that under the title "Lord of the Sabbath"—and the forgiveness of sins or to put it more positively, the gift of a new righteousness, which we can look at under the title "the salvation of man".

Lord of the Sabbath

In the second chapter of his Gospel, Saint Mark shows Jesus involved in a controversy with the scribes over the Sabbath, and he indicates that this was one of the main factors initiating the process that led to his crucifixion. Outside the Syn-

[4] Ibid., p. 142.

optic tradition, this is confirmed by Saint John, who gives a hint that the Sabbath controversy really involved Jesus' entire claim to messiahship and indeed divinity. "This was why the Jews sought all the more to kill him, because he not only broke the Sabbath but also called God his Father, making himself equal with God" (5:18). In the Judaism of our Lord's time, there was growing a powerful link between Sabbath observance and the messianic age. In one fairly contemporary Jewish document, the Mishnah, the Last Day is described as the "Day that is all Sabbath, when . . . the righteous are seated with crowns on their heads and are refreshed in the glory of the Shekinah", in the radiance of the divine glory. God rested on the first day of creation, yes, but he goes on working, preparing creation for the arrival of his Kingdom. Only then will the perfect Sabbath of God begin. Jesus' arguments with the scribes over the appropriateness of his Sabbath healings need to be seen in this context. The scribes held that healing activity was acceptable on the Sabbath if it was a life-or-death affair. If, on the other hand, the medical aid required could wait a day, then wait it should. Why then did Jesus insist on such healings as of the man with a withered hand happening on the Sabbath? Surely, the scribes were right that waiting another twenty-four hours would not matter when somebody had already been waiting for half a lifetime. Jesus' attitude seems to have been that it was not a question of in what precise circumstances healing might be allowed on the Sabbath. It was a question of the intense appropriateness of the Sabbath for healing of all sorts.

This is understandable if he believed that the Sabbath was to be regarded as the messianic day par excellence, and that he himself had come to Israel as her Messiah. In that case, it was only to be expected that he would "seize on that day as the great day, of all the seven, for the work of healing".[5] When Jesus refers to David in order to show why he can allow his disciples to break the Law about harvesting on the Sabbath (an offense which, in Israel's criminal code could lead in certain circumstances to the death penalty), his argument is that David could act as one above the Law because he was a type of the Messiah who when he comes will be above the Law. He *has* now come, he is Jesus, and so the era that began with Moses and the original gift of the Torah on Sinai is at an end. "Now that the Lord of the Sabbath is come, those who know Him will rejoice in His presence; and the prohibitions proper to the pre-Messianic Age pass away. Now that the true Sabbath is here, the shadow Sabbath is not needed."[6]

That is not to say that the Law must not be kept up until the time when it is perfectly fulfilled by him, which, as we shall see, will be through his sacrificial death. It is must go on being kept and kept carefully "until the time comes when it is fulfilled, and transcended, in the new order which completes it".[7] That is why in Christianity the weekly rest on the transferred Sabbath, the day of the Resurrection, cannot have the same meaning as in Judaism. The Jews keep the Sabbath as an act of anticipation looking forward to the future. But to the Church the hoped-for Sabbath rest is something on which she has in part already entered, by receiving its first fruits, the Holy Spirit. This is the peace of God which, in the Gospel, has accordingly a deeper meaning than the prophets were able to allot it.

[5] Ibid., p. 152.
[6] Ibid., p. 155.
[7] Ibid.

The Salvation of Man

The other striking telltale sign of the fulfillment of the Old Testament in Jesus' ministry concerns the forgiveness of sins and the gift of a new righteousness. Abrogating as he did the law of ceremonial defilement, which, as we have seen, was really a kind of pedagogy enabling ancient Israel gradually to grasp the horror of sin itself as rejection of God's holy will, our Lord turns his attention instead to the root of sin in man. As he puts it in Mark 7: "There is nothing outside a man which by going into him can defile him; but the things which come out of a man are what defile him" (7:15). This is what Saint Paul will call "the mind of the flesh", at enmity with God, not just a proneness of man's nature to sin but the actual corruption of the nature of the offspring of Adam. Our Lord envisages the messianic Kingdom as the restoration of the innocence of Paradise. "Truly I say to you, unless you turn and become like children, you will never enter the kingdom of heaven" (Mt 18:3). That is why he especially attacks self-righteousness, since this sin of which at any rate the publicans and prostitutes are not guilty, is the deadliest enemy of humility and love. Saint Paul discovered at his conversion that all along his zeal for the Law had never given him peace, but it had led him into the great sin of trying to destroy the infant Church, the "ecclesia" of God. But sin typified him in union with the rest of mankind, and it took a stupendous divine intervention in human affairs to reverse the Fall from Paradise. As he writes in Romans 5:8: "while we were yet sinners Christ died for us." This is how the forgiveness of sins and the gift of the new righteousness were de facto obtained. This brings us to the climax of any account of the fulfillment of the Old Testament hope: the paschal mystery or sacrifice of the Messiah.

The Sacrifice of the Messiah

The accounts of the Last Supper in the Gospels indicate plainly enough that Jesus interpreted his death sacrificially. It is not difficult to trace back his words as given by the Synoptics and Saint Paul to a common formula, which a German scholar has helpfully paraphrased as follows: "I am the sacrificial victim whose blood is poured out for you, that is, for the believing people, to seal a new covenant with God, and whose body is slain for you."[8] In the accounts of the institution of the Mass (which simultaneously *are* the Lord's interpretation of his own dying as sacrifice), the emphatic "my", especially in the phrase "my blood"— mine, not some other's—is important. Two covenants of God with man are being compared. The first was under Moses, at Horeb, where animal blood was spilled, and divided into two parts, part sprinkled on the altar and part on the people after they had assented to the words of the "Book of the Covenant". The second is the covenant of the Messiah, ratified by his blood soon to be shed on the Cross. The Holy Eucharist is one act with this sacrifice and interprets its meaning. "He is saying, This is My Sacrifice, whereby the Messianic Covenant of God with man is made."[9] And the words telling us it is offered "for many", by recalling the prophecy of the Suffering Servant who in Isaiah 53:12: "bears the sins of many", identify this sacrifice as explic-

---

[8] H. Lietzmann, *Messe und Herrenmahl: Eine Studie zur Geschichte der Liturgie* (Bonn, 1926), p. 221.

[9] Hebert, *Throne of David*, p. 189.

itly an offering for sin. In Saint Paul's version of the words, the phrase "New Covenant" occurs and irresistibly calls to mind not Isaiah but Jeremiah and the prophecy of the coming covenant to be written on men's hearts. Hence we might paraphrase the words of institution of the Eucharist, "This is the ratification of the new and spiritual covenant by the sacrifice of the Messiah." Taken together—the displacement of the ancient blood sacrifices and the announcement of a New Covenant à la Jeremiah, what this means then is that the entire Mosaic system of sacrifice is now fulfilled and superseded.

This is the moment Jesus has been looking forward to in his prophecies of the Passion, which also tell of the way he will go to his triumph. This death is, as Peter says at Pentecost, "by the determinate counsel and foreknowledge of God" (Acts 2:23). Its necessity—which, we can suppose by his acquired knowledge, the Word incarnate gained humanly through discernment of the prophetic accounts of what it costs to be the Servant of the Lord—receives its seal from the actual course of events during his ministry. The cup he must drink is at once a cup of woe, such as that which Jeremiah was commanded to take from the hand of the Lord and give to all the nations of western Asia to drink (25:15–33) and which Isaiah claimed Israel herself had drunk to the dregs in her conquest and Exile (51:17–23), a cup of woe and also (cf. Ps 96:13; Ps 16:5; Ps 23:5) the cup of salvation, which the psalmist desires to offer in thanksgiving to God.

Jesus interprets his Passion as an act of purchase: buying back the lives of men, an act of which they were incapable themselves, and doing so redemptively by a kind of New Exodus—a passing through death waters to new life—to which is joined the New Sinai of the making of the New and everlasting Covenant. The Gospels identify the hour of the Passion as Jesus' hour par excellence, when the glory he had with the Father before the world began was revealed through reckless self-giving. This self-giving shines out in the Son-of-Man sayings—such as that he has come not to be served but to serve—and is recommended to the disciples in the Great Sermon, which we know best as the Sermon on the Mount.

From the Passion and death we must be careful, in any account of the sacrifice of the Messiah, not to separate the Resurrection, Ascension, and Session. In the Mosaic sacrifices, the immolation or death was not the climax. The purpose of the immolation was not to destroy life but to transform it in such a way that it could be the medium of atonement. It was for this that blood was sprinkled on the altar and the people at Sinai. That is why in the Letter to the Hebrews the author treats Jesus' life and death as *preliminary* to his heavenly priestly activity in his risen and ascended state when he comes to sit at the "right hand of the throne of the Majesty in heaven, a minister in the sanctuary and the true tent which is set up not by man but by the Lord" (8:1–2).[10]

The Eucharistic Liturgy expresses this when the Church's offering of bread and wine is consecrated to be the Body of the Messiah and his Blood of the covenant, according to his institution. As Hebert writes, beautifully:

> That this may happen, it is necessary that the action pass from earth to heaven; for it is in heaven that the Eternal Priest is celebrating His own timeless Sacrifice. On earth, the celebrant acts in His Name, standing at the head of the worshipping Ecclesia; but mystically the whole Church is met together,

[10] See J. van der Ploeg, O.P., "L'Ancien Testament dans l'Epître aux Hébreux", *Revue Biblique* (1947), pp. 187–228.

and the one Priest celebrates for us all His one full, perfect and sufficient Sacrifice.[11]

This is expressed in a key formula of the Roman Canon that probably expresses the most ancient notion of eucharistic consecration of any of the Church's liturgies:

> We humbly beseech thee, Almighty God, bid these things to be carried by the hands of thy holy Angel [Christ] to thy altar on high, in the sight of thy divine Majesty; that all we, who by the communion of this altar shall receive the holy Body and Blood of thy Son, may be filled with all heavenly benediction and grace.

The sacrifice belongs to earth and to heaven because in it all sacrifice finds fulfillment, since here man's salvation is seen as complete. As von Balthasar puts it, "The dispersed are indeed reunited, but the reunion is now Eucharistic, reunion in the body of Christ which is his Church".[12]

That brings me in conclusion to "The Gospel for all nations".

The Gospel for All Nations

That the gift of salvation is now in principle fully given in turn explains why the infant Church so quickly realized the moment for the "Calling of the Gentiles" had come. During the public ministry there were some openings to this, in the encounter with the Syro-Phoenician woman and the Roman centurions, and in those Parables where a coming in of the Gentiles is in mind, for instance the Parable of the Wicked Husbandmen (Mk 12:1–12), where the Kingdom is

[11] Ibid., p. 208.
[12] Von Balthasar, *Martin Buber and Christianity*, p. 82.

given to a nation bearing the fruits thereof, and in the Parable of the Wedding Feast (Lk 14:17–24) where the guests
invited from the "highways and hedges" may well be the
Gentiles. Jesus' abolition of the law of ritual uncleanness and
his teaching that the true righteousness is not righteousness
from the keeping of Torah point in the same direction. So,
and most especially, does his cleansing of the Temple, the
house of prayer for all nations, since when the sanctuary is
purged and fitted to gather Israel around her Messiah, Zion
can then become the place where all the nations shall come
as to their spiritual home. At the trial of Jesus in Saint Mark's
Gospel, it was said against him that he threatened to destroy
the Temple and replace it with another not made by hands.
Saint John claims to give the true interpretation of this gar-
bled report. The Temple he had cleansed was symbolic of
the spiritual temple, Israel. By his death and Resurrection,
the spiritual temple that is his Mystical Body, the true Israel,
the remnant of the people of God, would be raised to life.
It is to the Messiah himself in his Church body that, in the
words of Matthew 8:11, "many shall come from the east
and from the west and sit at table with Abraham, Isaac, and
Jacob in the kingdom of heaven." In the fourth Gospel, he
told the woman of Samaria that the hour was coming when
neither on Mount Gerizim (the Samaritan sanctuary) nor
in Jerusalem would men worship the Father (4:21). It was
to Jerusalem that his entire ministry had gravitated, and at
Jerusalem that the Church had been founded.

Yet now "Zion" is losing its geographical meaning, precisely because the center of the messianic Kingdom, the true
temple and sanctuary, is where the Messiah himself is, at the
right hand of the Father. The Letter to the Hebrews tells
Jewish Christians now in the Church:

You have come to Mount Zion and to the city of the living
God, the heavenly Jerusalem, and to innumerable angels in
festal gathering, and to the assembly of the first-born who
are enrolled in heaven, and to a judge who is God of all,
and to the spirits of just men made perfect, and to Jesus, the
mediator of a new covenant, and to the sprinkled blood that
speaks more graciously than the blood of Abel (12:22–24).

Similarly, in the Book of the Revelation, where the Lamb
is standing, surrounded by the 144,000 of the redeemed, is
Mount Zion (14:1), since Zion is now defined as where the
Lamb is. And because the King is never without his Kingdom, the worship of God in spirit and in truth is not now
localized in the geographical Jerusalem but can happen instead in every place where the ecclesia, the true Israel, the
Church, is.

Israel in Corinth and Philippi and Ephesus looks up to the
Jerusalem which is above and is free. Wherever the ecclesia
is, there mankind can come to Zion, the Zion from which
Torah [instruction] goes forth, and the word of the Lord from
Jerusalem. The Center of Unity for mankind is Jerusalem in
the mystical sense: it is the Messiah and His Kingdom.[13]

We might say with von Balthasar: "The clarity of the final
result reflects the clarity of the Origin which has directed
the whole process."[14]

---

[13] Hebert, *Throne of David*, p. 232.
[14] Von Balthasar, *Martin Buber and Christianity*, p. 96.

PART THREE

Two Important Presuppositions

7

GOD AND HIS SELF-MANIFESTATION

Here we have the central motif joining together the Old Testament and the New: the call and the fulfillment of Israel. It is time now to turn and look at some of the other very important Old Testament themes that are presupposed by this or give it its context. The first of these is God and his self-manifestation.

One writer has embarked on this subject in the following words: "The Old Testament is a book about God. [But] *prima facie*, on first reading, the Old Testament seems to be the history of ancient Israel."[1]

He resolves his own self-set dilemma a few pages later in these words:

> The Old Testament is a book about God. But the Old Testament is also a book about God and Israel as they confront each other in a special relationship and for a special purpose. The theology of the Old Testament is thus observable and discoverable as we watch the historical unfolding of the purpose of God which becomes "incarnate" in, with, and through the working of God's Spirit upon that one nation, which in his wisdom God chose to use for his mighty purposes.[2]

[1] G. A. F. Knight, *A Christian Theology of the Old Testament*, 2nd ed. (London, 1964), p. 17.
[2] Ibid., p. 19.

This does not mean, however, that the Church cannot draw out of the Old Testament Scriptures important concepts as well as images for service in the construction of the doctrine of God.

Divinity as Such

First, it may be helpful to call to mind the Church's teaching, formulated at the First Vatican Council, that the existence of God as source and goal of creation is a truth that should be naturally available to man's mind. In and of itself it does not require revelation to confirm it. Rather, the existence of divinity—the divinity that, as Shakespeare puts it in *Hamlet*, "shapes our ends, rough-hew them how we will"—is more like a presupposition of revelation, something that should be, and normally is, in place before revelation starts its work. I say this because, with this reminder, we shall be less surprised to learn that the fundamental name of God, in Old Testament usage before Moses but also to a considerable degree after him, is shared with the pagan religions surrounding Israel. It is the name *El*, which can also be found in a plural form: *Elohim*. In the words of G. A. F. Knight, *El* "appears, for example, in the Ras Shamra documents of the fifteenth pre-Christian century as the name of the chief divinity of the Canaanite pantheon. With the exception of Ethiopic, all the Semitic languages employ this word as the root form of their word for God, and it is known to the general public even today in the Arabic name for God, Allah."[3] In our English Bibles it is customarily translated—and quite rightly—"God". It is especially common in the Psalter and the Book of Job, but can also be found in interesting compound formulas in, for example, the patriarchal sagas in the Book of Genesis.

[3] Ibid., p. 61.

Distance and Relationship

The origin of the word *El* is contested, but it seems to come from one of two roots, which mean, respectively, "to be strong" and "to bind". In either case, the noun form—*El* itself—could reasonably be translated "the Mighty One", or "the Governor". As one Old Testament scholar has observed:

> It is worth noting that whichever of these meanings we adopt stresses the distance between God and man. In this they are in conformity with a basic characteristic of the Semitic concept of God, namely, that what is of primary importance is not the feeling of kinship with the deity, but fear and trembling in the face of his overwhelming majesty. Another point which it is necessary to remark is that they do not identify the Godhead with any natural object, but describe it as the power which stands behind Nature or the overruling will manifest in it.[4]

That statement, assuming it is a fair description of the ancient Semitic use of *El*, already brings us across four millennia into a preliminary contact with the already-mentioned teaching of the ecumenical council. However, as the same scholar goes on to say, what is distinctive about the occurrence of the word *El* for God in the patriarchal narratives is the way that God is designated by a special—one could indeed almost say "intimate"—relation with each one of the patriarchal figures. He is the "*El* of Abraham" (Gen 31:53), or the "Fear, *Pachadh*, of Isaac" (Gen 31:42), or the "Mighty One, *Abhir*, of Jacob" (Gen 49:24), or, rolling all these designations into one, he is "*El* of the fathers"— of all the patriarchs together. This is a God who has drawn

[4] W. Eichrodt, *Theology of the Old Testament*, vol. 1 (London, 1961), p. 179.

close to particular people, who thus become the first recipients of a special—later theology will call it a "supernatural"—revelation. God bends down to concern himself with the life projects of the patriarchs, and this is reflected in the theophorous names common in ancient Israel, such as "God is merciful", "God helps" or "God judges". This is, then, not a God who as source and goal of nature and man's life is simply a backcloth, albeit an exceedingly important one, to man's existence. It is a God who involves himself with men's lives by establishing bonds that are not simply the general linkage between what is divine and what is not. It should be stressed, however, that this is done without in any sense suppressing that note of the tremendous majesty of divinity the name *El* always carries. The Jewish philosopher Martin Buber held that two German words sum up Israel's sense of God: *Urdistanz*, "primordial distance", and *Beziehung*, "relationship". We see that in the version of the divine name *El Shaddai*, used by Abraham in Genesis 17:1 and elsewhere, for this can be translated "God the Exalted", or again, and virtually synonymously, "*El Elyon*", "God the Most High", a phrase that also occurs on Abraham's lips, in Genesis 14:22, in Abraham's speech to the king of Sodom. It is used in the same chapter of that book by the priest-king of Salem, Melchizedek, one of the Old Testament's "holy pagans", who blesses Abraham with the words,

> Blessed be Abram by God Most High,
> maker of heaven and earth (Gen 14:19).

A Latin Catholic, wishing to get the sense of these terms might think of that great cry of the Church to God in the *Dies irae: Rex tremendae majestatis*, "King of fearful majesty".

To call God *Elyon*, the Most High, was something especially common in the last phase of Old Testament revelation in the Greco-Roman period. Its implications of sublimity and almightiness were useful to Jews trying to express to others the character of their faith, just as to speak of God as source and goal of the world is useful to Catholic Christians for the same apologetic and missionary purposes today. As has been said:

> The title commended itself in such circumstances as a convenient means of indicating a kind of halfway stage between Judaism and paganism because of its universality and lack of definition; and by using it instead of anything more nationalistically Israelite, it was possible to establish a link with the loftier heathen concepts of God which was of the greatest convenience especially for the Jewish Diaspora.[5]

That is presumably why this version of the name of God is used as many as fifty times in the Book of Ecclesiasticus, for the later Wisdom literature was precisely on the cusp between the Jewish and the pagan worlds. Another compound version of the general divine name *El* is *El olam*, the "God of ages", "God of ancient days", or "God of eternity". This names God as the One exalted not merely over the world at large but over time, transcience, and change in particular. This designation is also found in Genesis, albeit at just one point, Genesis 21:33, but it became very popular among the prophets, in the Psalms, and in the deuterocanonical literature. Here in this later literature, possibly because its authors were so aware of the vulnerability of Israel's nationhood to the ravages of a changing world, there are "frequent references to the eternal God, whom the stars obey, and before whom this fleeting world cannot but tremble, to the everlasting King, who puts the false gods to shame; to the eternal Governor, exalted over the world and time."[6]

[5] Ibid., p. 182.
[6] Ibid., p. 183.

We must now turn to the very significant plural form of *El*, namely, *Elohim*. At one level, this term functions as what has been called a "plural of intensity", which serves to reinforce the concept implied in the singular. So in our case, this would mean: "the God who is—really and truly —utterly divine". It is likely that, at least sometimes, God would have been named this way polemically, over against other religions. The Lord God of Israel is not simply one *el* among many, "a" god. Rather is he the summation of all deity, Godhead pure and simple, and as such he rules out the invocation of other gods. That was the issue in, for instance, Elijah's struggle with the prophets of Baal in the First Book of the Kings.

The One and the Many

On the other hand, the sense that *Elohim* was a true plural never died out among the Old Testament writers, and this is part at any rate of what is involved when a twentieth-century, theologically minded exegete can produce a book entitled, *The One and the Many in the Israelite Conception of God*.[7] God has a "council", he is known through his "family", the *benei elim* or "sons of *Elohim*". These latter appear in, for instance, Psalm 89 as what the psalmist calls [God's] "holy ones".

> Let the heavens praise thy wonders, O LORD,
>   thy faithfulness in the assembly of the holy ones!
> For who in the skies can be compared to the LORD?
>   Who among the heavenly beings is like the LORD,

---

[7] A. R. Johnson, *The One and the Many in the Israelite Conception of God* (London, 1942).

a God feared in the council of the holy ones,
> great and terrible above all that are round about
>   him (Ps 89:5–7).

These "heavenly beings" are of course the holy angels. This psalm text is very clear about the vast difference between the angels and God. It would not be difficult to find parallels for this particular psalm. We might think of Isaiah's call vision in the book that bears his name, where Isaiah sees how the Lord is utterly distinct from the angelic host who, rather, serve him as ministers to the Holy One of Israel.

> In the year that King Uzziah died I saw the Lord sitting upon a throne, high and lifted up; and his train filled the temple. Above him stood the seraphim; each had six wings: with two he covered his face, and with two he covered his feet, and with two he flew. And one called to another and said, "Holy, holy, holy is the LORD of hosts; the whole earth is full of his glory" (Is 6:1–3).

But this "conception of otherness than, and lordship over, the angels is only one aspect of God's relationship to his angels."[8] Even in this chapter of Isaiah there is a disconcerting alternation between the use of the singular, "I", and the plural, "we" or "us". Thus the prophet hears from the lips of the Lord pronouns of both these kinds simultaneously: "Whom shall I send, and who will go for us?" (6:8). And this may well remind us of the various passages in the Pentateuch, and in "The Former Prophets", where a like alternation is the order of the day in references to the Lord himself on the one hand and to his angel messengers on the other. In Genesis 16, for instance, from the Abraham cycle, we are told that "the angel of the Lord" finds Hagar in the

---

[8] Knight, *Christian Theology of the Old Testament*, p. 65.

wilderness and addresses her. She, however, recognizes it is the Lord himself who is speaking and gives her visitor the title "the God who sees". More famously, not least from the iconography that illustrates this episode in the Russian Christian tradition, at the oaks of Mamre Abraham is surprised, so we are told in Genesis 18:2, by a visit from three men. But in the very next verse all three are addressed by the title "my Lord", in the singular, as if they were one personality. (The icon illustrating this is often called—on the basis of the exegesis practiced by the Fathers of the Church—"the Old Testament Trinity".)

Of a number of other examples that could be chosen, we select just one: the call of Moses in Exodus 3. In verse 2 of that chapter, we hear that in the theophany of the burning bush it was an angel that appeared to Moses, but in verse 4 we read, "When the LORD [Yahweh] saw that he [Moses] turned aside to see, God [*Elohim*] called to him out of the bush." So in these passages, and others like them, the God who is the Lord identifies himself with the angels he has made. As members of his creation, they sing his praise (thus Ps 148:2—"Praise him, all his angels, praise him, all his hosts!"). Yet when he acts in history to attain his purposes he can limit himself by acting through them. We might well see this as a sign of the humility of the God of Scripture, a foretaste of the stooping down he will carry out in the Incarnation of his Word.

Noting how in Psalm 104:4 the inspired writer calls the angels "flames of fire", G. A. F. Knight attempts an exposition of this image that will throw light on the relation between the angels and God in the Old Testament understanding:

> A flame has no root of existence in itself. It is born from the glowing mass of burning timber, or it is seen to emerge from the radiant ball that is the sun. As the flame leaps forth from

out of the fire, however, it actively bears the power of the fire, which is the will to burn. The flame is identical with the fire, yet the flame is not the fire in itself. In doing the "will" of the fire, the flame is compelled to separate itself from its source, and continues to perform this task in its state of separation. Yet when its task is done, the flame ceases to exist as an entity in its own right. While it was in action as a flame, however, there was a species of family relationship between it and the other flames, and between it and the parent fire.[9]

This is pictorial theology, of course, and as such is necessarily imperfect. The angel does not cease to exist when its particular divine mission is over, but it ceases to operate in the mode that enabled it to be representative of God himself.

The Name

The burning bush episode is of importance for more reasons than concerns A. R. Johnson's *The One and the Many*. It is the moment of the gift to Moses of a new and more revealing divine name, or perhaps, if we follow some commentators, a new and more revealing explication of a name already known. We glanced at this in the opening chapter on the Pentateuch. There is a lack of clarity as to whether it is the Tetragrammaton, the name "Yahweh", which is revealed to Moses at this juncture or rather the explanation of a name already known to the patriarchs. At any rate, we can say with certainty that the explanation is new, and the Hebrew phrase in which it is given is pregnant with meaning, thanks to the genius of the Hebrew language. "I AM WHO AM"—the translation we have from the Fathers and the medieval Schoolmen will serve—except that "being"

[9] Ibid., p. 69.

here is not mere existence but dynamic being, and, owing to the fact that the Hebrew imperfect denotes simply ongoing action, the key verb can refer to the future as well as to the present. Then if we add to the equation the way that, two verses earlier, God replies when Moses asks why he of all people is the witness and the commissioned one, with the words, "I will be *with you*" (Ex 3:12), we reach the complex outcome that in this text God is not only indicating his own mystery as the One who simply is in total dynamic actuality but, more even than that, he is: "offering to make himself known to Moses through personal nearness to him. And being 'with' Moses, the [humanly speaking] . . . 'redeemer' of Israel, God himself will share in all that is to come, i.e. in the redemption from Egypt, the Covenant at Sinai, the entry into the Promised Land, and the whole future development of Israel."[10]

We notice how, later, in the writing prophets, the phrase "I am" recurs in the divine speaking, just as it will in the Gospel of Saint John on the lips of Jesus. And as in the fourth Gospel it does not, generally speaking, stand alone. Rather is it accompanied by verbs that indicate how the living God is in action in judging and saving his people. Thus in Isaiah 43:13 we read:

> I am God, and also henceforth I am He;
> there is none who can deliver from my hand;
> I work and who can hinder it?

We might sum this up by saying "God's being is for Israel", so long as we bear in mind that, not least for the Book of Isaiah from which these words are taken, God is not only the Savior of Israel but also the Creator of all things. Only the One who sustains all things in being can be the Holy

[10] Ibid., p. 40.

One of Israel with effect. That is what we read in Isaiah 45:11–12:

> Thus says the LORD,
>   the Holy One of Israel, and his Maker:
> "Will you question me about my children,
>   or command me concerning the work of my hands?
> I made the earth,
>   and created man upon it;
> it was my hands that stretched out the heavens,
>   and I commanded all their host."

The Trinity in the Old Testament

But before leaving the topic of God and his self-manifestation and moving onto that of God and creation, it is very much worth adding, from a Christian theological perspective, that the issue of the unity of God in the Old Testament does not concern simply the relation between the Lord and his angel-messengers. It also concerns the interrelation of the Word and the Spirit of God with God himself.[11] When God utters his Word, he manifests a reality and sends that reality out into the world. Isaiah 55 has the great text on this:

> For as the rain and the snow come down from heaven,
>   and return not thither but water the earth,
> making it bring forth and sprout,
>   giving seed to the sower and bread to the eater,

---

[11] So, in keeping with a long line of Fathers and Doctors, Pope John Paul II declared of the trinitarian revelation that "although fulfilled completely in the New Testament, [it] is already in some way anticipated and foreshadowed in the Old", cited in *The Trinity's Embrace: A Catechesis on Salvation History* (Boston, Mass., 1996), p. 315 (from the General Audience of February 5, 2000).

so shall my word be that goes forth from my mouth;
    it shall not return to me empty,
but it shall accomplish that which I purpose,
    and prosper in the thing for which I sent it.

(Is 55:10–11)

Connected with the doctrine of the Word of God—which
is at once his own Word and yet acts for him, on his behalf,
in the realm of creaturely reality—is the notion of God's
name conceived as the way in which he makes this or that
finite place his dwelling on earth. He does so, as the Book
of Deuteronomy especially emphasizes, by putting his name
there. Those are the terms in which the Moses of Deuteronomy commends to the Israelites recourse to a central sanctuary for the tribes: "You shall seek the place the LORD your
God will choose out of all your tribes to put his name and
make his habitation there; thither you shall go . . ." (12:5a).
The early Church Fathers find in such texts cryptic prefig-
urings of the Incarnation since the Word is the Father's self-
revelation—enigmatically so for the faith of Israel, but visibly, tangibly so to the apostles when born in time.[12]

Finally, God is active in creation and salvation not only
by the sending of his Word and name, but also through the
sending of his Spirit. The Hebrew word for spirit, *ruach*,
means "wind" or "breath", and we can say: "In the same
way that the Word does not return unto God void, neither
does the Spirit of God blow without effectively bearing the
will of God."[13] This is so in creation, as the psalmist recognizes in Psalm 33:6:

---

[12] Thus for example, Tertullian, *The Demurrer against the Heretics*, 13.1; St.
Hilary of Poitiers, *The Trinity*, 3.42; St. Basil the Great, *Against Eunomius*,
2.18.
[13] Knight, *Christian Theology of the Old Testament*, p. 78.

> By the Word of the LORD the heavens were made,
>   and all their host by the breath [*ruach*] of his mouth.

Saint Irenaeus, often called the first Catholic theologian owing not least to his comprehensive grasp of biblical revelation, loves to repeat that God created the world with his
"two hands": not the Son only but the Spirit too.[14] In the
prophecies of Ezekiel and the later chapters of the Isaiah
collection, the economy of the Divine Spirit extends to salvation as well. It is the Spirit of God who is God's "intelligible, purposeful, effortlessly powerful activity with which he
continues to maintain and nurture the life of his people."[15]
Thus the Spirit stirs up the judges of Israel, comes upon
her prophets, and, in the hope for the future, rests on the
messianic King and Suffering Servant in the scrolls of Isaiah
(11:1–3, 61:1–3).

These, we can say, are proto-trinitarian references and by
that very token they are used in such a way as to guard,
not jeopardize, the unity of God. "Hear, O Israel, the LORD
our God is one LORD" reads Deuteronomy 6:4, meaning
not only that the God of Israel is unique, but that he is the
exhaustive source and bearer of all divinity. Israel's faith is
a monotheism and has been since the time of Moses, who
lived in an age when, as it providentially happened, there
were currents of thought moving toward monotheism in
both Egypt and Mesopotamia. Those movements miscar-
ried, but, owing to the investment of divine agency in Israel, Moses' did not. Israel's monotheism is still recogniz-
able in the triune monotheism of the Church.

---

[14] Irenaeus of Lyons, *Against the Heresies*, 4.4.4; 4.7.4; 5.1.3; 5.5.1.
[15] Knight, *Christian Theology of the Old Testament*, p. 79.

8

GOD AND CREATION

The second most important theme subjacent to the principal theme common to the Old and New Testaments, the theme of the messianic hope, must surely be the theme of *creation*.

Creation in the Beginning

In the Book of Nehemiah, we are given the text of the great sermon preached by Ezra the scribe when, with the consent of the Persian rulers, he initiated in Jerusalem a revived life together under the Torah for the survivors of the Babylonian invasion and the returnees from Exile. (That came up in our opening "overview" as a key moment in promulgating the canonical or authoritative status of the Books of Moses and possibly in finalizing the text as we have it.) It begins with the words:

> Thou art the LORD, thou alone; thou hast made heaven, the heaven of heavens, with all their host, the earth and all that is on it, the seas and all that is in them; and thou preservest all of them; and the host of heaven worships thee. Thou art the LORD, the God who didst choose Abram and bring him forth out of Ur of the Chaldeans . . . (Neh 9:6–7).

In other words, Ezra speaks of creation as the work of God before he goes on to talk about the formation of Israel as

153

a people and the consequent implanting of the great hope. This is, as the opening words of the entire Bible tell us, creation "in the beginning": that is, at a moment that is the first moment of time. The world has a beginning, a middle, and an end. The most important events in the middle are those exhibiting what we have been calling the "pattern of revelation"—the events leading from the call of Abraham, through the making of Israel in the Exodus, at Sinai and the entry into the Land, through all her subsequent trials and tribulations with their hard lessons, to the "Christ event", by which we mean the Incarnation and the paschal mystery and the way these stupendous happenings are received in the corporate mind of the apostolic Church. It is that pattern, with its amazing issue, which points us to the end. But first there is the beginning. There is the act of creation. As one scholar has said:

> In the Bible's own beginning, the act of creation is identified as the beginning. This need not have been the case. The act of creation might have been preceded by all kinds of eso-teric histories purporting to explain its possibility; Gnostic mythologies rewrite the Genesis narrative along these lines. Alternatively, the act of creation might have been conceived as an eternal event incapable of the narrative rendering an-nounced by the opening reference to "the beginning". Or the creation of heaven and earth might have been identified with the single, constantly-unfolding world-process, the work of a God who never ceases to create, who does not rest on the first Sabbath and whose creative activity therefore cannot be confined to "the beginning".

And Francis Watson continues: "The content of the familiar opening verse of the Bible is in fact anything but obvious. It represents a choice of one particular rendering at the expense of all other possibilities, whether exotic and far-fetched or plausible and reasonable. The chosen rendering rests upon the presupposition that God's activity, in creation and beyond, is appropriately depicted in narrative form."[1]

Plotting History

As Watson explains, the divine-human history recounted in Scripture corresponds to Aristotle's definition of a plot in his treatise the *Poetics*. "Well-constructed plots must neither begin nor end in a haphazard way".[2] So it is that "The biblical narrative concludes with an imaginative rendering of the event in which the heavens and the earth established in the beginning pass away and are no more, superseded by new heavens and a new earth: an absolute end to all worldly occurrence which transcends all the relative endings that we experience and narrate, corresponding in the comprehensiveness of its scope to the absolute beginning."[3] A universal beginning is joined to a universal ending through a highly particular—we might even say *narrowly* particular—middle consisting of Abraham, Christ, and the Church. All of which manifests the difference, incidentally, between the biblical revelation and pagan religiosity. As R. K. Harrison puts it: "The Old Testament can never be regarded as a typical mythology in part or in whole, because it proclaimed God as the Lord of history in contradistinction to the polytheistic patterns that made life and history in general dependent upon the rhythm of natural forces."[4]

---

[1] F. Watson, "Creation in the Beginning", in *Text and Truth*, p. 225.
[2] Aristotle, *Poetics* 1450b.
[3] Watson, "Creation in the Beginning", in *Text and Truth*, p. 226.
[4] Harrison, *Introduction to the Old Testament*, p. 457.

The Setting for Redemption

In the beginning, then, this universal and absolute beginning, God, according to the first chapter of Genesis, brought into existence day and night, the sky, sea and dry land, which are to serve as permanent structures for the foreseeable future. He also bestowed on plant life, animal life, and finally human life the creative power to secure its own future reproduction. And in the second chapter of the book, we are shown how God put in place a human environment in such a way that in this description every imaginable human place and time is included in advance. In the succeeding Noah sequence —which emphasizes, in the new circumstances of the Fall and its consequences, the stability of this all-encompassing world created by God—the divine determination not only to create but also to preserve what has been created is described as a "covenant". The covenant with Noah is a forerunner of the covenants with Abraham, Moses, and David and typified by the same divine faithfulness to what has been promised as will mark those later covenants also.[5]

> I establish my covenant with you, that never again shall all flesh be cut off by the waters of a flood. . . . And God said, "This is the sign of the covenant which I make between me and you and every living creature that is with you, for all future generations: I set my bow in the cloud, and it shall be a sign of the covenant between me and the earth" (Gen 9:11‑13).

This beginning, the original act of divine creation and its reaffirmation in the covenant with Noah, is the decisive theological presupposition for all that follows. The rainbow,

---

[5] For the importance of the Noachic covenant, see R. Rendtorff, *Canon and Theology: Overtures to an Old Testament Theology* (Minneapolis and Edinburgh, 1993).

as it were, hangs over all subsequent landscapes in Scripture. When in Genesis 12 the Lord tells Abram to leave Haran and to migrate to the land that will be inherited by his descendants, the God of Abraham can do that because he is also the Creator who separated land from sea and to whom all land whatsoever accordingly belongs. Again, in Genesis 15, when the Shield of Abraham promises the patriarch descendants as numerous as the stars of heaven, this is only feasible because he is also the divine Creator with the power to bless mankind with the ability to "be fruitful and multiply", as the first of the two Genesis accounts of creation puts it. And above all, the original creation of man in God's image, in God's likeness, tells us that there is a unique affinity between the Creator and this particular creature, the human creature. That is in the first creation account, but in the second, we discover how this entails for men the possibility of real dialogue with God, as we actually hear when God addresses the protoparents, Adam and Eve, in the Garden. That is of prime importance because, as Francis Watson, again, remarks: "This possibility of divine-human dialogue and interaction is fundamental to the concept of the covenant, in which God's speech or action evokes responsive human speech or action."[6] Without that, it is impossible to see how the rest of the story of the divine concern with Israel could go forward. The "middle" of the plot, the pattern that revelation took there, would be impossible and so accordingly would the disclosure of the ending of the story as a whole. That the Redeemer God of the Exodus and Sinai events is indeed the same as the Creator is a point made very simply in Exodus 20, in the recital of the Decalogue, the Ten Commandments, at verse 11, where, harking

---

[6] Watson, "Creation in the Beginning", in *Text and Truth*, p. 232.

back to the first creation account, the writer substitutes the name "Yahweh" for the divine title *Elohim* found in Genesis 1. It is the One who made heaven and earth, the sea and all that is in them, who met Moses in the burning bush and proved powerful to save. In his book, the prophet Amos initially describes the divine source of his prophetic oracles in terms of the Exodus: "Hear this word that the Lord has spoken against you, O people of Israel, against the whole family which I brought up out of the land of Egypt" (3:1). But a little later he defines the Lord in terms not of divine redemptive action but of its creative counterpart and predecessor.

> For lo, he who forms the mountains and creates the wind,
>   and declares to man what is his thought;
> who makes the morning darkness,
>   and treads on the heights of the earth—
> the LORD, the God of hosts, is his name! (Amos 4:13).

Creation, then, is the stable foundation of the covenant or covenants, from beginning to end.

New Testament Confirmation

This is confirmed in the New Testament. The Letters of Paul speak of our gracing by Jesus Christ as a new creation (thus Gal 6:15, and similar language appears in Rom [4:17], Eph [2:10, 15] and 2 Cor [5:17]), but that does not mean that the foundational beginning, the created order itself, ceases to be of significance. As we saw when looking at the fulfillment of the "pattern of revelation", the covenants of old culminate, so far as history is concerned, in the New Covenant in Jesus Christ and his blood. But intimate, continuing links between the Gospels and the creation narrative of Genesis 1 show that, in all this, creation is still the presupposed foundation of everything that happens—as Catholic theology has often had to maintain over against much of its Protestant and some of its Orthodox competitors.

This is not only vital. It is also so simple an aspect of the Gospels that, except with simple people perhaps, it can easily be overlooked. The way the Gospels, especially the Synoptics, describe the fulfillment of the messianic hope underscores the real creatureliness of the Redeemer. Emmanuel has visited his people, mighty to save, but he has done so through the Word of God becoming one of his own creatures, inhabiting that foundational reality of the world that Genesis shows was put in place when God spoke "in the beginning". Thus, on the first day of creation God set in motion the regular alternation of day and night. We see in the Gospels how Jesus is subject to this. At the opening of his ministry in the Gospel according to Mark, the sick are brought to him at sundown (1:32), and often in the morning before dawn he rises and goes to a lonely place to pray (1:35). At the end of his earthly career, Joseph of Arimathea arranges for his burial, according to the same Gospel, "when evening [has] come" (15:42), and the Savior arises from death in Mark 16 "on the first day of the week, [before] the sun [has] risen". Again, on the second day of the Genesis creation narrative, God created the firmament of heaven, and we notice in the Gospels how much of Jesus' ministry is open to this sky—on the lake and the lakeside, on the open road, or in the mountains. True, he is sometimes found within enclosed spaces—in houses or synagogues, but in Saint Matthew's Gospel he tells people he has no fixed dwelling but must often sleep under the sky. Unlike foxes and birds, the Son of Man has "nowhere to lay his head" (8:20). On the third day, God separated the sea from the dry land. We frequently hear of Jesus on the shore that marks this division, and he takes as his first disciples people who belong to both land and sea—fishermen. It was on the third day likewise that God created plants and trees, which, so it later emerges, are to provide food for animals and men. Jesus speaks of sowing and harvest in his parables, he knows of fruit-bearing trees, and he admires vegetation not just for its usefulness but for its beauty. "Consider the lilies of the field. . . . I tell you, even Solomon in all his glory was not arrayed like one of these" (Mt 6:28–29). On the fourth day the divine Creator made the sun, moon, and stars. Jesus tells of a time when the sun will be darkened, the moon will not give its light, and the stars will fall from heaven (Mk 13:24–25). But that time is not yet. In the meanwhile God makes his sun, he says, to shine on the evil and the good indiscriminately (Mt 5:45). On the fifth day, God created the living creatures in the sea and the air. Jesus deals with fish—twice securing for his disciples a miraculous catch (Lk 5:1–11; Jn 21:1–8), dividing two fish between more than five thousand people (Mk 6:41), and after his Resurrection both cooking and eating fish (Lk 24:42–43; Jn 21:9–13). He bids his hearers observe "the birds of the air", which, though "they neither sow nor reap nor gather into barns" are fed by the heavenly Father (Mt 6:26), and though they are of little value in the marketplace "not a [single sparrow] will fall to the ground without your Father's will" (Mt 10:29). On the sixth day, God made the land animals and created mankind, male and female, to have dominion over all creatures of the sea, the sky, and the land alike. Jesus is aware of this relationship in various forms— not only the fishermen and fish (Mk 1:16–20) but also the shepherd and his sheep (Lk 15:3–7; Jn 10:1–18), and indeed his own riding a colt into Jerusalem (Mk 11:1–7). He also knows that the human creature, made uniquely in the image of God, is of more value than all other creatures. On the seventh day, God rested from his labors. And though, as we have seen, Jesus envisages a transformation of the Sabbath since now the messianic rest is at hand, nonetheless, until all things are fulfilled Israel's faithful are to "share in the Creator's rest and hear the law and the prophets read to them, and [in that way] they will find themselves reminded, week by week, of the ultimate source, norm and goal of their labours."[7]

Cosmos and Chaos

In case we begin to think of the manner of the Incarnation as an idyll, a Galilaean springtime, the Passion narratives with which each of the four Gospels ends are there to rub our faces in the fact that the Old Testament's doctrine of creation is far from sentimental. As Watson puts it, if we cannot say with certainty of all the relevant texts that they teach "creation from nothing", *creatio ex nihilo*, we can definitely say that they teach "creation *against* nothing", *creatio contra nihilum*. The Old Testament speaks of a world with terrors, which is only a cosmos, an ordered world, because divine action is capable of victory over the terrors, the chaos, that constantly threaten to break in. The chaotic waters of *tehom*, the primal ocean—a piece of Babylonian imagery typical of the peoples of the Mesopotamian plain—were mastered in the original act of creation (thus Gen 1:1, 6–7). But they are still present to human life. "God is undoubtedly in control of the chaotic ocean, yet just as undoubtedly he permits it

[7] Ibid., p. 239.

to remain as part of his created universe. At any moment the 'windows of heaven' could open, and the fountains of the great *tehom* . . . could well up from below."[8] It is only through God's mercy that the catastrophe of Noah's time is not to be repeated for all the known world, but it may recur for parts of it, not least for individual persons. "That is why, when the waters close over his head, the individual Israelite, crying 'out of the depths' (Psalm 18:16; 130:1), is fully aware that he can have no help save in God who controls those very waters."[9]

As symbols of the enemies from whom the psalmist hopes to escape, these waters represent the "war" that God has waged from the beginning with the Deep and that became visible in the history of the nation when the Lord overthrew Pharaoh at the Red Sea. So Psalm 89:8–10 tells us:

> O LORD God of hosts,
>> who is mighty as thou art, O LORD,
>> with thy faithfulness round about thee?
> Thou dost rule the raging of the sea;
>> when its waves rise, thou stillest them.
> Thou didst crush Rahab like a carcass,
>> thou didst scatter thy enemies with thy mighty arm.

Calling Egypt, or the Egyptian king "Rahab" is to equate him with the monster that either was or inhabited chaos in the non-Israelite Near Eastern mythologies. "Rahab" is also "Leviathan", as in Psalm 74:14—"Thou didst crush the heads of Leviathan, / thou didst give him as food for the creatures of the wilderness", and under both names he is paralleled with the *tannin*, the Serpent or Dragon of which we read in the previous verse of that psalm: "Thou didst

---

[8] Knight, *Christian Theology of the Old Testament*, p. 106.
[9] Ibid.

divide the sea by thy might; / thou didst break the heads of the dragons on the waters." For, says Psalm 93:4, "Mightier than the thunders of many waters, mightier than the waves of the sea, the LORD on high is mighty", to which one might append the Song of Solomon 8:7—"Many waters cannot quench love." Hence therefore the expectation of the Book of Daniel that, at the end of days, at the turn of the ages, when all things are fulfilled, those kingdoms that have emerged from the chaos waters—Daniel writes of the "great beasts [coming] up out of the sea" (7:3)—God will utterly cast down. There is reason to think that the enormous receptacle for water that stood in the precincts of the Solomonic Temple as the Second Book of Kings tells us, the so-called "Brazen (or "Bronze") Sea" (2 Kings 16:17; 25:13), and for which the Old Testament gives no clear rationale, actually symbolized this great truth about which so many of the psalmists sang. When the seer responsible for the last book of Scripture declares, "I saw a new heaven and a new earth; for the first heaven and the first earth had passed away, and *the sea was no more*" (Rev 21:1; emphasis added), it is surely not the idyllic Lake of Gennesaret that is meant, though even that could have its storms, as the disciples well knew, and Jesus' stilling of them is a pre-fulfillment of the Lord's mastering the chaos waters and an anticipation of the final victory over chaos still to come in his Resurrection and Parousia. All potentiality, with its possibilities of frustration and disorder, is actualized in the New Jerusalem.

Once again, we may leave a last word to von Balthasar, who writes:

> If the existence of Israel in the world since Christ, and quite particularly in the world of today, has a meaning and consequently a purpose, a precise significance, we should not be far wrong in regarding the defence of the natural order, to which

Israel seems called, as an essential element in its mission. Israel is the temporal image of the whole earthly and heavenly Kingdom of God, whose coming "in mirrors and riddles" is the Church of Christ. The Church must fulfil both tasks simultaneously; it must embody the Word of God and the flesh of Jesus Christ more fully in the temporal order, and at the same time uproot and transplant the world as a whole into the Kingdom of Heaven and time into the dimension of eternity.[10]

All of which raises the issue of typology, or the typological interpretation of Scripture, which must absorb our attention next.

---

[10] Von Balthasar, *Martin Buber and Christianity*, p. 107.

PART FOUR

THE TYPOLOGICAL INTERPRETATION
OF THE OLD TESTAMENT

9

PRINCIPLES

We have been saying that the principal characteristic of Scripture is the revelation of greater and greater promises—and not just "revelation" of them but, in considerable part, fulfillment as well. That means of course that at each stage of its development, as well as in the pattern it exhibits overall, the structure of the Bible is one of promise and fulfillment —even though the final, definitive fulfillment of the divine design remains by the end of the scriptural narrative still at the level of hope, a divinely founded hope, of course, which is pictured in those texts speaking of heaven and the age to come. The fundamental promise-fulfillment format of the Bible is why the kind of exegesis we call "typological" is the sort that best befits its unique genius. That is something recognized within Scripture itself, since in the Old Testament the prophets interpret typologically the founding events of the history of Israel, and in the New Testament, the various inspired writers interpret typologically both the ancient Old Testament history and the comments on that history made by the writing prophets.

The Fathers of the Church will continue this typological reading of the Bible, which was found in the official catechesis taught by the bishops, notably to those preparing for Christian initiation by baptism, chrismation (or confirmation) and first Holy Communion.[1] Indeed, such typological exegesis is the chosen method of understanding Scripture found in the liturgy itself. Nor is this in any way surprising: in numerous concrete aspects the liturgy is a gift to us of the Fathers of the Church.

The Promise-Fulfillment Scheme

Given the way that Catholic theology accords a special place to the Fathers and the liturgy (or at any rate ought to do so), it is not surprising that Catholics, along with Anglican High Churchmen, took the lead in the scholarly rediscovery of typological exegesis in the twentieth century. And just because, for internal reasons, the biblical literature is best construed on the promise-fulfillment scheme, Protestant exegetes of the Old Testament with no special confessional—denominational—predilection for typology have been known to follow suit. Such is the case with the distinguished Lutheran exegete Gerhard von Rad, who died in 1974.[2] About a quarter of the second volume of von Rad's *Old Testament Theology* is devoted to the relation between the two Testaments, a topic which, von Rad rightly notes, is quite neglected in most modern biblical studies. The development of separate departments of scholarship, said von Rad, has left many important theological questions about the Bible in a "no-man's-land" between the Testaments. In

---

[1] Appropriately, then, the Fathers are at pains to describe these sacramental actions themselves in terms of biblical typology, as "the expression of the constant modes of the divine action . . . ; their sacramental theology is a biblical theology." J. Daniélou, *The Bible and the Liturgy* (London and Notre Dame, Ind., 1960), pp. 7–8.

[2] See on this figure J. Crenshaw, *Gerhard von Rad* (Waco, 1978).

this situation, he sponsors a return to the topic of typology. As has been noted in a survey of his contribution, for von Rad, "[p]recisely when 'understood in its own terms', the Old Testament itself raises the question of its relation to the New. Old Testament theology is characterized by a dynamic of promise and fulfillment in which the fulfillment does not exhaust the content of the promise but, on the contrary, discloses that dimension of the promise that transcends the present and points towards the future."[3] That is why Israel is constantly reinterpreting her own traditions and doing so, it may be said, typologically, as with the projection into the future of an intensified Exodus imagery in the second half of the Book of Isaiah.

Von Rad considers the Old Testament to be crowded with continually self-fulfilling divine promises. Such promises underlie the whole of the Pentateuch and the Book of Joshua.[4] All six of those books come to their climax in the editorial comment in chapter 21 of Joshua: "The LORD gave them rest on every side just as he had sworn to their fathers. . . Not one of all the good promises which the Lord had made to the house of Israel had failed; all came to pass" (vv. 44–45). And yet, as the rest of "The Former Prophets", with the very same editorial direction, suggest, the promise is by no means exhausted in this fulfillment. That is the key to "The Deuteronomic History" of the Israel of the monarchical period in the Books of Kings. There the Word of the Lord does not only function as a law that directs and, where it meets resistance, punishes, but also as the promise to David

[3] Watson, "Old Testament Theology as a Christian Theological Enterprise", in *Text and Truth*, p. 197.
[4] G. von Rad, "Grundprobleme einer biblischen Theologie des Alten Testaments", *Theologische Literatur Zeitschrift* 68 (1943): p. 228.

that brings forgiveness and salvation. The Divine Word continually presses events toward a further fulfillment.[5] Despite the possession of the Land, and the achievements of David and Solomon, the promise of rest remains open. We already noted in connection with Jesus' attitude to the Sabbath and the claim of the author to the Hebrews that "there remains a rest for the people of God" (4:9).

But then, looking beyond "The Former Prophets", in the writing prophets, the "dynamic of promise and fulfilment" takes new forms. The classical prophets looked to a future where a catastrophic divine judgment would show all sense of security based on the traditions of election from the past to be insufficient. That was the negative message. But it also had two very important positive elements. First, those prophets also maintained that: "Beyond this judgement lies a definitive, eschatological act of [the Lord] on behalf of his people, sometimes glimpsed as if from afar, sometimes rendering in glowing colours."[6] Then secondly, there is no question of absolute discontinuity with Israel's past. In von Rad's words: "The specific form of the new thing which [the classical prophets] herald is not chosen at random; the new is to be effected in a way which is more or less analogous to God's former saving work."[7] And so those prophets speak of a new entry into the Land, a new David, a new Zion, a New Covenant, a New Exodus. True, in the Book of Isaiah, Israel is told:

---

[5] G. von Rad, "The Deuteronomic Theology of History in 1 and 2 Kings", in *The Problem of the Hexateuch and Other Essays* (London and Edinburgh, 1966), pp. 205–21.

[6] Watson, "Old Testament Theology as a Christian Theological Enterprise", p. 201.

[7] Von Rad, *Old Testament Theology*, 2:117.

Remember not the former things,
   nor consider the things of old.
Behold, I am doing a new thing.

(Is 43:18–19)

But this is clearly not meant literally, since in the three previous verses the God who promises this new thing is described as:

The LORD, your Holy One,
   the Creator of Israel, your King . . .
   who makes a way in the sea,
   a path in the mighty waters,
who brings forth chariot and horse, army and
   warrior;
they lie down, they cannot rise,
   they are extinguished, quenched like a wick.

(43:15–17)

In other words, he wants to continue to be known or identified as the God of the original Exodus!

Typological Thinking

And this is where von Rad brings in typology. For von Rad, typology is a kind of analogical thinking. More specifically, the basic claim that typological exegesis of the Old Testament makes is that the Christ-event—the Incarnation, the paschal mystery, and the reception of those by the apostolic Church—constitutes, in his words, "the only analogy which is relevant for a theological interpretation of these texts"[8]. It is not a question of saying that typological interpretation

---

[8] Von Rad, "Typologische Auslegung", p. 31.

is one means among others that the Church can make use of if she wishes because she finds this helpful in showing the continued pertinence of the Old Testament to the lives of the faithful. Von Rad makes a much stronger affirmation than this. For him, typological exegesis is what these texts—the Old Testament—positively "require if their true nature is to be brought to light".[9] In the term favored by many theologically minded Catholic exegetes, the texts carry a "plenary sense".[10]

For a Christian, the goal toward which the restless movement of the Old Testament is directed is Jesus Christ, and, appropriately enough then, what traditional typology, as found in the Fathers and the liturgy, seeks to do is to indicate a way of displaying the relation to Christ of the main events of Israel's story. The typological method cannot be called an extraneous imposition on the Old Testament, since, on the contrary, it grows out of the Old Testament from within. Its connection with the Old Testament is organic and inherent. In his commentary on the Book of Genesis, von Rad,

[9] Watson, "Old Testament Theology as a Christian Theological Enterprise", p. 205.

[10] One can usefully distinguish here between (a) the sense an Old Testament text possesses when read in the context of the entire canon of Scripture, Old and New, as received in the tradition of the Church: the Louvain Old Testament scholar Joseph Coppens called this "the total or 'perichoretic' " plenary sense; (b) the sense an Old Testament text possesses when it enjoys a homogeneous historic continuity with some New Testament text—for Coppens, the "historic-typical" plenary sense; (c) the sense an Old Testament text possesses when its authors used it to give provisional expression to their grasp of the later—or final—outcome of revelation, termed by Coppens the "prophetic-typical" plenary sense. See J. Coppens, *Les harmonies des deux Testaments: Essai sur les divers sens des Ecritures et sur l'unité de la Révélation* (Paris-Tournai, 1947). Coppens admits that the latter is only available via tradition, where its certitude, in particular cases, is guaranteed by the Magisterium of the Church. That implies, then, that some aspect of the literal sense of the Old Testament cannot be found by historical methods alone.

despite his heavyweight status as a historical-critical scholar, roundly declares that: "We receive the Old Testament from the hands of Jesus Christ, and all exegesis of the Old Testament therefore depends on whom one thinks Jesus Christ to be."[11] Or as Joseph Ratzinger, with rather more nuanced sophistication, writes:

> Nowadays it is the fashion to attack typology as doing violence to the text, and certainly there have been inappropriate applications of typology. But the central and quite justified significance, the essential message, of typology is absolutely clear right here: there is a line running through the history of faith and worship. Inwardly, things corresponds to this—there are deviations, but there is also a path in a particular direction; the inner harmony with the figure of Jesus Christ, with his message and his existence, cannot be ruled out, in spite of the variety of historical contexts and stages.[12]

Reverting to the stance proper to dogmatics, Francis Watson declares with exemplary forthrightness: "The 'Old Testament', as Christian scripture, only comes into existence in the moment of absolute newness represented by Jesus, and should be interpreted on the basis of its moment of origin; only the antitypes make the types visible as such."[13] We must look now at some concrete examples of how that works.

---

[11] G. von Rad, *Genesis: A Commentary* (London, 1972), p. 43.

[12] J. Ratzinger, *Truth and Tolerance: Christian Belief and World Religions* (San Francisco: Ignatius Press, 2004), pp. 96–97.

[13] Watson, "Old Testament Theology as a Christian Theological Enterprise", p. 207.

10

CONCRETE EXAMPLES

In his eucharistic sequence, the *Lauda Sion*, Saint Thomas Aquinas does not confine himself to generalities in his typological exegesis of the biblical basis of the eucharistic sacrament. True, he does offer a generalized statement, in the verse beginning "*In hac mensa novi Regis*", or "within our new King's banquet hall". That verse continues:

> the Old is by the new replaced;
> the substance hath the shadow chased;
> and rising day dispels the night.

But a few verses later, after hailing the Blessed Sacrament as "the bread of angels sent for pilgrims in their banishment", and summing up some New Testament references to this nourishment ("The bread for God's true children meant, / That may not unto dogs be given"), Thomas gets down to concrete examples of Old Testament types.

> In figuris praesignatur,
> Cum Isaac immolator:
> Agnus paschae deputatur:
> Datur manna patribus.

In the English translation in my Burns, Oates, and Washbourne Missal of 1952:

Oft in the olden types foreshowed;
In Isaac on the altar bowed,
And in the ancient paschal food,
And in the manna sent from heaven.

All three of his examples: the sacrifice of Isaac, the Passover from Egypt, and the manna of the desert wanderings—are of course taken from the Pentateuch, the first from the Abraham cycle in Genesis and the second two from Exodus. It is indeed in the Pentateuch or the Pentateuch together with the first book of "The Former Prophets", Joshua, that the typological interest in the Old Testament literature of the Fathers and the Liturgy is chiefly focused, following in this not least the example given by Saint Paul.

Father (later, Cardinal) Jean Daniélou in his study *Sacramentum futuri* ("The Sacrament of the Future"), which was translated into English under the rather less striking title *From Shadows to Reality*, takes principally four types much exploited in the Church of the Fathers. And these are Adam, and notably the sleep of Adam; the Flood; the sacrifice of Isaac; and the Exodus, culminating as this does in the entry into the Promised Land.

Adam and His Slumbers

Let us take each of these examples in turn. First, Adam and especially the sleep of Adam—that is, the sleep during which Eve was drawn from the side of our protoparent, the first man. Saint Hilary of Poitiers, sometimes called "the Athanasius of the West", writing in the fourth century, in his *Tractate on the Mysteries* says that all the outstanding persons and leading events of Scripture can be considered both stages preparing the mystery and also rough outlines prefiguring the mystery that is one day to be fulfilled in Christ. He calls them *sacramenta*, signs, as the sacraments of the Church are signs. And of these, he goes on, the very first to be mentioned is "the sleep of Adam". The thinking is that, just as Eve, Mother of all the living, was drawn by God from Adam's side, so the Church, the Mother of all the supernaturally living, came forth from the side of Christ as he slept on the Cross—namely, through the blood and water that flowed from his opened heart when he died, according to the testimony of Saint John's Gospel (19:34–35).

The Letters of Saint Paul, and especially the Letter to the Romans, already make the point that Adam, the Head of the old humanity, is a type of Jesus Christ, who is Head of the new. Saint Paul specifically calls Adam *typos tou mellontos*, "a type of the One who was to come" (Rom 5:14). There is a likeness between Adam and Christ, since both are primary originators in a genealogy, whether physical or spiritual. There is also a difference between them, as Paul explains when he sums up the spiritually progenitive power of Christ as the free gift of grace and sums up the physically enlivening power of Adam as at the same time a deviation from the divine design insofar as it passed on to us a nature wounded by sin and destined for death. "The free gift is not like the trespass. For if many died through one man's trespass, much more have the grace of God and the free gift in the grace of that one man Jesus Christ abounded for many" (Rom 5:15).

Implicitly, that way of construing Christ in terms of Adam, and Adam in terms of Christ, is present also in the Gospels. In the Synoptics, in the story of the temptation of Jesus, the temptation of Adam is relived but with an opposite outcome. This is underlined especially in Saint Mark's Gospel, where after his temptations, Jesus is described as enjoying mastery over the animals and being served by the angels. In Genesis, the animals were brought to Adam to name, which was a sign of that mastery, and likewise the ancient Jewish commentaries on Scripture, the Midrash, speak of angelic ministrations as a feature of Adam's existence before the Fall, even if Genesis itself fails to advert to this. Whereas Adam's obedience wrecked the original divine vocation of mankind to enter into God's communion, his endless life, God himself takes up this task again in Jesus Christ who, as the Second Adam, leads mankind, this time definitively, into the Paradise we lost in our first father. Saint Paul has his own way of expressing that in 1 Corinthians 15:45. There he says (I paraphrase somewhat) that, mankind began with the Adam who became, as Scripture tells us, a living soul. It is fulfilled in the Second Adam (Christ) who has become for us a life-giving spirit. In the Letter to the Ephesians, Paul applies to Christ and the Church the text in Genesis that founds the covenant of marriage: "a man shall leave his father and mother and be joined to his wife, and the two shall become one" (Eph 5:31, with reference to Gen 2:24). In other words, the union of Adam and Eve, who, despite their lack of a human father and mother, were nonetheless the first married couple, represents the union of Christ and the Church. Already in the Old Testament, the Song of Solomon portrayed the union of the Lord with Israel in a paradiselike setting. Now Paul is revealing that this union is actually fully realized in Jesus and his Bride.

What the Fathers do, then, is to take this Adam-Christ typology, with its combined likeness and difference, one step —or more than one step—further. Here is how Daniélou presents the key text from Saint Hilary. "Eve, born of Adam's flesh [is a type of] the Church born of the Word made flesh, since it is first from the pierced side of Christ, sleeping on the cross, as from the pierced side of Adam, that blood and water flowed out, symbols of Baptism and the Eucharist, giving birth and life to the Church—and this communication of life is continued by the sacramental life, through which the flesh of Christ received in communion continues to sanctify the Church." "This theme", explains Daniélou, "is at once Christological and sacramental": here we have "the mystery of Christ himself, prefiguring the mysterious bond between his Passion and the birth of the Church."[1] Daniélou emphasizes that this is not simply an imaginative insight on the part of some individual—and therefore possibly isolated—theologian. It is found in Tertullian, in North Africa; in Saint Methodius of Olympus, in Greece; in Gregory of Elvira (near Granada), in Spain; in Saint Zeno of Verona, in northern Italy: four writers who between them span the whole of the period from the subapostolic age to the Council of Nicaea and the entire Mediterranean world where the Church came to birth.

Saint Zeno's account is especially rich because it brings "the sleep of Adam" theme into connection with other aspects of the Adam-Christ, Eve-Church typology. He writes:

As the devil by his plausibility had found a way into the ear of Eve, inflicting a deadly wound, so Christ, entering the ear of Mary, brushes away all the heart's vices and heals the woman by being born of the Virgin. Adam is circumcised on the Lord's cross, and as it was through a woman who alone had touched the deadly tree that both the sexes had found death, so in an inverse fashion by this man who hung on a tree the whole human race has been redeemed. And lest the beginning should fail to appear as totally restored to its earlier

---

[1] J. Daniélou, *From Shadows to Reality: Studies in the Biblical Typology of the Fathers* (London, 1960), pp. 52–53, with reference to St. Hilary of Poitiers, *Tractate on the Mysteries*, 1.3.

condition, man on the cross is first offered [in sacrifice] but then during that blessed sleep his side is pierced by a lance. Yet it is not a rib that is removed, but through water and blood, signifying Baptism and martyrdom, the spiritual body of a spiritual woman issues forth in such a way that while Adam is renewed by Christ, Eve is renewed by the Church.[2]

Here we are listening to the authentic sacramental catechesis of the teaching Church, the teaching given, especially at Christian initiation, not just to inform people about Christian doctrine but to insert them into the Christian life in depth. It is, we can say, *mystagogical* teaching, teaching that is aimed at profound spiritual initiation.

In his own very full Adam-Christ typology, Saint Irenaeus of Lyons makes Christ the "recapitulator" of Adam. In his writings, this term has a complex sense. Christ realizes aright the plan spoiled in Adam, "rerunning the episode", so to speak, and this time getting man's part right. He does not merely, however, do well what Adam was meant to do but did badly. In so doing—all this is contained in the "recapitulation" idea—he also brings the entire divine design to perfect fulfillment. One way the wider Church tradition put this was to say that the mystery of baptism is one of reentry, but this time definitive reentry, into Paradise. We saw how the messianic hope, *sensu lato* ("broadly conceived"), includes among its intrinsic aspects a return to Paradise. The baptismal life is—we hardened folk of the storm-tossed Church of the early twenty-first century may be surprised to hear—the paradisal life. As Saint Gregory of Nyssa tells the catechumens: "You are outside Paradise, catechumen, as sharing in the exile of Adam our first parent. But now that the gate has been opened once more, enter in again."[3]

---

[2] St. Zeno of Verona, *Tractates*, 1.13; translation modified.
[3] St. Gregory of Nyssa, *On Baptism*, (Migne, *PG* 46:418c).

As Daniélou organizes the patristic references to this, the realization of Paradise is brought about first by reentering through baptism; secondly, by entering more deeply through the mystical life; and finally, by completing this process in our deaths, something more clearly seen in dying as practiced by the martyrs.[4]

The Great Flood

The water symbolism of Scripture is, however, ambivalent, as we see from our second "concrete example", the great Flood. Baptism, after all, is not only positive, the renewal of our arid selves by the life-giving waters of divine grace. It is also negative, a divine judgment on sin. Indeed, we can say, baptism is able to be positive only because it is first negative. Divine judgment on us on account of our sinfulness is a necessary presupposition of mankind's renewal by saving grace. We can see from the frescoes in the Roman catacombs how the baptismal imagery of the early Church took as its main resource the great Old Testament miracles of deliverance celebrated by the synagogue in its worship. That includes the saving of Noah from the catastrophe in which God virtually destroyed a sinful world. In Saint Peter's first Letter, which may be based on a baptismal homily, Noah's survival of the Flood is used as a type both for the descent of Christ into hell and for the Christian's descent into the baptismal waters. In early Christian exegesis (so Daniélou again):

> The Flood appears first as the figure of Christ's triumph over the sea dragon through his descent into Hell: he is the true Noah who has experienced the turbulence of the waters of

[4] Daniélou, *From Shadows to Reality*, p. 25, with references respectively to St. Cyril of Jerusalem's *Procatechesis*; St. Ambrose, *On Paradise*, 1.1; and the *Passion of SS. Perpetua and Felicity*, 1.

death, and has been delivered by God to be the beginning of a
new world; [the Flood also] represents . . . Baptism wherein
the Christian is buried with Christ in the waters of death
through the symbol of the baptismal waters, figuratively undergoing the punishment due to sin and being freed with
Christ and henceforth belonging to the new creation, to that
eighth day which is the life of the world to come, already
present in mystery.[5]

That reference to the "eighth day" is an allusion to the notion of one of the apostolic Fathers, Saint Justin Martyr, that
because Noah and his wife, his three sons and the wives of
his sons form together the number eight, they are a type
of the eighth day, the day of the manifestation of the Resurrection. Compare 1 Peter 3:20, for which in the ark it
is worthy of mention that specifically eight persons were
"saved through water", and 2 Peter 2:5 which calls Noah,
significantly, "the eighth man, the preacher of righteousness", were we to translate this literally.

The original Flood, then, had meant both condemnation
and salvation. The early Fathers see the type of the Flood
fulfilled not only in the paschal mystery and its sacramental
expression in baptism, but also eschatologically, in what will
befall at the world's end. Baptism is not only an efficacious
memorial of Christ's death and Resurrection, it is also an
efficacious prophecy of our own eschatological death and
resurrection. Baptism is a sacramental anticipation of the
Final Judgment. And all three actions—Christ's death and
Resurrection, our baptism, and the Final Judgment—are for
the Fathers prefigured in the Flood. The Last Judgment will
inevitably have negative aspects, but these will be much soft-
ened for those who by faith and *the* sacrament of faith, holy
baptism, throw themselves on the mighty mercies of God.

---

[5] Daniélou, *From Shadows to Reality*, p. 83; translation slightly modified.

The early ecclesiastical writers stress that the wood of the ark is a type of the wood of the Cross. But they also hold that the ark itself is a type of the Church, which saves us on and in the waters. This too is the common teaching of the tradition. We can cite here Tertullian's treatise on baptism:

> As the dove was sent forth from the Ark after the Flood—the world's baptism, so to speak, purifying it from all iniquity— and that dove, returning with an olive branch, a sign (even among gentiles) of peace, announced peace upon earth, so in the same way, but on a more spiritual level, the dove of the Holy Spirit came down upon earth, that is, upon our flesh when it comes forth from the font after the washing away of its former sins, bringing the peace of God, coming forth from the heavens to where the Church is, prefigured by the Ark.[6]

And Saint John Chrysostom remarks in his homilies: "The story of the flood is a mystery and the details are types of the future. The ark is the Church, Noah is Christ; the dove the Holy Spirit, the olive branch the divine philanthropy."[7] But the difference, adds Chrysostom, is that whereas the ark took in brute animals and kept them as such, the Church takes in beastly people and transforms them.

The Sacrifice of Isaac

What of the sacrifice of Isaac, our third example? Though Abraham is the first and preeminent patriarch, something recognized not only in rabbinic tradition but also by the Jews reported in the Gospel of Saint John who say, "we are children of Abraham" (Jn 8:39), and Jacob was revered by Christian readers of the Old Testament not least for his

[6] Tertullian, *On Baptism*, 8.
[7] St. John Chrysostom, *Homily on Lazarus*, 6.

other name "Israel", which means "He who sees God", it is the intermediate patriarch, Isaac, the son of Abraham and father of Jacob, whose saga is most used typologically by the Fathers. Scholars are not in agreement as to whether the Jewish theology of Isaac's sacrifice was a response to the Christian typological appeal, or something that preceded and prepared for that appeal. Either way, it was a very high theology of Isaac's significance. Owing to a tradition preserved by the Jewish historian Flavius Josephus, a contemporary of Jesus, to the effect that Isaac had consented voluntarily to his sacrifice by Abraham,[8] the episode was seen by Jews not so much as a testimony to Abraham's faith but more as a redemptive work accomplished by Isaac. In Christian circles, the example of Isaac was of intense interest. In the Letter of Barnabas, the author goes so far as to remark, "Christ had to die for our sins, so that the type of Isaac's sacrifice might be fulfilled" (7.3) The Letter to the Hebrews was the first to draw attention to it, unless with some commentators we can find a veiled allusion in Romans 8:32, speaking of the Father of Jesus: "He that spared not his own Son". Hebrews 11:17–19 has this to say:

> By faith Abraham, when he was tested, offered up Isaac, and he who had received the promises was ready to offer up his only son, of whom it was said, "Through Isaac shall your descendants be named." He considered that God was able to raise men even from the dead; hence he did receive him back and this was a symbol.

Daniélou comments:

> The author notices first the essential motive of the trial: Isaac being the fruit of God's promise, God appears to destroy his own promise. But more significant still for us is the conclu-

---

[8] Josephus, *Antiquities of the Jews*, 1.232.

sion. Abraham offers his son, thus destroying the promise, which is a type of the Passion, and an apparent defeat: but he believes that God is powerful to raise him, and because of his faith in God's power he receives him back, which is a type of the Resurrection.[9]

So a twofold type is involved: there is a foreshadowing of the Passion, but there is also a foreshadowing of the Resurrection. Tertullian for his part, in his treatise *Against Marcion* (3.18) notes that the fact that the sacrifice was proposed but not actually carried out suggests its typical status: it would be actually performed only by Jesus Christ.

Tertullian, who considers the episode the most important type of the New Testament fulfillment that the Old Testament contains, expresses the wider tradition when he draws attention to two things—first, to the way Isaac carries wood for his own sacrifice, as the Lord his Cross, and secondly, to the fact that, when God himself provided, in place of Isaac, a ram for the sacrifice, this was a beast, so Genesis informs us, that had been caught by its horns in a thornbush. In Latin, a possible word for the ends of the crossbeam is the "horns" of the Cross, so we can appreciate why Tertullian writes: "So in due course Christ bore the wood on his shoulders, being hung from the ends, *cornibus*, of the Cross, with a crown of thorns on his head."[10] The scene of the sacrifice of Isaac was so popular in early Christian art that Saint Augustine could say: "The deed is so celebrated that, hymned in so many languages, painted in so many places, it strikes the ears and the eyes even of those who seek to fly from it."[11]

---

[9] Daniélou, *From Shadows to Reality*, p. 123; translation slightly modified.
[10] Tertullian, *Against the Jews*, 13.
[11] St. Augustine, *Against Faustus* 22.73.

The Exodus

Our final example is the typology of Moses and the Exodus, leading up to the entry into the Land. As Daniélou writes: "Universal Christian tradition has seen, in the people, events and institutions of the Exodus, types of the New Testament and the sacraments of the Church."[12] To take, with the distinguished Jesuit patrologist, the most obvious aspect: "There is a very evident continuity between [first] the first-born of the Jews, saved by the avenging Angel because they were marked with the blood of the Lamb; [secondly] Christ, the first-born of the new creation, conqueror of death through his blood, the blood of the true Lamb, and [thirdly] the Christian saved from the death due to sin because he was marked at Baptism with the blood of that Lamb [Jesus Christ]."[13] The great prophets, notably Isaiah and Jeremiah, had held up to the Jews of the captivity the future God had in store for them, presenting it as a New Exodus of which the earlier Exodus from Egypt was the type. This New Exodus will be superior to the Exodus of old, as Isaiah insists in chapter 43 of his book.

> Thus says the LORD,
> who makes a way in the sea,
> a path in the mighty waters . . .
> "Remember not the former things,
> nor consider the things of old.
> Behold, I am doing a new thing;
> now it springs forth, do you not perceive it?"
>
> (43:16, 18–19)

[12] Daniélou, *From Shadows to Reality*, p. 153.
[13] Ibid.

It will also have a more spiritual character, as Jeremiah assures us in his book likewise:

> Behold, the days are coming, says the LORD, when I will make a new covenant with the house of Israel and the house of Judah, not like the covenant which I made with their fathers when I took them by the hand to bring them out of the land of Egypt, my covenant which they broke, though I was their husband, says the LORD. But this is the covenant which I will make with the house of Israel after those days, says the LORD: I will put my law within them, and I will write it upon their hearts; and I will be their God, and they shall be my people (31:31-33).

Did the return from Exile fulfill these prophecies? At best, it sub-fulfilled them: fulfilled them only in part, for the Old Testament writers record the disappointment of contemporaries that the temporal and spiritual achievements of the Return were not greater, and in the last of the prophets, Malachi, it is strongly implied that the New Exodus has not yet been achieved, since Elijah is to be sent to prepare the way—evidently, for the Lord who is to come once again across the waters and through the wilderness.

Not surprisingly, the Judaism of the time of Jesus, following the prophetic tradition, represented the time of salvation in terms borrowed from the Exodus: the Messiah will replicate all the main features of the person and role of Moses; Israel will be fed once again on manna and living water. This salvation will take place in the springtime, as did the Passover.[14]

The New Testament authors, above all Saint Matthew, show these expectations to be fulfilled in Christ. Saint

---

[14] L. Goppelt, *Typos: Die typologische Deutung des Alten Testaments im Neuen* (Gütersloh, 1939; Darmstadt, 1969), pp. 30-34. This book was photographically reproduced at Darmstadt in 1969.

Matthew's Gospel is permeated with allusions to the Exodus. Matthew presents the life of our Lord in the framework of the New Exodus foretold by the prophets. As an infant, Jesus leaves Egypt, following the death of Herod. He is the herald prophesied by Malachi in John the Baptist (Mt 11:10), whose message is, "Prepare the way of the Lord" (3:3). The first Gospel goes on to show us what this way is. Immediately after his baptism, which corresponds to the crossing of the Red Sea, Jesus is led by the Spirit into the wilderness, where, after crossing that Sea, the Jewish people underwent various trials. Jesus too is tempted, for forty days, parallel to the forty years of the original Exodus experience (and the forty days of Moses' fast). The character of his endurance is surely modeled on Deuteronomy 8:2–3, where we read:

> And you shall remember all the way which the LORD your God has led you these forty years in the wilderness, that he might humble you, testing you to know what was in your heart, whether you would keep his commandments, or not. And he humbled you and let you hunger and fed you with manna, which you did not know . . . ; that he might make you know that man does not live by bread alone, but that man lives by everything that proceeds out of the mouth of the LORD.

Jesus cites this text in response to the first temptation, while Matthew links the second temptation—to put the Lord to the test—to the "murmuring" of the people against the Lord at Massah and Meribah as described in the Books of Exodus and Numbers, about which Moses in Deuteronomy drew the lesson: "You shall not put the LORD your God to the test, as you tested him at Massah. You shall diligently keep the commandments of the LORD your God, and his testimonies, and his statutes, which he has commanded you"

(6:16–17). The final temptation on the high mountain recalls Sinai, not least because Christ's answer to Satan is taken from the Decalogue revealed there: "You shall worship the Lord your God and him only shall you serve" (Mt 4:10). So Jesus, the true Israel and the new Moses, both in the desert and on the mountain top, offers the contrast of his own fidelity to the waywardness shown by Israel.

As the story line of Matthew's Gospel unfolds, Jesus' resemblance to Moses intensifies. We see that in the Sermon on the Mount, which shows Jesus as the Lawgiver of the New Covenant. Again, as Moses passed through the sea, commanding the waters, so Jesus "crosses" the sea, commanding wind and waves. As Moses distributed manna in the desert, so Jesus gives bread to the multitude. As Moses chose seventy elders to assist him in governing the people, so Jesus chooses and sends out seventy disciples. The parallel between Moses and Christ culminates in the Transfiguration, with its numerous allusions to the Exodus: the presence of Moses himself, the cloud, the divine voice, and the booths that Peter offers to make in line with a Jewish practice on the Feast of Tabernacles, the liturgical commemoration of Israel's dwelling in tents during the Exodus journey.[15]

Saint John's Gospel prolongs Saint Matthew's in this respect. From its outset, in the Prologue, the Word appears as the Shekinah, the true abode of God's glory, which in the desert filled the tabernacle the people had constructed there at the Lord's command (Ex 40:34–38). Then he reveals himself as the Serpent lifted up in the desert, healing those who look on it (Jn 3:14); as the Manna come down from heaven to feed God's people (Jn 6:32–35); as the Spring gushing forth water for them (Jn 7:37b); as the

---

[15] See H. Riesenfeld, *Jésus transfiguré* (Uppsala, 1947), p. 122.

Pillar of Fire following the people (Jn 8:12), and as the Paschal Lamb whose blood not only protects from deadly danger but now takes away the sins of the world (Jn 1:29; 19:36).

No doubt the fourth Gospel already has the Church's sacraments in view, but the chief apostle to spell this out is Saint Paul, who in 1 Corinthians tells his readers that the crossing of the Red Sea is a type of baptism, and the water gushing from the rock a type of the Holy Eucharist. Saint Peter in his first Letter manages to condense into his description of baptism at least six features of the Exodus narrative: the girding of the loins, the rejection of the fleshpots of Egypt, freedom from bondage, the blood of a lamb without spot or blemish, the rock of living water, and the description of the people of God as "a royal priesthood, a holy nation, God's own people" (1 Peter 2:9; cf. Ex 19:5–6).

Finally, among all the texts that might be cited, we can look briefly at the Johannine Revelation. The Revelation describes the life of the Christian people in Exodus terms. Under the gaze of the sacrificed Lamb, the punishments meted out to the enemies of God are repetitions of the plagues of Egypt, worked by Moses to secure the liberation of the people. The deliverance of the "number of the sealed"— the 144,000, based on the twelve tribes of Israel who now represent the Church—is a new crossing of the Red Sea, as we hear in Revelation 15:2–3: "And I saw what appeared to be a sea of glass mingled with fire, and those who had conquered the beast . . . standing beside the sea of glass with harps of God in their hands. And they sing the song of Moses, the servant of God, and the song of the Lamb." In other words, the Exodus is fulfilled in Jesus Christ and the people he redeems.

In their own typological exegesis, the Fathers of the Church build on these foundations. They are particularly keen to show how, through the paschal mystery, the Exodus is the type of the sacraments by whose means the power of God continues to bring about man's redemption. That is why we find patristic typology at its most developed in texts designed for catechetical instruction and the purposes of liturgical worship. The principal theme is the Exodus and Christian initiation, but within this we find a number of themes covered. The same motifs recur in different Fathers in both East and West at the same time, but to illustrate them we need to have recourse, obviously enough, to individual texts.

In the West, Saint Ambrose provides two major sources: his treatise *On the Sacraments* and its companion volume, *On the Mysteries*. Ambrose discovers pertinent types in the pillar of light that preceded the Israelites and the pillar of cloud that followed them; in the episode in Exodus 15 when Moses sweetened the waters of Marah, and of course in the Red Sea crossing itself. First, then, in *On the Sacraments*, Ambrose finds in the pillar of light a type of Christ pouring his truth into the minds of those undergoing Christian initiation. He finds in the pillar of cloud a type of the Holy Spirit who once overshadowed the Hebrews as later the Spirit would the Virgin Mary and now the same Spirit throws the shadow of his presence over the baptized.[16] Next, at Marah, thirsty Hebrews on the march found water, but it proved bitter to the taste. Moses threw his staff into the waters, and the waters turned sweet. For the Ambrose of *On the Mysteries*, this is a type of the waters of baptism, sweetened by the Cross. "Water, without the preaching of the Lord's Cross,

---

[16] St. Ambrose, *On the Sacraments*, 1.6.2.

is of no value for salvation, but when it has been sanctified by the mystery of the saving Cross, then it is ready to be used as a spiritual bath and healing drink. As Moses cast his staff into the spring, being a prophet, so does the priest proclaim over the water the Lord's Cross and it is replenished with grace."[17] And lastly, the crossing of the Red Sea is the most fundamental motif as Ambrose himself points out, this time in, once again, *On the Sacraments*. "What is more important [for the Old Testament] than the fact that the People of the Jews passed through the sea? Yet the Jews who passed through all died in the wilderness. But he who passes through the font, that is from earthly to heavenly things— for this is the *transitus*, that is, the Passover, a passing from sin to life, from guilt to grace . . . he who passes through this font does not die but rises again."[18]

In the East, Saint Cyril of Jerusalem in his *Mystagogical Catecheses* contextualizes the crossing of the Sea within the setting of the Passover from Egypt as a whole. "You must know [he tells the catechumens] that this type is found in ancient history. For when that cruel and ruthless tyrant Pharaoh oppressed the free and high-born people of the Hebrews, God sent Moses to bring them out of the evil thralldom of the Egyptians. The doorposts were anointed with the blood of the lamb, that the Destroyer might pass by those houses which had the sign of the blood. And so the Hebrew people was marvellously delivered." Now Cyril invites people to institute a comparison, old with new.

Now turn from the ancient to the recent, from the type to the reality. There we have Moses sent from God to Egypt, here Christ sent by his Father into the world; there, Moses had to

[17] St. Ambrose, *On the Mysteries*, 3.14.
[18] Ambrose, *On the Sacraments*, 1.4.12.

lead forth an oppressed people out of Egypt: here, Christ rescues mankind when overwhelmed by sin; there the blood of
the lamb was the spell against the Destroyer; here, the blood
of the unblemished Lamb, Jesus Christ, puts the demons to
flight; there that tyrant pursued to the sea the people of God,
and in like manner this brazen and shameless demon follows
the people of God to the very waters of salvation. The tyrant
of old was drowned in the sea, and the present tyrant is destroyed in the saving waters.[19]

Saint Gregory of Nyssa, in his *Life of Moses*, thinks not so
much of assault by the evil angels as trouble from our own
disordered passions (though these two are interconnected).
"Do you not see that the Egyptian army, and all its forces,
horses, chariots of their riders, archers, slingers and foot-
soldiers—all these powers cast themselves into the water after the Hebrews whom they pursue? But the water, by the
power of the word of faith and of the luminous cloud becomes the beginning of life for those who seek refuge there
and the beginning of death for their attackers."[20]

Whether in West or in East, whatever the precise way the
"typical" relation—the relation of type to antitype, type to
fulfillment—is presented, there is some kind of appropriate
proportion involved. As Saint John Chrysostom explains in
a commentary on a "dictum" in Saint Paul's Letters: "The
type must have something in common with the antitype, or
there would be nothing typical. But the type must not be
identical with the antitype or it would be the reality itself.
There must be that proportion, so that it neither possesses
all that the reality has, nor is it entirely deficient. . . Do not
expect the Old Testament to explain everything. If you find
certain enigmas, which are difficult and obscure, learn to

---

[19] St. Cyril of Jerusalem, *Mystagogical Catecheses*, 19.3.
[20] St. Gregory of Nyssa, *The Life of Moses* (Migne *PG* 44.361c).

be satisfied."[21] Chrysostom's own example here is the food and drink of the manna and desert water that prefigure the Holy Eucharist. "Just as you . . . coming up out of the bath of water, hasten to the table, so did they, coming up out of the sea, find a new and wonderful table, I mean the manna. And just as you have a wondrous drink, the blood of the Savior, so did they; for even when there were no springs, or running waters, an abundance of water gushed forth from a dry and barren rock." That the water from the rock can typify either the eucharistic chalice or holy baptism shows Chrysostom is right to caution his hearers, "Do not expect me to explain everything, but when you consider the various events bear in mind they are only part of a rough outline".[22] Typology means "both continuity and disparity".[23]

The Entry into the Land

The Exodus-Sinai events end with Joshua and the entry into the Land. In the Letter to the Hebrews, there is just a hint that Joshua is a type of Christ who leads the people into the true Promised Land (cf. Heb 4:8 and 4:14). But when the Fathers take up the theme, the first point they emphasize is the significance of Joshua's name: *Iêsous*, "Jesus". Saint Justin Martyr, in his *Dialogue* with the Jew Trypho comments on the fact that in Exodus, when the Lord instructs Moses to tell the people God is sending his angel to bring them into the Land he has prepared for them "for my name is in him" (Ex 23:20), it was actually Joshua who—humanly speaking,

[21] St. John Chrysostom, *On the Apostolic Saying, "I Would Not Wish You Ignorant"*, 4.
[22] Ibid.
[23] Daniélou, *From Shadows to Reality*, p. 199.

at any rate—led the people into the Land.[24] Saint Justin in-
fers that "Jehoshua" or "Iêsous" is a name of the Word of
God, and Joshua himself the prophetic type of Jesus Christ.
Furthermore, as others of the Fathers propose, Joshua's victory over Amalek is a type of Christ's victory over principalities and powers. Just as Joshua divided the land between
the tribes, so Jesus Christ distributes the inheritance of salvation to the elect. When Joshua re-circumcises the people
and renews the covenant by reading the words of the Law,
he shows the incompleteness of the patriarchal and Exodus-
Sinai events and thus points to the future completion of what
they promise. When the spies Joshua sends out to explore
the Promised Land are saved from capture by the enemy
king of Jericho thanks to the efforts of the pagan harlot Rahab, she is told to dangle a scarlet cord from her window so
that when the Israelites arrive to take the city she and her
household will in turn be saved from slaughter.

The Fathers give this last episode a prominent place in
the typological exegesis of the Book of Joshua. As Justin,
again, explains to Trypho: "The sign of the scarlet thread,
which the spies sent to Jericho by Joshua, son of Nave, gave
to Rahab the harlot, telling her to bind it to the window
through which she let them down to escape from their enemies, also manifested the symbol of the blood of Christ, by
which those who were at one time harlots and evil persons
out of all nations are saved, receiving remission of sins and
continuing to sin no longer."[25] Origen of Alexandria, interpreting Rahab's name as meaning "breadth", thinks of her
as a notorious sinner who was filled with the Holy Spirit
and prophesied when she said to Joshua's men, "I know that

---

[24] St. Justin Martyr, *Dialogue with Trypho*, 75.1-2.
[25] Ibid., 206.3-4.

the LORD has given you the land" (Josh 2:9a). Followed by Saint Hilary and other Fathers in the West, he treats her, accordingly, as a type of the Catholic Church, which is also broadly spread, once a sinner and now a prophetic voice. As he says in his homilies on Joshua:

> She who was formerly a harlot receives this injunction: All who shall be found in thy house shall be saved. . . . If anyone wishes to be saved, let him come into the house of her that is a harlot. Even if anyone of this people (the Jewish) wishes to be saved, let him come into this house to obtain salvation. Let him come into this house in which the blood of Christ is the sign of redemption. Let there be no mistake, let no one deceive himself: outside this house, that is outside the Church, there is no salvation. If anyone does go forth, he is the cause of his own death.[26]

That homily is the first place, incidentally, where the words "outside the Church is no salvation" make their appearance, before they are taken up, more influentially, by Saint Cyprian in his treatise *On the Unity of the Church*.

One reason why the Cyprianic version was more influential than Origen's was the dishonor into which Origen's name fell. Great exegete as he was, he came to be considered, rather, a speculative theologian who had not fully respected the limits of the Church's discourse. Certainly he was willing to innovate on the catechetical tradition he had received, and a pertinent case is his typological reading of the Red Sea and River Jordan events. For Origen, the crossing of the Red Sea, which took place in fear while on a forced march, is a type of entry into the catechumenate, merely. It is the crossing of the River Jordan, which was joyful and serene, that is for him the true type of baptism.

[26] Origen, *Homilies on Joshua*, 3.

Similarly, he takes the manna in the desert to be the bread of the imperfect, ill-suited to be a type of the eucharistic Food. It was the bread Joshua got the people to bake in the Land that is the real type of the divine Eucharist. That was too sharp a wrench from Church tradition to be acceptable. Yet Origen was responsible for the fuller development of a Joshua-typology in others, such as Saint Gregory of Nyssa, who writes in his oration on baptism: "Imitate Jesus the son of Nave. Bear the Gospel, as he bore the ark. Leave behind the desert, that is, sin: cross the Jordan, and hasten to the life according to the commands of Christ. Hasten to that land which brings forth fruits of joy, where flow, as was promised, milk and honey. Overturn Jericho, your former way of life, and do not let it be built up again. All these things are types for us, all prefigure truths which are now revealed."[27] Yes, the texts reviewed confirm the judgment of the Pontifical Biblical Commission: these are meanings "expressed by the biblical texts when read, under the influence of the Holy Spirit, in the content of the paschal mystery of Christ and the new life that flows from it."[28]

[27] St. Gregory of Nyssa, *On Baptism* (Migne *PG* 46, 420d–421a).
[28] Pontifical Biblical Commission, *The Interpretation of the Bible in the Church* (Vatican City, 1993), 2.B. 2.

PART FIVE

FATHERS AND DOCTORS INTERPRET

11

AUGUSTINE ON GENESIS

Even when Origen's name fell under a cloud, the example
of his exegesis, his way of reading the Old Testament—by
and large, not in all of its particulars—had a considerable
impact. Quite simply, he was the most learned, prolific,
and profound commentator on the Old Testament in the
ancient Church. Very many, though not all, of his homilies
on the Old Testament have come down to us. Apart from
developing an important *moral* way of reading the Old Testament—using it as a sourcebook, generously interpreted,
for constructing models of ethical behavior, he also exem-
plified by his preaching the three basic aspects of the typological approach—Christological, mystical, and eschatological. Moreover, not only can these dimensions be found
richly in his writing, he has a clear sense of their order and
interrelation. For him they are not three different things,
but "three successive points of development in a single typology": namely, Christ considered in his historic life (the
Christological antitype), Christ considered in his Mystical
Body (the mystical antitype), and Christ considered in his
final Parousia (the eschatological antitype). We find this
again in Saint Augustine, where it appears as the three ad-
vents of Christ—in the flesh, in our souls, and in glory.
That—even taken by itself, before we have begun to fill
out its content—makes an important doctrinal point about

the Bible: "Not only does the Old Testament as a whole prefigure the New, but equally the coming of Christ in the flesh and in the Church prefigures the final Parousia."[1] So one modern student of the exegesis of the Fathers can say about Augustine's biblical interpretation when he is preaching: "We are in the ambit of the traditional typological and more generally allegorical reading of the Old Testament, the one best able to develop the text read in Church in such a way as to instruct the faithful and encourage them in Christian commitment."[2]

We can examine this by seeing how Augustine deals with the first book of Scripture, the Book of Genesis. Let me note first that Origen found it extremely difficult, but not impossible, to get beyond the Prologue to the Gospel according to Saint John. Likewise, Augustine found it difficult to get beyond the Genesis account of creation and the Fall—even though he made three attempts to write a commentary on this book. I shall be concentrating on the earliest commentary, which he wrote as a refutation of the Manichees: the heresy—a better description would be the alternative religion—to which he himself had been attracted as a young man, because it seemed to have a plausible answer to the problem of evil. It was a heresy that in its medieval form, Catharism or Albigensianism, aroused Saint Dominic's zeal for teaching the orthodox faith and led him to the notion of an Order of Preachers.

---

[1] Daniélou, *From Shadows to Reality*, p. 277.

[2] M. Simonetti, *Biblical Interpretation in the Early Church: An Historical Introduction to Patristic Exegesis* (Edinburgh, 1994), p. 106.

Augustine and Creation

Before we launch into Saint Augustine's commentary we can raise and answer the question: Why did Augustine's mind return so often to the subject of creation—not just in these commentaries but in the *Confessions* (books 10–12), in the *City of God* (book 11), and at many other places? And the answer surely is that the reality of the relation between the creature and the Creator underlies all religious actions of whatever kind—even, or especially—those based on grace. As one scholar has written:

> During his break with Manicheism . . . and his final turn to the Church, he realized ever more fully and deeply that he had been created by God and that he possessed his own being only within a relationship to the Creator. . . . In Augustine's view creation is destined to find its fulfillment through a return to God. The Creator awaits the free response of his creature. . . . Only by turning to the Creator, by contemplating God, by praising the light which God is, does the creature achieve its true form and become in fact that which it ought to be according to God's plan, but which it can become only through a free choice.[3]

Augustine will in fact trace a spiritual itinerary for us individually, based on the six days of creation, at the end of his commentary on the opening chapter of Genesis.

Augustine's study of Genesis "against the Manichees" was written in 388 or 389, soon after his journey home to Africa following his baptism in Milan. It is an important doctrinal monument. It amounts to an elucidation of Catholic faith, carried out as an apologia for the Old Testament against

[3] M. Fiedrowicz, "General Introduction", in J. Rotelle, O.S.A., ed., *The Works of Saint Augustine*, I/13, *On Genesis* (Hyde Park, N.Y., 2002), pp. 14–15, 21–22.

its detractors. Specifically, the Manichees rejected the Old Testament on the grounds that its foundational texts, the Genesis creation accounts, were intrinsically incoherent. By denying this charge, Augustine was not only—negatively—defending the Old Testament and defending it as a whole since its account of the Creator/creature relation is so basic and essential. More than this he is also—positively—expanding the Church's intellectual patrimony through careful thinking about the Genesis creation stories themselves. That is what we expect Doctors of the Church to do—first to receive the revealed Word of God with the obedience of faith, but then, by thinking that is bold and ambitious yet always controlled by that same Word, to increase the Church's understanding of the faith once delivered to the saints.

The Manichee objections were as follows. According to Genesis, a time came when God created heaven and earth. Is it, they asked, an acceptable hypothesis to say that a God exists who suddenly decided to create the world after not doing so previously through all eternity?[4] And did he really create everything? The text of Genesis itself implies a preexisting chaotic earth—preexisting matter, then—and the darkness that covered the abyss. Behind these objections lay the Manichees' own mythological system.

> In the primeval beginning, before any history, there existed originally a dualism formed of two natures, that is, Light and Darkness or Good and Evil or God and matter. Manicheism combined this doctrine of the two natures with a doctrine of three periods or times. The "time of the beginning" was the time in which two unadulterated principles existed in opposition to one another. This first time was replaced by the "middle time" in which the attack of the world of darkness

[4] St. Augustine, *On Genesis, against the Manichees*, 1.2.3.

on the world of light led to a mingling of the two principles. The "third time" is the final state in which the dualism will be overcome.[5]

At least in Africa, the Manichees identify the Old Testament Creator with the evil principle, contrasting that God, as Marcion had done, with the good God of the New Testament. They rejected the created world because, as a mingling of light and darkness, it could only be the outcome of aggression by the evil God. In criticizing these beliefs, Augustine was also seeking to amplify, through his reflections, the Church's grasp of her own faith, though he himself puts it far more humbly when he writes at the opening of his treatise (the highly readable translation is by the Cambridge Dominican Edmund Hill):

> There is no part of Scripture . . . which it is not the easiest thing in the world to find fault with, to the dismay of those who do not understand it. But that is precisely why divine Providence permits so many heretics to come along with various errors; it's so that when they taunt us and shower us with questions we do not know the answers to, we may at least in this way be shaken out of our mental sloth and start longing to become acquainted with the Scriptures.[6]

To know Scripture with greater intimacy, or at a greater level of depth, *is* to amplify, to extend, one's sense of the faith if it be true as Saint Thomas thinks, that all divine revelation is contained in Scripture *in some way*. (That may of course be tacitly or allusively, in a fashion that needs the other monuments of tradition to bring out.)

[5] Fiedrowicz, "General Introduction", pp. 32–33.
[6] Augustine, *On Genesis, against the Manichees*, 1.1.2.

Defending Creation

Augustine begins his commentary by considering the Manichee objection to the phrase "in the beginning". So creation was in time, then, was it; and if so, what was God doing beforehand? In the *Confessions*, Augustine remarks about the same question, "I will not respond with that joke someone is said to have made: 'He was getting hell ready for people who inquisitively peer into deep matters!', for this is to evade the force of the question."[7] Augustine explains that time began together with heaven and earth. It only makes sense to speak of "before" and "after" once heaven and earth had come to be, so the Manichee question is what Oxford philosophers call a "category mistake". They mistake the force of the expression they challenge. More profoundly, perhaps, Augustine also maintains—and here is an example of the Old Testament being read within the unity of the entire canon of Scripture, Old and New—that if we are to speak of the creative act as made "in" anything it is not *time* in which it is made but *Christ*, since he was "the Word with the Father, through which and in which all things were made". In Augustine's Latin Bible, when in John 8:25 the Jews ask Jesus, "Who are you?" he does not reply as in our usual English translations, "Even what I have told you from the beginning . . ." but—and perhaps this *is* the implicit force of the Greek—"The beginning, as which I am also speaking to you. . . ." It is our Lord Jesus Christ who is "the beginning" in which God made heaven and earth.

Why, then, did God create? For Augustine, this question reposes on another category mistake. As he writes: "You see, they are seeking to know the causes of God's will, when

[7] St. Augustine, *Confessions*, 11.12.14.

God's will is itself the cause of everything there is. . . . Anyone . . . who goes on to say, 'Why did he wish to make heaven and earth?' is looking for something greater than God's will is; but nothing greater can be found."[8] We might not necessarily agree fully with Augustine on this particular point. Can we not say in the light of revelation that God created so as to communicate his goodness? Or, to put that more elaborately, to enact in nothingness his own perfection as the blessed Trinity? But Augustine is right to insist that these considerations are not something other than a description of God's will.

Next, when Genesis says (in Edmund Hill's translation) at 1:2, "the earth was invisible and shapeless" (in the Revised Standard Version this reads, "without form and void", and in the New American Bible "a formless wasteland"), does not the Old Testament writer actually concede that God created by working on preexisting matter? How, then, can what God did accurately be called "creation"? Augustine replies: All that is said in Scripture is that the earth God made was invisible and shapeless—*before*, that is, God "distributed the form of all things in their proper places and settings with their duly arranged differences", and, not least, before he said, "Let light be made."[9] But what about the "darkness" over the "abyss"? Doesn't this mean that God was in darkness before he made light? Augustine insists that, just because there was no physical light, that does not imply God did not exist in the uncreated Light of his own radiance.

These people, you see, know of no light except the kind they see with the eyes of the flesh. And that is why they worship this sun which we share the sight of not only with the bigger

[8] Augustine, *On Genesis, against the Manichees*, 1.2.4.
[9] Ibid., 1.3.5.

animals, but also with flies and worms; and they say that it is
in a particle of the sun's light that God dwells. But we for our
part should understand that there is another light in which
God dwells, from which comes that light about which we
read in the gospel: "That was the true light, which enlight-
ens every person who comes into this world" (John 1:9).
I mean, the light of this sun [the sun of the solar system]
does not enlighten every *person*, but just the human body and
its mortal eyes; and here we are completely outclassed by
the eyes of eagles, which are said to be able to gaze at the
sun much better than we can. That other light [the light the
Johannine Prologue celebrates], however, does not feed the
eyes of birds, but the pure hearts of people who trust and
believe God and turn from a love of visible and time-bound
things to the fulfillment of his commands.[10]

In any case, the darkness that Genesis speaks of before light
was made is not a thing. It is not "something" at all. Rather,
it is an absence of something—an absence, in fact, of light.
Here Augustine draws out the meaning of Genesis with the
help of reflective thought. Not every referring term, such as
the words "darkness", "silence", "emptiness" here, indicates
a positive reality. These terms may draw attention instead to
the way some positive reality—such as: light, sound, something—*is not*.

On Augustine's account of Genesis, and it makes sense,
when in the beginning God made heaven and earth he made
what was able to be heaven and earth. If Augustine's treatise had
been more widely read in the nineteenth century, or the
twentieth or even the twenty-first century for that matter,
there would not have been such a colossal clash between
Christians and the defenders of Mr. Darwin. As Augustine
explains: "It's as if, when we examine the seed of a tree, we

[10] Ibid., 1.3.6.

were to say that the roots are there, and the trunk and the branches and the fruit and the leaves, not because they are in fact already there, but because they are going to come from there."[11] In our everyday language, he points out, when absolutely certain that what we are expecting will happen, we say, "Take it as already done." It wasn't absurd to call the formless matter "earth" because of all the world's elements, earth seems to have less specific form than the rest (air, water, fire). Nor was it absurd to call it water because "everything that is borne on the earth, whether animals or trees or grasses", starts off by being "formed and nourished from moisture".

Genesis 1:3–4 (again, in Hill's translation) reads, "And God said: Let light be made, and light was made, and God saw the light that it was good." What, exclaim the Manichees, God didn't know the light was good before he made it? Don't be silly, replies Augustine. These words indicate, not that some unfamiliar good suddenly dawned on God, but that something perfectly finished gave him satisfaction. But how about verse 5: "And God called the light 'day' "? Did he perchance use Hebrew in so doing, or did he prefer, say, Greek, or Latin or some other language? To this sardonic query, Augustine responds, Of course not. "With God there is sheer understanding, without any utterance and diversity of tongues." So why does Genesis say God *called* them this or that? It means, says Augustine, "he caused to be called", since he "so distinguished and arranged all things as to make it possible for them to be told apart and given names".[12]

Once the sea and the dry land are formed from the chaotic

---

[11] Ibid., 1.7.11.
[12] Ibid., 1.9.15.

material called first earth and subsequently water, we hear in verses 11 to 13 of the earth sprouting grass for fodder and fruit trees producing fruit. Oh then, comment the Manichees, so who gave orders for thorny and poisonous plants to grow, and trees that bear no fruit into the bargain? Augustine claims such plants come into existence only with the Fall, which is indeed what Adam is told in Genesis 3:17–19, "Cursed is the ground because of you . . . thorns and thistles it shall bring forth to you." Whatever we, heirs of modern natural science, make of this, we can certainly profit from the way Augustine reads Genesis as teaching that, in the plan of God, creation, not least after the Fall, is a spiritual ecology, an environment packed with lessons for us. As he explains, the thorns came to be so that earth: "might always be setting the criminal nature of human sin before people's very eyes, and thus admonishing them to turn away at some time or other from their sins and turn back to God's commandments."[13] And by unfruitful trees: "human beings are being mocked and taunted, to make them understand how they should blush for shame at lacking the fruit of good works in the field of God, that is, in the Church, and to make them afraid, because they so neglect unfruitful trees in their fields and do nothing by way of cultivating them, of being neglected in their turn by God and left uncultivated."[14]

Next comes the creation of the two "lamps", the lesser—the moon, and the greater—the sun. The Manichees asked what occurs to bright children in catechism classes today: How come we're now on the fourth day of creation, and yet we're only just about to have a sun, when it is the sun that measures days in the first place? Augustine's reply is so-

[13] Ibid., 1.13.19.
[14] Ibid.

phisticated. He writes: "The actual changes from one work to the next were given these names: evening on account of the completion of the finished work, and morning on account of the next work to come, from the similarity with human work, which for the most part begins in the morning and ends in the evening."[15] Augustine invokes an important principle of interpretation when he adds: "The transference, you see, of words from human matters to express things divine is common form with the divine Scriptures."[16]

After the creation of the birds and sea creatures, which Augustine thinks are bracketed together on the fifth day because the water content of the atmosphere supports birds in their flight (and so in a sense both are aquatic), we come to the sixth day and the making of the land animals. Of these, the Manichees wanted to know: Why so many kinds, many quite superfluous and some downright horrible and nasty to us, too ? Augustine responds "When they say things like that, they are failing to understand how all these things are beautiful to their maker and craftsman, who has a use for them all in his management of the whole universe which is under the control of his sovereign law."[17] And he goes on in a justly famous passage:

> I must confess that I have not the slightest idea why mice and frogs were created, and flies and worms; yet I can still see that they are all beautiful in their own specific kind, although because of our sins many of them seem to be against our interests. There is not a single living creature, after all, in whose body I will not find, when I reflect upon it, that its measures and numbers and order [a phrase based on Wisdom 1:20] are geared to a harmonious unity. Where these should all

[15] Ibid., 1.14.20.
[16] Ibid.
[17] Ibid., 1.16.25.

come from I cannot conceive, unless it be from the supreme measure and number and order which are identical with the unchanging and eternal sublimity of God himself.[18]

And he concludes:

Yes, of course all living creatures are either useful to us, or pernicious or superfluous. Against the useful ones they have nothing to say. Those that are pernicious are either to punish us or to put us through our paces or to frighten us, so that instead of loving and desiring this life, subject to so many dangers and trials, we should set our hearts on another, better one, where there is total freedom from all worries and anxieties, and get moving along the road to gaining it for ourselves by meritorious devotion.

As for the superfluous ones, what business is it of ours to call them into question? If you object to their not being of any use, be thankful they do no harm, because even if they are not needed for our homes, at any rate they contribute to the completion of this universe, which is not only much bigger than our homes, but much better as well; God manages it after all, much better than any of us can manage our homes. So, then, make use of the useful ones, be careful with the pernicious ones, let the superfluous ones be.[19]

The events of the sixth day culminate in the making of man in God's image, in his likeness—a very important Genesis text. It is "important" not only because Genesis 1:26 is foundational for the theological anthropology, or doctrine of man, in Scripture and the Church's teaching, but also because Augustine's comments raise the wide-ranging question of the anthropomorphic or humanlike way the Old Testament speaks of God. Augustine's remarks on this are, at the present stage of his treatise, adequate but not com-

[18] Ibid., 1.16.26.
[19] Ibid.

prehensive. We shall find in a moment that, having seen off
the Manichee objections to the "Hexaemeron", the six-day
creation account in Genesis, and spoken of the significance
of God's seventh-day rest, he will revisit the entire text in
the spirit, this time, of typological and not philosophical exegesis. That will enable Augustine to complete the analysis
more in relation to Christ and the Church.

The Manichees taunted Catholic Christians, who held to
the inspiration of the Old Testament, for saying man was
made in God's image. Presumably, they cackled, God has
high teeth and a beard, then, since your Scripture certainly
mentions his eyes, ears, lips, and feet? Augustine replies that
"in the Catholic school of doctrine the faithful who have a
spiritual understanding do not believe that God is circum-
scribed in a bodily shape." These names refer not to body
parts but to spiritual powers. Moreover, man's being an image of God consists in his Godlike dominion in relation to
other creatures, and this in the interior man, where reason
and intelligence are found even though, to be sure, the body
shares to a degree in divine imaging inasmuch as it walks
erect, signifying that "our spirit also ought to be held upright, turned to the things above it, that is, to eternal, spiritual realities."[20] We miss here—as yet—any notion that the
imaging of God in man is fulfilled in Christ whom the New
Testament declares to be "the image of God". We also miss
any notion that there is in the divine foreknowledge a plan
to become man, and in that sense a kind of protohumanity
in the divine mind, for God the Word was always to become man, and the anthropomorphic language of the Old
Testament is best seen in that perspective. This is what Tertullian had maintained against Marcion, defending the Old

[20] Ibid., 1.17.28.

Testament thereby only a few miles from where Augustine was living, but doing so two centuries earlier.

So what about that "rest" of God on the Sabbath, which, predictably, the Manichees mocked, asking, Was he tired out, then? For Augustine, when God is said to rest from all his works, which he had made very good, what is at stake is the rest God is going to give *us* from all *our* labors—*if* we have done good works.

Six Ages of the World

This response is adequate, remarks Augustine, so far as it goes, but conscious, maybe, that this supposed climax of his treatise is slightly banal compared with the Christian vision of salvation history and its outcome in the New Jerusalem, he now revisits the six-day creation and its issue on the Sabbath, looking at this typologically, basing himself on the larger picture of Scripture in its overall developmental scheme. As Augustine explains, what he sees "throughout the whole tapestry of the Scriptures is some six working ages . . . , like those six days in which the things were made which Scriptures describes God as making".[21]

Day One of creation is like Day One of history from Adam to Noah. The day when God made light is a type of the early development of our race from its infancy, when it first saw the light of day, to the Great Flood, because man's infancy, we ourselves find, is blotted out by a sort of "flood" of oblivion. Day Two of creation when the solid structure was put in place between the waters above the heavens and the waters below, can be compared, Augustine suggests, to the childhood of the human species, between the "morn-

[21] Ibid., 1.23.35.

ing" of Noah, whose ark was just such a solid "structure",
and the "evening" of the Tower of Babel. The key to this
epoch, for Augustine, is that, just like children, our ancestors were unable to procreate—unable, that is, to procreate
the people of God.

That is why, if the plan of God was to go forward, a
new morning had to come with Abraham. And so the third
age follows, comparable with Day Three of creation when
the dry land was separated out from the waters. Augustine
writes:

> All the nations, you see, are aptly signified by the name of
> "sea", unstable in their errors and tossed about by the doc-
> trinal futilities of idolatry as if by the winds of heaven. So
> then from these futilities of the nations and the storm waves
> of this world the people of God was separated through Abra-
> ham, like the earth which appeared as dry land, thirsting, that
> is, for the heavenly showers of God's commandments. This
> people by worshipping one God, like earth watered to make
> it capable of producing beneficial crops, received the holy
> Scriptures and prophecies.[22]

This age runs from Abraham up to (but excluding) David,
covering the patriarchal and Exodus-Sinai sequences, the entry into the Land, and the time of the Judges up to Samuel.
Its evening was the "sins of the people by which they trans-
gressed the divine commandments" up until what Augustine calls, rather harshly, "the malice of that worst of kings,
Saul".

The fourth age is the young adulthood of the chosen people, the time of its monarchy, opening with the "morning"
of the reign of David. This corresponds to Day Four of creation when sun, moon, and the lesser lights of heaven were

[22] Ibid., 1.23.37.

made, since, as Augustine asks rhetorically: "What, after all, more manifestly signifies the splendours of kingship than the majesty of the sun? And the splendour of the moon indicates the people complying with the royal authority like the synagogue itself, and the stars represents its leaders, and all of them on the stable foundation of the kingdom as in the solid structure of heaven."[23] But evening falls on that kingdom with the sins of its kings, for which it was deservedly taken into captivity and enslaved.

The fifth age reaches from the Exile to the birth of Christ. It corresponds to the growing enfeeblement of the adult, or, in this case, of the Jewish people. Augustine focuses on the phenomenon of the Jewish Diaspora, which very probably (not that Augustine knew this) reached a total of between three and four million people, such that, for instance, the city of Alexandria is thought to have been perhaps one third Jewish at the time of our Lord's birth. That fits well enough, typologically speaking, with Day Five of creation when God made the sea creatures and birds. How so? Congruently, it was the time when the Jews "started to live among the Gentile nations as in the sea, and to have an unsettled and unstable residence, like flying birds. But clearly [here Augustine thinks surely of the Maccabee leaders] there were also great whales there, that is, those great men who were able to dominate the stormy waves of the world rather than submit to the slavery of that captivity. You see, they were not corrupted by any terror into worshipping idols."[24] Like the sea creatures and flying creatures, the Jews multiplied in the Diaspora, yet evening fell, because their iniquities also so multiplied that they failed to discern the Messiah when he came.

[23] Ibid., 1.23.38.
[24] Ibid., 1.23.39.

The sixth day is the old age of Jewry but also the day when the "new man" is born. In the Book of Genesis, a great deal is happening on the sixth day. In verse 24 of the opening chapter, the Latin Bible offers as a translation of the Hebrew "Let the earth produce live soul" (in English Bibles, this creation of the land animals is more likely to read, as with the Revised Standard Version, "Let the earth bring forth living creatures"). For Augustine, the Latin text is pregnant with significance. The "live soul" that was born on Day Six was the new man of the Gospel, "alive with the life in which a longing for eternal realities is beginning to show itself". And just as on that action-packed day in Genesis, man too was made "according to the image and likeness of God" (1:26–27), so our Lord was born in the flesh. Indeed, just as man came to be, male and female, so too in this age not only did Christ come to be, a person in human nature in the male gender, but there originated also the womanly Church. We saw how for Augustine man's dominion over the animals is a primary consequence of his being made in God's image. Well, this leads him now to write:

> The man is put in charge in that [sixth] day of cattle and snakes and the flying things of heaven, just as in this age Christ rules the souls that defer to him, which have come to his Church partly from the Gentiles, partly from the people of the Jews. They have come so that people may be tamed and domesticated by him, whether they had been given over to fleshly concupiscence like cattle, or had been groping in the darkness and murk of curiosity as if they were snakes, or soaring up on the wings of pride as if they were birds.[25]

What about the evening of the sixth day? There *is* one, or as Augustine says "a sort of one", and he goes on, "I hope

[25] Ibid., 1.23.40.

to goodness it doesn't overtake us, provided that it hasn't already begun, because it's the one about which the Lord says, 'Do you suppose when the Son of Man comes he will find faith on the earth?' (Lk 18:8)." After this evening, so Augustine continues: "There will be made morning when the Lord himself is going to come in glory. Then those who are told, 'Be perfect like your Father who is in heaven' (Mt 5:48) will take their rest with Christ from all their works. Such people, you see, do works that are 'very good'; after such works a rest is to be hoped for on the seventh day which has no evening."[26]

Personal Applications

That might seem to be that. But Augustine doesn't want to end his commentary on Genesis 1 without trying to apply all of this to the individual believer. That is very Origenian of him: the whole tradition of adapting typology to the individual Christian, where it becomes spiritual allegory, the story of the soul, was given a tremendous boost by Origen's work. As one historian of patristic exegesis has written: "Most often . . . [Origen] individualises traditional typology, in the sense that he refers the sacred text to the relationship between the Logos and the soul of each Christian. [For Origen] corporeal things are types of spiritual realities and historical events are types of intelligible realities."[27] That is why Origen was strong on moral, ascetical, and mystical applications of exegesis, and now Augustine in effect, by closing Book 1 of *On Genesis, against the Manichees*, tries to emulate him, albeit in brief compass. As Augustine puts

[26] Ibid., 1.23.41.
[27] Simonetti, *Biblical Interpretation in the Early Church*, pp. 46–47.

it: "We also, one and all, have those six days in our personal lives, distinguished from each other in good works and an upright way of life, after which we should be hoping to rest."[28]

Day One, then, of our ongoing creation as Christians is marked by the light of faith, when we believe first the material world as telling us about its Maker and secondly the visible humanity of the God who deigned to appear to us in material form, in our nature. On Day Two, a solid structure appears. That is when we start to distinguish between things of the flesh and things of the spirit, in this way separating (so to speak) the lower from the upper waters. On Day Three: just as the dry land was set apart from the disturbances of the sea, so we individually are called to separate our minds from the "slippery slope and stormy waves of fleshly temptations". It was on this day that the crops appeared, so we too should now be able to bring forth the fruits of good works. On Day Four, when the lights of heaven were made, is a phase in our personal lives when, having started to discern spiritually on the basis of a "solid structure of discipleship", we now go on to: "see what unchangeable truth is, which shines in the soul like the sun; [moreover, we then find] the soul made a participant in this truth itself, and bestowing order and beauty on the body, like the moon lighting up the night." Is there a comparison here with the stars as well? Certainly. "Like all the stars, twinkling and shining in the night, we have those spiritual perceptions in the foggy darkness of this life." Day Five is the day when aquatic creatures and the birds of heaven emerged. That corresponds to our next state when, "strengthened and given courage by awareness of these unchanging spiritual realities", we "begin to

---

[28] Augustine, *On Genesis, against the Manichees*, 1.25.43.

produce results" by apostolic action in this turbulent world. Such apostolic deeds could be the "reptiles of live soul" of the Latin Bible—that is, evangelical works that benefit human souls, or they could be that the Bible's "great whales" —the "bravest kinds of action which contemptuously smash their way through the stormy waves of the world". Or again they might be the Latin Scriptures' "flying things of heaven" —Gospel voices by which heavenly truths are proclaimed like the song of birds. Day Six, penultimately, is for the cosmos at large the day of the land animals and man, when the earth yielded "live soul". We too, says Augustine, who by this stage of our personal Christian development already have the spiritual fruit of good thoughts and ideas, should now direct all the movements of our spirit to make of it truly a "live soul" in the service of divine truth, divine righteousness. And just as man was made in God's image and made such "male and female", so we have to practice both action (which presumably Augustine considers more masculine) and understanding (which, as receptive, could be deemed more feminine). Understanding and action need to be "maritally" united if we are ever to fill the earth with spiritual offspring—to do all the things that pertain to human perfection.

Then after these works we should be hoping for everlasting rest and appreciate what it means to say that God rested on the seventh day from all his works (Gen 2:2), because at the end of these works God "bestows himself on us as our rest".[29] He himself will be our eternal Sabbath in the heavenly Jerusalem.

[29] Ibid.

12

GREGORY THE GREAT ON JOB

Our next port-of-call is Saint Gregory the Great, Pope from 590 to 604, on the Book of Job. Gregory's *Morals on Job* is an enormous work, in thirty-five books, which has baffled many students. Studies of the Gregorian *Moralia* might lead us to believe that Gregory wrote about everything *but* Job. It is true that in Job's story as presented by the biblical author Gregory found every conceivable topic touched on, from the virtues of marriage to the Christology of the Council of Chalcedon. Though historians have noted the importance for the Western medievals of what Gregory has to say about the three "senses of Scripture"—what he calls the historical, the typical, and the moral—the *Moralia* has served mainly as a source for his theology, spirituality, and mysticism: not for enlightenment about the Book of Job. However, while the *Moralia* was read for varying purposes throughout the Middle Ages, the fact is that Gregory's treatise was the principal work on this Old Testament book until Saint Thomas came along with his more "literal" commentary in the thirteenth century.

Gregory's View of the Book of Job

How, basically, does Gregory see the Book of Job?[1] He takes it to be a work about a holy man divinely struck down.

[1] I am indebted throughout this chapter to S. E. Schreiner, " 'Where Shall

Neither Job nor Job's friends understand that the scourges sent from God are meant to increase Job's merit, rather than purge his sins. In the biblical book, Job compares his sufferings with his possible offenses and cries out—quite correctly —that it is not possible for his sins to have drawn down on him the wrath of God since there were none worth mentioning. Job is confused about the real cause of his afflictions. In the course of his trials, as Gregory interprets Job's speeches, Job's virtue, unacknowledged by his friends, in effect lifts him above the temporal vicissitudes of earthly life. By coming to despise transient or temporal goods, Job is in fact yearning for eternity—as one deeply should. As he describes Job rising above the temporal realm, Gregory analyzes the emotions, dispositions, and states of mind required for such a renunciation of earthly things in favor of the transcendent Good. To a degree, the historical and the moral sense of the Book of Job coincide at this point. Job, just because of what he lived through, is a moral example for us. We shall return in due course to my phrase "to a degree" and explore both its justice and its limitations. Meanwhile, we can ask how, if at all, this involves the third of the "senses of Scripture" in Gregory's scheme of biblical interpretation, the typical sense. He certainly finds a basis for it in the figure of Job. Job is a historical character, but he also typifies Christ and the Church. His sufferings foretell the Passion of Christ and the persecution of the Church on her earthly pilgrimage.

Actually, Gregory wants to go further than this and say that Job *prophesies* that Passion and those sufferings in persecution. That is a statement not about what Job will rep-

Wisdom Be Found?' Gregory's Interpretation of Job", *American Benedictine Review* 39, no. 3 (1988): pp. 321–42.

resent for the future without realizing it, but about what at some level of consciousness—"superconsciousness" we might call it, rather than the murky subconscious—is going through Job's mind as he lives. Why Gregory feels licensed to say that is something we must also investigate.

Job's Comforters

The other characters in the Book of Job—apart of course from God, and in the Prologue, Satan—are Job's comforters. These are the friends who try to reason with him by arguing that he must be repressing the memory of his past misdeeds or else all this sorrow would never have come upon him. The phrase "Job's comforters" has passed into English idiom with an ironic meaning attached to it. "Job's comforters" are people who while seeking to encourage us just give us worse news than we had already. And there is about that phrase a hint too that they take pleasure in this. They are indulging in what the Germans call *Schadenfreude*, a secret delight in the misfortunes of others by contrast with which our own happier position can be the better appreciated. As we shall see, that understanding of the phrase "Job's comforters" is very close to the way Gregory himself interprets the role of the friends with whom, incidentally (and here I think he goes wrong at an important juncture) he associates the young man Elihu. Be that as it may, the "comforters" are key to Gregory's reading.

For Gregory, the companions are, on the historical level, the friends of Job, but "typically", by their mixing together of truth and error in their addresses to him, they represent the "heretics" who persecute the Church.[2] Gregory offers

[2] St. Gregory the Great, *Morals on Job*, preface, 9.19.

a convincing explanation of their speeches. What is true about those speeches is the formally correct nature of the general propositions they contain. What is false about them is the way the "friends" apply those propositions to Job's case. Gregory admires the friends for their ethical orthodoxy at the level of universal principle. He has no wish to deny that, citing extracts from their speeches, God does "great and marvelous things", that God "does not pervert justice", that man cannot be "pure before his Maker", that "the exulting of the world is short", or that "the innocent shall be saved".[3] There is a huge amount of moral wisdom on the surface of the sayings of Job's companions. The problem with them—and why despite such formal orthodoxy they typify *heretics*—lies in the faulty way they apply these truths to Job. For Gregory, this is not merely a pardonable mistake, or series of mistakes, in applied ethics. It is the evil fruit of pride. It is owing to their lack of humility that the friends lack the insight to pierce through the outer circumstance of Job's predicament to the deeper inward reality. Their mistake reveals a deep-seated problem in their own life situation. Job's friends have not reached Job's level of inward transcendence. They overestimate the significance of temporal blessings because they are too stuck in time and unable, accordingly, to penetrate to inward truth. Unlike Job, they place their love in the temporal realm. Gregory draws the moral lesson for us from their case:

> When the soul is in no way rooted in the love of the eternal world, it slips away together with the very objects in which it is centred. For no one can attach himself to the moveable and remain unmoved. For he that embraces transitory things

[3] Schreiner, " 'Where Shall Wisdom Be Found?' ", p. 337.

is drawn into movement by the mere fact that he is entangled with things running out their course.[4]

The friends are just too attached to the passing goods of this world—too attached by their own fault—to be able to apply their otherwise excellent principles aright. And as a consequence they misdescribe the nature and purpose of God's providence in Job's case. Thus the divine reproof to them, despite their orthodoxy, in Job 42:7. "The Lord said to Eliphaz the Temanite: 'My wrath is kindled against you and against your two friends: for you have not spoken of me what is right, as my servant Job has.'"

Of course the mixture of truth and error in what the friends say is a challenge to the reader of the Book of Job. But, says Gregory, now at the typical level, that is what you always find with heretics. Just because heretics synthesize truth with error, the reader's task is to sift their words and sieve out the valid elements from the pernicious by penetrating to the inward meaning. On this basis, Gregory acclaims the truths taught by the "heretical" Eliphaz, Bildad, and Zophar about man's lack of purity, his false love of praise, the dangers of anger, the importance of right intentions, and, ironically enough, the deceitfulness of hypocrisy.

The Virtuous Job

But back to Job himself. Naturally enough, it is in the person of Job that Gregory's interest is focused—in keeping, surely, with the intention of the author of the book that bears Job's name. The "bottom line" of Gregory's interpretation is God's praise of Job's discourses in the Epilogue to

[4] Gregory, *Morals on Job*, 8.42.69.

the book: that text just cited in chapter 42. Gregory takes
the divine words here to be a reaffirmation of statements
in the Prologue where the Lord says to Satan: "Have you
considered my servant Job, that there is none like him on
the earth, a blameless and upright man, who fears God and
turns away from evil? He still holds fast his integrity, although you moved me against him, to destroy him without
cause" (Job 2:3; cf. 1:8). For Gregory, the Prologue and the
Epilogue together give us the clue to the interpretation of
the person of Job and, not least, his speeches. If, writes Gregory, we say that Job "erred amid the blows, in his speech,
we assert what it is impious to imagine, namely, that God
was mistaken in his pledged word."[5] For Gregory, then, *all*
Job's speeches are worthy of the divine blessing. None of
them can rightly be taken as expressions of despair, or rebellious challenges to the divine justice.

Now this creates a real exegetical challenge of its own.
It will be interesting to see how Gregory rises to meet it.
After all, he has to account in this perspective for such texts
as Job 3:1–2:

> After this, Job opened his mouth and cursed the day of
> his birth.
>   And Job said,
>
> > "Let the day perish wherein I was born,
> >   and the night which said,
> > 'A man-child is conceived.'"

Or again, Job 3:20–21:

> Why is light given to him that is in misery,
>   and life to the bitter in soul,

[5] Ibid., 2.8.13.

> who long for death, but it comes not,
>   and dig for it more than for hid treasures . . . ?

Or, most succinctly of all, Job 7:16: "I loathe my life; I would not live for ever." In Gregory's eyes, these statements are neither complaints about Job's present suffering nor accusations against divine providence. Rather are they insights into the radical futility of all temporal existence *when taken as ultimate*. These laments, which are seemingly so negative, are actually full of positive meaning. They embody a longing for the light of eternity. What Job desires is that, in Gregory's words, *dies mutabilitatis pereat, lumen aeternitatis erumpat*: "the day of change may perish and the light of eternity burst forth".[6] When we read that Job "gives up hope", we should take that to mean he forsakes earthly objects of desire, transcends the goods of the present life, comes to a proper distrust of the temporal realm of existence, suppresses the tumult of passions, and advances toward eternity in the inner man. Job gives voice to the tragedy of all earthly existence.

> Has not man a hard service upon earth,
>   and are not his days like the days of a hireling?
> Like a slave who longs for the shadow,
>   and like a hireling who looks for his wages . . .
>
> (Job 7:1-2)

Life is "hard service", and like a hired man, Job longs for the reward of his toil: namely, eternity. As a holy person, Job, in the words of Gregory, "reckons the present life his road, not his country", *viam, non patriam*; it is "a warfare, not the palm of victory", *militiam non palmam*.[7] "In his transcendence

[6] Ibid., 4.1.4.
[7] Ibid., 8.17.12.

over his own misfortune, Job sees that the finitude of life means that no one can keep anything of the past."[8] On Gregory's reading, Job's references to the "blooming" yet subsequent "ruin", at the moment of death, of the wicked prove that prosperity in the present life no more promises eternity than it testifies to righteousness.[9]

The exegesis of Job's laments and complaints shows us how Gregory sees the virtue of Job. Like all righteous men, Job remains unattached to the temporal goods that came into his hands and just as quickly slipped out of them. External circumstances leave his interior nature untouched. His desire to "argue" with God does not imply some inner confusion, but the contrary, namely, that his soul remains fixed on God throughout. Job's inner eye is firmly focused on the heavenly country. And so while what Gregory calls the "infirmity of the flesh"—which presumably includes, then, those emotions that have their seat in the body and the imaginative life insofar as it reflects those emotions—suffers disquietude, Job nonetheless still rests in the "security of a holy mind".[10] We all know something of what Gregory means here. Strangely, we can be content at some deep level even when our nerves are strained, or even shattered, by events or circumstances around us—to a certain extent, at any rate, and presumably the range of that "extent" increases with growth in holiness. The decisive criterion—not that this identifies a state we shall ourselves reach since it turns on the ontological constitution of the God-man—is Jesus on the Cross. At Calvary Jesus enjoys, according to Saint Thomas, the beatific vision at the "apex" of his soul, yet at

---

[8] Schreiner, " 'Where Shall Wisdom Be Found' ", p. 332.

[9] Cf. Job 21:7–9, 13.

[10] Gregory, *Morals on Job*, 12.16.36–37.

every other level of mind (and not just body) he undergoes, for the same Thomas, the greatest suffering ever known.

Job as Type and Prophet

This glance ahead to the thinking characteristic of the last "Father and Doctor" we shall be looking at brings me to Gregory's view of the relation between Job and Christ. In Gregory's view, to repeat, it is not sufficient to make of Job the unwitting type of Jesus Christ. Gregory considers Job to be a great prophet who foresees all the mysteries of Christ's Incarnation and atonement. For Gregory, it is not enough that Job offer, in the contours of his life, a rough outline—to use the language of Saint Hilary—of the life of Christ, in this way prefiguring the Coming One. As an innocent sufferer, his life is not only a sign of Christ. More than this, precisely by virtue of the total way he transcends the vicissitudes of historical existence he is granted the spirit of prophecy and gains a glimpse of the entire structure of the plan of God, the whole divine economy.

Now there is in the Book of Job one passage of which the Hebrew text is very uncertain, but where many exegetes have found indeed, at the level of the "literal"— what Gregory calls the "historical"—sense a Christological prophecy. More specifically, it is a prophecy of the Incarnation and, through the Incarnate One, the resurrection of the body. That passage is Job 19:25–26, wonderfully set by Handel, in a slightly different version, in *Messiah*:

> For I know that my Redeemer lives,
>   and at last he will stand upon the earth;
> and after my skin has been thus destroyed,
>   then from my flesh I shall see God.

But, according to Gregory, the reader of Job should be aware that for Job time collapses as his mind ascends to God through the Spirit of prophecy. Job is able in that way to look down on the vast expanse of history and trace there the thread of the redemptive divine action snaking its way through our world of change, the realm of time. *What* it is Job sees cannot, by and large, be discovered from the literal sense of the text. But it can be discerned on the deeper, typical level where there are prophecies, predictions, and not only prefiguring acts. Thus, for instance, when Job cries, "Naked I came from my mother's womb and naked I shall return" (1:21), he is depicting Christ leaving the synagogue his mother and manifesting himself to the Gentiles. When he asserts that he is suffering "without cause" (9:17b), Job prophesies the Passion of Christ who will suffer without sin. When he comments that "the earth is given into the hands of the wicked" (9:24), he is predicting the crucifixion of Christ by the devil and his legions, the principalities and powers behind the political and religious leadership of the day. And of course he foreknows the Resurrection, in the passage already cited.

Influenced by Augustine, whose overall theological vision he reflects, Gregory holds that things that are true of Christ can also be maintained in some manner of the Church. In Augustine's much-favored formula, the "total Christ", *Christus totus*, is Head and members together. So from Job's laments, and from his vindication, we can also gather impressions of the persecution, suffering, and purification of the earthly Church. So Job foresees not only the vices and virtues of the patriarchs and the formulation of the messianic hope, and not only the Incarnation and the paschal mystery that are that hope's fulfillment but also the mission of the apostles, the development of the Church—and, more somberly, the work of the Antichrist.

For Gregory all this is feasible not just because God gives prophets extraordinary gifts, but also owing to the nature of the human mind itself. By a process of interior conversion, the mind can be turned toward eternal being, and the reality of this world glimpsed *sub specie aeternitatis*, in the perspective of eternity. Or, as Gregory himself writes: "What was to follow [in salvation history, Job] saw as present in [God] whom neither things future come to, nor things past go from, but all things are present at once and together before his eyes."[11]

As readers of the Book of Job will recall, chapters 38 to 41 are taken up by an extraordinary piece of rhetorical prose, the Lord's speech from out of the whirlwind. The literal sense of the passage is that when we look at the wild and wonderful, terrible yet beautiful beasts in nature, we are overcome by a sense of the mystery of God, and this ought to warn us not to suppose we can scrutinize or get to the bottom of God's judgments. But in a *tour de force* of typical exegesis, Gregory finds in this menagerie of animals that God puts on show for Job's benefit an evocation of all salvation history and notably of the virtues of past and future saints. It is a warning of another kind—a warning to Job not to rely on his own limited virtue, real though that is.

From out of the whirlwind, God speaks too, in this zoological language, of the increasing horrors of the Antichrist and Satan—the Behemoth and Leviathan, those ancient sea monsters that in Job's menagerie become the hippopotamus and crocodile and are thus somewhat reduced in scale though not by any means deprived of all lethal power. More significant still are the temptations yet triumphs of the elect as history draws to its end. Gregory's Job falls down before the Lord and confesses that the goodness of his life pales before

[11] Ibid., 11.20.31.

the virtue of all saints and the mighty wisdom that sacred history displays. Having thus been granted a transcendent view of God's actions throughout history, Job contemplates finally the New Jerusalem as the Church rests on the eternal Sabbath in the "contemplation of eternity".[12]

Gregory in Question

Gregory's spirituality—and above all his account of the time-eternity relation, not least in the *Morals on Job*—was enormously influential in the later Latin Church, so much so that at some point difficult to define it ceased to be recognized as a distinctive influence. In his great study of medieval spirituality, *The Love of Learning and the Desire for God*, Dom Jean Leclerq wrote: "His ideas and his expressions have passed into the doctrine and language of countless spiritual writings, generally after having lost any connection with their original context. Without knowing it, we are living, in great measure, on his modes of expression, and on his thought, and for that very reason they no longer seem new to us."[13]

Those words were originally written in the 1950s. As it happened, the following two decades in much of the Western Catholic Church saw a revolt against this subterranean Gregorian influence. It was said that Gregory's writings were too influenced by themes of withdrawal from the world or even contempt for the world; excessively dominated by allusions to man's frailty and the need for dependence on God; overdetermined by considerations of sin and divine judgment, the presence of evil in the world, the need for penitence and mortification.[14] But the Pope who summoned the

---

[12] Ibid., 35.20.48.

[13] J. Leclerq, O.S.B., *The Love of Learning and the Desire for God: A Study of Monastic Culture* (London, 1978), p. 33.

[14] The liturgical reform of the late 1960s and 1970s affected the Roman

Second Vatican Council, Blessed John XXIII, in a speech to doctoral candidates at the Lateran University told his hearers: "If you wish to learn wisdom, if you wish to taste what will forever raise up your spirits, be assiduous readers of the thirty-five books of the *Moralia* of St. Gregory the Great."[15] That is something easier said than done, even for doctors in theology. But we must presume the Pope meant it seriously, since when he began to occupy the papal suite in the apostolic palace in the course of 1958 he had Gregory's writings sent up to his bedroom. After the Second Vatican Council, however, it was said that Gregory had fostered spiritual individualism, that his theology was insufficiently paschal, and instead of directing Christian life to the transformation of human society he had diverted his readers' attention away from that central arena of God's will which is the here and now.

A historical problem arises there. The same man who was so targeted happened to be an ecclesiastical statesman and practically minded pastor who in the absence of any effective civil power in central Italy, took over, amid the ruins of ancient civilization, not only ecclesial but civil responsibilities,[16] as well as preparing the way, as many historians would argue, for the new civilization of the Middle Ages. So far as the accusation of passivism is concerned, he held that higher even than the contemplative life is the "mixed" life in which the pursuit of contemplative union with God is blended with an active life in the service of one's neigh-

---

rite not least by toning down such themes or transferring them to the season of Lent.

[15] Cited by F. Clark, "St. Gregory the Great, Theologian of Christian experience", *American Benedictine Review* 39, no. 3 (1988): pp. 261–76, here at p. 263.

[16] J. Richard, *Consul of God: The Life and Times of Gregory the Great* (London, 1980).

bor for God's greater glory. On the other hand—and this is highly relevant to his commentary on Job, Gregory did consider awareness of man's sinfulness, starting with one's own, to be crucial, and along with it the humility to let God be God. His conviction that to give our love chiefly to this world in its totality is to "love wounds, not joys" is realistic, given life's sorrows and illusions. That he is the "doctor of divine desire" for whom the source of all human striving for the good should be a passionate love and yearning for God is to his credit, not otherwise. All these are perfectly biblical teachings. If in our preaching and catechesis we downplay them on the grounds that people wish to hear something more cheerful and more obviously community-building, we shall not be doing them a service.

In his commentary on the Song of Songs—our next and penultimate example of the Old Testament exegesis of Fathers and Doctors—the twelfth-century Canon Regular Hugh of Saint Victor is highly Gregorian when he remarks on the Bridegroom's repeated call, "Come away, come away" (Song 4:8):

> Why does he say, "come" twice? So that the person who is outside himself may first of all return to himself, and the person who is in himself may rise up beyond himself. First of all he is within us, and he warns transgressors to return to the heart; but then he is above us, that he may invite the justified to come to himself. "Come", he says, "Come". Come out inwardly to yourself! Come within, further within, wholly within, above yourself to me![17]

---

[17] Cited in R. A. Norris, Jr., ed., *The Song of Songs: Interpreted by Early Christian and Medieval Commentators* (Grand Rapids, Mich., 2003), p. 170.

13

ORIGEN ON THE SONG OF SONGS

Origen was not absolutely the first early ecclesiastical writer to comment on the Song of Songs, but he was the most influential, especially in the Christian West—and this despite the fact that out of his ten-volume commentary only four volumes have come down to us, in the early fourth-century translation into Latin by Rufinus of Aquileia.

A Taste of Alexandria

These four volumes take us up to the biblical book's chapter 2, verse 15, which in a translation closer to Origen's Greek text, reads, "Catch us the little foxes, that destroy our vines, and our vines will flourish." Those words Origen takes to be words of the Song's Bridegroom not to the Bride but to his own companions. He interprets the "little foxes" according to the *moral* sense as a reference to evil thoughts. Any thought of that kind, as he says, "should be caught and cast out while it is still immature and 'little' for otherwise, if it has become mature and deep-seated, it can no longer be got rid of". *Ecclesially*, the foxes will suggest, rather, teachers of heretical ideas. That is why, as he puts it, "a charge is given to Catholic teachers that while these foxes are still little and have not deceived many souls even though perverse doctrine has got a start, they [Catholic teachers] should make haste to censure such people and restrain them —and by opposing them with the word of truth to subdue and catch them with statements of the truth."[1]

I offer these two citations at the outset of this chapter to alert readers to the twofold path Origen follows in his exegesis of this particular biblical book. The Song of Songs readily lent itself to this dual approach. While in each case the Bridegroom is Christ the Word incarnate, in moral exegesis, the Bride is the individual soul, whereas in ecclesial exegesis, she is the Church. In practice, however, that distinction is not quite so sharp. For one thing, though these two sorts of interpretation are different in kind, Origen often intermingles them. And for another, ecclesial exegesis in a certain sense englobes moral exegesis, the reason being that —surely rightly—Origen sees the individual Christian soul as an *anima ecclesiastica*: a soul that has taken its orientation from the mystery of the Church and found its resources— biblical, sacramental, spiritual—in the Church. Such a soul, then, needs to be *referred to the Church* if its identity and itinerary is to be understood. Thus Origen's writing on the Song of Songs has much more about the Church than has, say, Saint Bernard's—unless we wish to say that in Bernard the abbot, whom Bernard describes as a spiritual mother, really represents the ecclesial body.[2]

Origen's commentary is generally dated to the 240s. The

[1] Origen, *Commentary on the Song of Songs*, 237. Origen's commentary and his two homilies are found in the "Berlin Corpus" of early Christian writings as *Griechische Christliche Schriftsteller*, vol. 33. An English translation is offered by R. P. Lawson, *Origen: The Song of Songs; Commentary and Homilies* (Westminster, Md., and London, 1957).

[2] For a comparison, see L. Brésard, *Bernard et Origène commentent le Cantique* (Forges, 1983).

Church historian Eusebius of Caesarea, who was born a generation or so after Origen's death, tells us that the first three volumes were written in Athens and the last seven in Eusebius' own home city, Caesarea, on the coast of Palestine, where Origen had been a kind of scholar-in-residence at the cathedral. We also have—again, only in Latin and this time translated by Saint Jerome, two homilies of Origen on the Song, as well as a few fragments in Greek collected by a Palestinian monk, Procopius of Gaza. What is amazing, considering how the lion's share of Origen's work is lost, is the richness of what remains.

The Nature of the Song of Songs

Given the primacy of ecclesial exegesis in Origen's approach to the Song, I propose to concentrate on that, making good use of a study by a French-Canadian Jesuit who has gone through the texts with a fine-tooth comb, drawing out Origen's meaning as clearly as he can, in a way that is theologically both powerful and subtle.[3] But first of all, let us set the scene. For Origen, the Song sets out to trace the spiritual journey followed by the heroine of the book, the "Spouse". As it opens, the Song presents a fiancée. Ardent and impatient, she is awaiting the arrival of a (royal) Bridegroom who has been delayed. Suddenly the Bridegroom arrives, interrupting the Bride in the very prayer she is making to implore his coming. That opening then releases the entire movement of this little mystical drama, the drama of the nuptials of a Bride and Groom. Origen lists the stages

[3] J. Chênevert, S.J., *L'Eglise dans le Commentaire d'Origène sur le Cantique des Cantiques* (Paris-Montreal, 1969).

covered, underlining both the speed with which the Bride advances and how, nonetheless, she still has quite some distance to travel. (Brief extracts from the Song of Songs in this chapter will echo the Greek rather than be cited from the RSV.)

He identifies four main stages. First, the Bride's entry into the chamber of the King, after exchanging with him a first kiss. That is at Song 1:4, which in the Greek Bible known as the Septuagint, the version Origen probably used, reads: "The King has brought me into his storehouse." The next major juncture is when the Bridegroom discloses he has at his disposal some secret meadowlands. The Bride asks at 1:7, "Where do you pasture? Where do you take your rest at noontide?" And she is told at 1:8, "If you do not know yourself, O fair one among women, go out in the footsteps of the flocks and pasture your goats by the shepherds' tents." The third key stage is the introduction into the house of wine, at 2:4, when the Bride beseeches the Groom, "Bring me into the house of wine: set love in order in me." Finally, what precipitates the climax is the appeal of the Bridegroom in 5:2 for the Bride to come forth for her definitive encounter with her beloved. Knocking at the door he calls:

> Open to me, my sister, my close one,
>   my dove, my perfect one;
> for my head is covered with dew,
>   my locks with the drops of the night.

Since we lack the full text of Origen's commentary, we do not know for certain whether he stayed faithful to this outline. But the consistency in what we *do* have makes it very likely.

As Origen portrays her, the Bride is already exceptionally advanced on the spiritual way. And yet Origen insists that, through these four stages, she must submit to a law of ongoing development or progress. In fact, Origen sees her as at one and the same time both perfect and imperfect. The significance of that should become plain as we delve further. It will emerge that throughout, Origen's perspective is principally eschatological. We explore his account of the ultimate goal to which the Church is called by looking at how he deals with four main themes: the preexistent Church; the Church of the Old Covenant; the Church and the Gentiles, the Church and the Word incarnate.

Phases of the Church

The Preexistent Church

The first topic—the preexistent Church—may seem a strange one. It is not an obvious feature of our customary doctrinal consciousness today. But for Origen it is highly important that the Church exists eternally in the divine counsel. The imperative to convert all nations, found at the end of Saint Matthew's Gospel, is not, he thinks, fully comprehensible unless this is a matter of a divine plan formed from all eternity, concerning the everlasting destiny of mankind. Origen sees the Church as preexistent not only in the mind and purpose of God, but also in the angelic world and even —so he suggests as a hypothesis, but this was *not* one of those ideas of his to which the Church rallied—in human souls before their entry into life in the embodied state. As he says in his commentary, the Church is a community gathered since the beginning of the age (in Latin, *saeculum*), a community whose origin precedes Christ's epiphany on earth.

In part, he is thinking here of historical time. The Fiancée of the Word was once a child under the supervision of a tutor, the Torah, and was taught by the prophets. In that period, she was already the same corporate personality she is now. In part, though, Origen has in mind an even earlier stage still, for *saeculum* here seems to mean the *entire* time of history.[4] Origen found himself stimulated to reflection thereon by Song 1:11-12: "We will make you necklaces in the likeness of gold, studded with silver, while the King remains plunged in his sleep." He interprets this text to mean the education that not only the prophets but also the angels gave the Church until the moment came when she was to receive teaching from the very mouth of God, the Word. Not only did the psalmist say, "Be mindful of your assembly, O Lord, which you called together from the beginning" (Ps 74:2)—which might refer simply to the Church as built on the foundation of Old Testament prophets as well as New Testament apostles. But in the Letter to the Ephesians Saint Paul goes further when he says that

> the God and Father of our Lord Jesus Christ . . . chose us in him before the foundation of the world, that we should be holy and blameless before him . . . destin[ing] us in love to be his sons through Jesus Christ, according to the purpose of his will, to the praise of his glorious grace which he freely bestowed on us in the Beloved (1:3a, 4-6).

The connecting link between the Church thus preexistent and the Jewish Church built on the prophets in the Old Testament is—*Adam*. Origen regards Adam as the first prophet since, as he writes, still in connection with the Song's "necklaces in the likeness of gold", Adam "prophesied the great mystery which is in Christ and the Church, saying: on account of this a man leaves his father and mother and cleaves

[4] Ibid., p. 18.

to his wife and both will become one flesh (Gen 1:24)".[5] That is a prophecy because it is of this text that Saint Paul says, "This is a great mystery, and I speak of Christ and the Church" (Eph 5:32). It helps to note that in Origen's Bible, unlike ours, the words about leaving father and mother are a continuation of the little speech by Adam in Genesis 1:23.

The Church, then, was from the beginning, when all things originated in the Word of God, when man was primordially made in God's image. Origen presents Adam as the type of Christ, Bridegroom of the Church, to whom all owe life. But like Paul, he also portrays him as the antithesis of Christ since whereas one introduced sin and death the other brought justification and eternal life. It would seem likely, by an obvious correspondence, that Eve will be for Origen the type of the Church, but the Church as falling, seduced by the Evil One, turned prostitute. Though much of the text of Origen's homilies on Genesis is lost, we know from another of the early ecclesiastical historians, Socrates, that in those sermons Origen *did* speak of Eve as representing the Church just as Adam represents Christ. This understanding, remarks Socrates, Origen found in "the mystical tradition of the Church"—which we can think of as finding expression in such very ancient Jewish-Christian texts as *The Shepherd of Hermas* and the Second Letter of Clement.[6] For Origen, from the very moment of the Fall, the Word begins to "leave his Father and Mother": that is, the Divine Father and the heavenly realm, the "Jerusalem above" of the choir of angels, in order to initiate the process of cleaving to his predestined Bride, so that the two may be one flesh.

In accord with his basically eschatological perspective,

---

[5] Origen, *Commentarium in Canticum Canticorum*, 157.

[6] Socrates, *Church History*, 3.7; on the Jewish-Christian texts see J. Daniélou, S.J., *The Theology of Jewish Christianity* (London, 1964), pp. 293–313.

Origen seeks to show that in the End things will be as they were at the Beginning—only more wonderfully so. When the Church of the absolute Beginning is reconstituted, it will be with men who are bodies and not souls only and who will have gained heaven through a drama of love in which the Word emptied himself to be united not only with the soul of Christ, which had "always" adhered to that Word, but also with fallen flesh. All for the sake of making a love-appeal to sinners.

The Church of the Old Covenant

Our second theme is the Church of the Old Covenant. As Père Chênevert remarks, "From the beginning of the Commentary properly so called [i.e., after completing the prologue], it is toward this Church of the Old Covenant that Origen turns his eyes."[7] The very first verse of the Canticle: "Let him kiss me with the kisses of his mouth", adverts, so Origen tells us, to the long preparation the Fiancée has received under the regime of the Old Covenant. The chief agents of that preparation were the Law and the prophets, though the angels and the patriarchs, starting with Noah, were involved as well. In the Song's *dramatis personae*, the Bridegroom's companions represent that group of educators —not excluding the angels who figure owing to the teaching of the New Testament letters that they were involved in mediating the Torah to Moses. Thus in Galatians 3:19 we read that the Law "was ordained by angels through an intermediary", a claim confirmed by Hebrews 2:2, "For if the message declared by angels was valid and every transgres-

[7] Chênevert, *L'Eglise dans le Commentaire d'Origène*, p. 79.

sion or disobedience received a just retribution, how shall we escape if we neglect such a great salvation [as is now offered in the Son]?"

Apart from their role in the promulgation of the Torah, the angels also prepared the Fiancée by the role they played in numerous mysteries witnessed in the Old Testament. Origen has in mind the many appearances of the angel of the Lord of the sort we noted at that major complementary theme in the pattern of revelation, "God and His Self-Manifestation". One of the most important for the young girl's formation, thinks Origen, was the visit of the Three (or was it One?) to Abraham at the oaks of Mamre, where there was brought to the holy patriarch, and so to his descendants, a first disclosure of the mystery of the Divine Trinity. The appearing of the angel of the Lord to Moses in the burning bush bulks large in this as well. Still, like every mediating action before Christ, the work of the angels was provisional. Its aim was to give the Fiancée—Israel, the proto-Church—the rudiments of doctrine, revelation's *initia*, so as subsequently to lead her toward perfection, which means "toward him whose presence will bring her the fullness of knowledge and charity".[8]

The Law and the prophets belong with this providential school. In the imagery of the Song, Origen considers their words a jar of spices whose aroma gives the Bride a foretaste —a "fore-smell"—of the heavenly perfume the One sent by the Father will spread abroad when the Father anoints him with that supreme Unguent, the person of the Holy Spirit. But above all, Origen sees the formation of Israel-Church as *preparation for a marriage*. God gives the Church as Israel

[8] Ibid., p. 81.

a dowry, and as Origen writes, "The dowry of the Church was the books of the Law and the prophets."[9] Origen has the Bride confess, "The words of the prophets made me know and showed me the Son of God, to whom they desired to marry me." They "spoke to me of his innumerable virtues and his immense works". But what she seems to have been most sensible to is the sketch the prophets traced for her of his "sweetness", and—above all—his *beauty*.[10]

The beauty of the Spouse occupies a crucial place in Origen's Old Testament-inspired mysticism. In his scheme, it expresses the well-nigh irresistible attraction for the spiritual universe of God the Word. Origen finds the explanation in the Christological hymn embedded in the text of Colossians 1: "He is the image of the invisible God [Origen writes, "the image and splendour of the invisible God"], the first-born of all creation, for in him all things were created, in heaven and on earth, visible and invisible" (Col 1:15, 16a). The perception of the Word's beauty arouses in the soul a spiritual, heavenly love, which only the presence of the Bridegroom himself can satisfy. As Origen says: "The soul is aroused by a heavenly love and desire once she has perceived the beauty and splendour of the Word of God, once she has been seduced by his attraction, once she has been struck as by an arrow and wounded in love."[11] And this happened, Origen maintains, through the envoys of the future Bridegroom, heroes of the Elder Testament.

As Chênevert points out, an important basis for this confidence is the "essentially sapiential and Pauline theme" of the sacred or—in a wide sense—sacramental nature of the cre-

[9] Origen, *Commentary on the Song of Songs*, 91.

[10] Chênevert, *L'Eglise dans le Commentaire d'Origène*, p. 82.

[11] Origen, *Commentary on the Song of Songs*, 67.

ated realm *as such.*[12] In such matters, Origen always appeals
to Scripture rather than philosophy: the Bible is his principal means for scanning the encoded meaning of the things
around us in the world. (When ferreting out the meaning
of the Song's comparison of the Bridegroom to a young
faun or a gazelle, Origen leafs through Scripture for reference to these animals "so as to speak not according to the
doctrine of human wisdom but according to the doctrine
of the Spirit, lighting up the spiritual by the spiritual".[13])
Still, we are looking to Scripture to help decode the *general* sacramentality of the world where, writes Origen, "the
least creature may have a point of resemblance with some
heavenly reality", citing the mustard seed of the parable.[14]
This, so Origen reminds us, is the sort of knowledge the
author of the Book of Wisdom said he had received, "as-
suredly showing that . . . every visible thing has some likeness, and some analogy, with an invisible reality".[15] People
living in the flesh have to start from the visible creation to
get an idea of what transcends the world. That is why we
have recourse to images for the expression of spiritual realities—something which, as Origen points out, the literary
texture of the Song of Songs brings home to us. So then,
grounded by the Wisdom literature of the Old Testament
and other pertinent sources, the Fiancée is led by the Spirit
through the works of creation, learning to read them and
go beyond them. She thus finds herself "at the gates of Wisdom itself", starting to practice what Origen in his prologue calls "inspective science". In such knowledge, carried

[12] Chênevert, *L'Eglise dans le Commentaire d'Origène*, p. 84.
[13] Origen, *Commentary on the Song of Songs*, 207–8.
[14] Ibid., 208.
[15] Ibid., 209.

beyond words, we "contemplate in a certain measure divine and heavenly things, doing so by spiritual means, since these realities are beyond bodily appearance".[16] As Origen writes: "These analogies recur not only in all creatures but the divine Scripture itself has been written, in some fashion, according to a comparable art and wisdom. Thus, it is in view of some hidden and mystical reality that one saw the people leave the earthly Egypt and take the road through the desert, with all that is recounted there of snake bites and scorpion stings, thirst in a waterless terrain, and so forth. All these things are the representation and image of some hidden mystery."[17]

We have heard Chrysostom speaking in like tones on typology. Types involve some kind of proportion or analogy —and it is always, in some way, to Jesus Christ and his work. All Scriptures' mysteries contribute in some way to preparing the Bride, revealing to her the qualities of her future Groom and the riches their union holds out. But where she can admire the purest reflections of this mysterious Bridegroom is in the types of Christ.

Old Testament types again. The type on which Origen concentrates most—understandably, given the title of the Song —is *Solomon.* (The Song, after all, is "The Song of Solomon".) Solomon, says Origen, was no stranger to concupiscence or sin. And yet he remains the type of Christ in two respects: first, when he is called "the peaceful one", and secondly, insofar as the queen of the South—often identified with a ruler from the southern Arabian peninsula or possibly present day Eritrea-Ethiopia—came from the "other end of the world" to hear his wisdom. Solomon's spiritual

[16] Ibid., 75.
[17] Ibid., 212.

wisdom, his penetration of the mysteries of God, gave him the privilege of prefiguring the Word incarnate, the "true Solomon and man of peace", our Lord Jesus Christ. The queen of Sheba's journey to hear Solomon prefigures in turn the Church coming from the ends of the earth to hear the new and veritable Solomon, Jesus.

Moses must be mentioned next. The excellence of his work and his extraordinary meekness (cf. Num 12:3) might be said to announce Christ, but he did that most fully through his privilege of speaking with the Lord "mouth to mouth" and seeing, albeit from "behind", his glory. The state of soul Moses reached surpassed, so Origen believed, the spiritual condition of every other man, no matter how advanced on the ways of the Spirit. His taking an Ethiopian wife gave the Church-to-be a prophetic image of the union to be realized between Christ and herself. Like the Ethiopian woman, the Church, sinful yet justified, would be "black but beautiful".

But for Origen all the prophets and holy men of the Old Testament, whether taken individually or together, carry the image of the Christ who is to come. They constitute the "mountains and hills" over which the Fiancée sees her beloved running. Origen exclaims: "He bounded indeed in the midst of the prophets as on the mountains, and in the midst of [Israel's] holy ones as on the hills, for they were in this world his image and prefiguration." [18]

Moreover, not just the human *figures* but the *events* of the Old Testament announce the works the Bridegroom will perform for the sake of the Bride. The events of the Exodus, of course—the blood of the paschal lamb, the crossing of the Red Sea, the cloud, the water from the rock,

[18] Ibid., 201.

the manna, but also the Jerusalem Temple and its utensils
and accoutrements or even such singular events as Judah's
relations with his daughter-in-law Tamar in the patriarchal
sagas or the imprisonment of Jeremiah in a cistern during
the build-up to the events of 587. All these, Origen argues,
are prefigurations of the Incarnation in its twofold aspect
of the self-emptying of the Word and the divine assumption
of human nature and, in dependence thereon, prefigurations
too of the effects of the grace of Christ—the redemption
of men in the waters of baptism, the gift of the Holy Spirit,
and the institution of the apostolic ministry, assuring grace's
sacramental transmission over time.

Preparing the Incarnation. Doubtless, concedes Origen, the
young Fiancée couldn't grasp the *total* meaning of all these
enigmas. But the Word of God succeeded in preparing her
heart for the full revelation of the mysteries. And so, when
the Incarnate One came, the Church had the feeling not
of learning absolute novelties but of *recognizing what she had
previously intuited obscurely.*

This Christological elucidation—which corresponds, of
course, to what we called in part two of this book the "fulfillment" of the "pattern"—was not the only formation little Israel was receiving. She was also getting a *moral* formation. That is the context in which Origen sees the trilogy of
Solomonic books: Proverbs, Ecclesiastes, and the Song itself.
Proverbs teaches the future Bride to correct her morals and
follow the commandments, while Ecclesiastes instructs her
about the vanity of the world and the fragility of the things
that pass away. Naturally, Origen is well aware that Proverbs
is not the only Old Testament book to offer moral purification—which is why he recommends to the Bride, and all
souls aspiring to equal her in perfection, the continued med-

itation of the Law and the prophets. The *Ecclesia ex gentibus* —the Church taken from the (pagan) nations—must gather up the heritage the Lord transmitted through Israel, and especially through Israel's faithful remnant (even though that remnant is *ultimately* expressed not in pre-Christian Jews but in the holy apostles). For Origen, ethical holiness normally conditions all entry into the mystical order and the progress of the soul toward full union with God. So this is pretty important. And of all the virtues the Fiancée can learn, charity is the chief. Charity is the sum of the others, since it implies one-hundred-percent faithfulness to the divine commands at large.

Learning from songs. Origen holds that, even before the writing of the Song of Solomon, the Old Testament knew six songs marking key stages on the Bride's journey. Angels and prophets sang them to accompany her on her way to perfection. He describes these six songs both in the commentary and in the homilies, though he changes his mind about the identity of the last one between the writing of these two works.

The first song consists of Exodus 15:1–18. It is the song of Moses and the people of Israel after crossing the Red Sea. Familiar to Western Catholics from the Easter Vigil in the Roman rite, it celebrates for Origen *basic conversion.*

> I will sing to the Lord, for he has triumphed gloriously;
>   the horse and his rider he has thrown into the sea.
> The Lᴏʀᴅ is my strength and my song,
>   and he has become my salvation (Ex 15:1b–2).

The second song is a very short one, found in Numbers 21:17–18. An acclamation of the desert journey, Israel sings in wonder at the Lord's fidelity to his promise to Moses to

find the people a well in the wilderness, in the Amorite bor-
derlands. According to Origen, its message for the newly
converted is *"Study the Scriptures!"*

> Spring up, O well!—Sing to it!—
> the well which the princes dug . . .
>
> (Num 21:17–18a)

The third song is far better known. It is the song of Moses
in the penultimate chapter of Deuteronomy as the journey-
ing people reach the edge of the Promised Land. Its theme,
thinks Origen, is *"Look toward heaven."*

> Give ear, O heavens, and I will speak;
>   and let the earth hear the words of my mouth. . . .
> For I will proclaim the name of the LORD.
>   Ascribe greatness to our God!
>
> (Deut 32:1, 3)

Origen's fourth song is the song of Deborah in the book
of Judges, a song commemorating Israel's struggle to pos-
sess her own heritage. Victory (with divine help) is contem-
plated, and a triumphant message passed on to others. It is
a celebration of *possessing the beginnings of salvation.*

> Tell of it, you who ride on tawny asses,
>   you who sit on rich carpets
>   and you who walk by the way.
> To the sounds of musicians at the watering places,
>   there they repeat the triumphs of the LORD,
>   the triumphs of his peasantry in Israel.
>
> (Judg 5:10–11)

The fifth song in Origen's list is the song of David after
his deliverance from the Philistines, and Saul, in 2 Samuel
22:2–51. "The LORD is my rock, and my fortress, and my

deliverer" (v. 2). Here the Bride's theme is *joy at deliverance from her spiritual foes*. As already mentioned, Origen hesitated about the sixth song. In the commentary, it is the song of praise David gave Asaph and the guild of cantors to sing in 1 Chronicles 16:8–36:

> O give thanks to the Lord, call on his name,
>> make known his deeds among the peoples! (v. 8).

A cue for pure praise, the theme of this song for Origen is *thanksgiving at the work of initial grace*. But in the first homily on the Song of Songs, Origen substitutes Isaiah's "song of the vineyard" in 5:1–30 of his book. Here the note of gratitude, "Let me sing for my beloved a love song concerning his vineyard" (v. 1) is muted by anxiety for the weaknesses of the people. The vineyard has only yielded "wild" grapes: tasteless or even bitter.[19] Either way, this and all the songs pale in comparison with *the* song, that song that pours forth from the Bridegroom at the moment when, present at last, he will take his Spouse whom he calls the "sole perfect dove". Origen comments:

> The Bride does not want any longer to hear the song of the friends of the Bridegroom, but desires to hear the very words of the Bridegroom present before her; that is why she says: Let him kiss me with the kisses of his mouth. Thus this canticle is preferable to all others. Indeed, the other canticles, the ones the Law and prophets sang, seem to have been for a bride who was still a child, who had not yet crossed the threshold of maturity. But this canticle is sung to a robust adult who is as strong as a man and able perfectly to comprehend the mystery. That is why she is said to be a perfect dove and unique. Perfect Bride of a perfect Spouse, she heard the words of the perfect doctrine.[20]

[19] Origen, *Homily 1 on the Song of Songs*, 27–28.
[20] Origen, *Commentary on the Song of Songs*, 80.

A spiritual understanding of the previous biblical songs enables us to see the Bride making magnificent progress and
reaching indeed "the chamber of the Bridegroom, the place
of the admirable tent, the house of the Lord, singing her joy
and faith in the midst of festive shouting; she reaches the
very chamber of the Spouse, as we have said, so as to hear—
and to utter—all that is contained in the Song of Songs."[21]

The importance Origen attaches to the moral formation
of the Bride is shown in his comments on 1:8 where she
is told to "know herself". This imperative Origen takes to
be telling her not only to attend to her moral state—her
dispositions, her habitual intentions—but also to know the
substance of her own mystery, the way she is fashioned in
the divine image, and so she must make her way to the
source of her own beauty there to discover, in her depths,
the imprint of the God who created her.

Old Testament strengths and weaknesses. For Origen, the Old
Testament, in these various respects, is both perennially valid
and yet severely limited. The Church today affirms its intrinsic value, which is now illuminated by Christ. In this
way, the Old Testament is—*even more than in its own era*—an
agent of communion with the Word of God. On the other
hand, precisely because the Old Testament marks a phase of
prophecy, it can only offer the "shadow of the good things
to come" (Heb 10:1). The "likenesses of gold" with which
the friends of the Bridegroom promise to adorn the Bride
during the sleep of her royal Spouse, these are precisely
shadows of spiritual reality as once projected by angels in
the Law or under the prophets. The true gold, the *vera*, the
only things that properly are realities, albeit invisible ones,

[21] Ibid., 83.

has only come into the possession of the Church via the presence of the incarnate Lord. Those visible goods once offered to the Fiancée, such as the Jerusalem Temple, are, though precious, simply figures, "copies", things made by the hands of man.

Inferior to the teaching of Christ, the religious formation offered by the Old Testament could only be suited to a young Church that was still imperfect. The maidens who follow the Bride are those "nourished only by elementary knowledge and food proper to beginners". They *are* old enough, however, to enjoy wine—in fact, to love the wine provided by their Old Testament tutors and guardians. That, though, does not make them old enough for the breast of the Bridegroom to arouse their love. When they mature and begin to experience what the "breast of the Bridegroom" really is, and to taste the riches of the Word of God, then "they will love the breast of the Bridegroom more than wine". "They will hasten more readily to the doctrine of Christ, this doctrine which is perfect and at every point brought to plenitude, than to that they thought they could draw from their 'common studies' [i.e. philosophy], or from the teachings of the Law and the prophets."[22] The Old Testament already has the strength of wine, but not the quality of the wine of Cana.

This contrast between Old Testament and New Testament is not an antithesis, in the manner of Marcionism. Indeed, Origen is strongly anti-Marcionite. From beginning to end, the two Testaments together make up one single communion in the Word of God. To compare the revelation of Christ with that of the prophets is not to counterpose good and evil but to set side by side better and good. The

[22] Ibid., 111.

essential value of the Old Testament for Origen is *to prepare the Church for her nuptial encounter with the Messiah.* Torah and the prophetic scrolls were given her as a foretaste of her Spouse and the joy he will bring. By leading the Fiancée to meet the Groom, the Old Testament brought the Church closer to the banquet of the Kingdom. On Song 2:4, "Bring me into the house of wine", Origen identifies the "wine cellar" as the banquet hall where Abraham, Isaac, and Jacob are waiting and whither the prophets are leading anyone who listens to them. It is the same "house of wine" that the Church too desires to enter.

In no way did Christ intend to blot out the memory of the Old Testament. On the contrary, he sought to immortalize it. As Origen's first homily on the Song puts it, commenting on Song 1:3, "Your name is perfume spread abroad":

> In the whole earth Christ is named, my Lord is publicized. His name is a perfume spread abroad. It is only now that one hears the name of Moses which before was enclosed in the narrow limits of Judaea. No one among the Greeks mentioned him and in no history of literature do we find anything written about Moses or the other [prophets]. But scarcely does Jesus begin to shine on the world than he makes the Law and the prophets stand out with him, and truly this prophetic word is accomplished, "Your name is a perfume spread abroad."[23]

The Church and the Gentiles

In the Old Testament, then, the Bride could not see her Spouse. But she was at least able to hear his voice. In that way she gained a perception of the One the Father had destined for her. The impression was fuzzy, but it was enough.

---

[23] Origen, *Homily 1 on the Song of Songs*, 4.

Once brought into his presence, she faces One by no means wholly unknown. Though her Old Testament understanding was limited, it was not *so* limited that she could not grasp something of his attraction. A desire was aflame in her heart, sometimes uncontrollably, to see the Bridegroom in person. The delay in his coming nearly exhausts her reserves of patience. She supplicates the Father no longer to speak to her by any other lips than those of his own Son. Hence Origen's expansion of the Bride's opening words in Song 1:1:

> For this reason I beseech you, Father of my Spouse, and pour out my prayer, that you will look with pity upon this love of mine and send him, so that now he may not speak to me any longer by any of his ministering angels and his prophets, but may come in his very own person and "kiss me with the kisses of his mouth"—may, that is, pour into my mouth the words of his mouth, that I may hear him speaking and see him teaching.[24]

And in his first homily on the Song, Origen has the Father hear the prayer of Israel and respond: "Because she merits to see accomplished in her the prophetic word: while you are still speaking I will say, Here I am, the Father of the Bridegroom hears the Bride, he sends his Son."[25]

But as we saw when looking at the "pattern of revelation", Israel's call to be bearer of a divine disclosure destined for all peoples—her call to "bring in" the Gentiles —was something she registered yet could not by herself fulfill. The throwing open of the covenant people to the pagans was, rather, a consequence of the fulfillment of that call in, specifically, the life, work, and, above all, the saving death of the Messiah, the Divine Servant. Origen speaks

[24] Origen, *Commentary on the Song of Songs*, 90.
[25] Origen, *Homily 1 on the Song of Songs*, 2.

enthusiastically of how the light of the Gospel has spread from Gentile province to province, kingdom to kingdom. But he is also aware that not all have received the name of Christ thankfully (how could he not be, since his father fell victim to Roman imperial persecution?). That is why, he thinks, the Bride in the Song does not say that all souls have received the name whose good odor has spread like perfume, but only that the *young maidens* so responded— meaning, souls capable of spiritual passion and already committed to the way of spiritual growth. Fortunately, these are numerous. "The flowers have appeared on the earth" (Song 2:12), the flowers of faithful peoples and newborn churches. At the center of this spring awakening is Christ himself, for the Bridegroom declares, "I am the flower of the field and the lily of the valleys" (2:1). These horticultural metaphors express the flowering of souls in communion with the love of Christ. The universal propagation of the Christian faith attests the attraction exercised by divine charity, of which Origen says that, since it defines the inmost essence of the Christian life, it conveys to those who participate in it the living model for their own behavior.

The hope for Israel. God's plan was from the start universal, but it had to pass through the narrow place of Israel. Among that elect nation there were always those deaf to the Word of God. Yet it was in Israel that God chose to make men open to his Spirit. It was on these righteous Hebrews that he bestowed his greatest spiritual gifts and the mission to transmit salvation to others, since "salvation comes from the Jews" (Jn 4:22). Israel's election is historical fact. But it is also the gift of God. Origen continued to hope for the salvation of Israel in Christ, basing himself on Paul's words in Romans

11:29: "The gifts and the call of God are irrevocable." He accepted the apostle's teaching in the same letter that once the totality of the Gentiles had "come in", Israel too would be saved. Hans Urs von Balthasar will praise Origen for his —alas, exceptional—awareness that "dazzling eschatological light" falls on Jewry from the eleventh chapter of Romans.[26] Though he rejoices in the international diversity of the Church of the Gentiles of which he is a member, conscious that the "true Israel" is without distinction of Jew and Greek, he knows that the Church cannot have her full integrity unless there is joined to her those "from whom Christ was descended according to the flesh" (cf. Rom 9:5).

Origen is strong on the kinship of Church and synagogue. What is the nature of their bond? Song 1:5, "I am black but beautiful, O daughters of Jerusalem", gives the key. Here the bridal Church, which by overwhelming predominance is a Church of the Gentiles, responds to reproaches from (Christianly) unbelieving Jews. The Church, so understood, recognizes her lowly origins when compared with the noble title "descendant of Abraham". She does not, she must admit, descend from spiritually illustrious fathers instructed by God. Origen takes her plea further. She is not a daughter of Abraham, but nonetheless she has acquired Abraham's soul, imitating him in the spiritual adventure initiated by his call. Like him, she has uprooted herself from the pagan culture of the Gentile nations, the house of her ancestors. Furthermore, says Origen, the Gentile Christians too have been through the exodus of baptism, the escape from the dominance of sinful powers. As chiefly a Church of the Gentiles, the Bride has not, to be sure, enjoyed the benefit of

---

[26] Von Balthasar, *Martin Buber and Christianity*, p. 12.

the lengthy religious education God gave the Jews. Yet her attitude is a lesson to Israel.

> Her faith in Christ demonstrates that, contrary to the assidu-
> ous readers of Moses, she has well perceived the true meaning
> of the entire educative economy. She has understood how its
> essential aim was to restore to the soul, through adhesion to
> God's living Word, that lost beauty of the image implanted
> in every son and daughter of Adam without distinction of
> race.[27]

And Origen goes through all those passages of the Old Testament that point to the future entry of the Gentiles, just
as we ourselves did when considering that key aspect of the
pattern of revelation.

Beauty and the bride. The Bride is now not only "black"
but "beautiful"—indeed, in the title of this book, "lovely,
like Jerusalem" (Song 6:4). She has undergone a threefold
beauty treatment, which Origen sums up as *conversio*, *paen-
itentia*, and *confessio* (or *fides*). This triplet is at once a sum-
mary of New Testament teaching and a reference to baptismal practice in the ancient Church: the preparatory ascetic
discipline and instruction of catechumens ("conversion"),
the disavowal of past ill behavior through contrition and
humility ("penitence"), and the profession of the Christian
faith and commitment to live by imitation of Christ in the
future ("confession" or "faith"). So the black one—her natural skin color ruined—recovers her beauty by sharing in
the Image of God, Jesus Christ, as she is launched on a new
life. That is why Origen lists, on the Bride's behalf, those
titles of Christ that sum up what he is and does for her. "I

---

[27] Chênevert, *L'Eglise dans le Commentaire d'Origène*, p. 128.

received into myself the Son of God, I welcomed the Word made flesh. I drew near to him who is the Image of God, the First-born of all creation, the splendour of God's glory and the One who bears the very stamp of his nature. I became beautiful."[28]

This (in the broad sense) conversion is both a singular event and a lifelong process, for the event implies a perpetual progress to come. For Origen, the ideal representation of the faithful is Mary of Bethany sitting at Jesus' feet, since she stands for all those who search ceaselessly for the light of the Word, and so are "continually in his presence; not those who are sometimes there and sometimes not, but those who are before the Word of God continually, without interruption."[29]

Thanks to this habitual contact, the Bride is enveloped with a light that, little by little, transforms her utterly. The study of Sacred Scripture is indispensable here. When in 1:6 the Bride declares, "They set me to be a guard in the vineyard", the "vineyard" for Origen is the completed corpus of the Scriptures, Old and New Testaments alike, which the apostles have placed in the hands of the Church coming from the pagans. This is how the Bride will avoid, negatively, the temptation of turning back on her steps and, positively, will assimilate ever more the doctrine of Christ. After crossing the Jordan and entering the Land, there is still a long way to go, a number of stages through which to pass before attaining the summit on which Jerusalem stands. Only at the end of the Song, notes Origen, is the Bride declared radiantly white. (Of course the pigments here are wholly metaphorical.)

[28] Origen, *Commentary on the Song of Songs*, 114.
[29] Ibid., 121.

> Who is this woman that is coming
> . . . up, all whitened,
> leaning upon her Kinsman? (8:5).

The "Kinsman" is Jesus Christ.

The Church and the Word Incarnate

And this brings us to our final heading. In the course of his commentary, Origen often invokes the mystery of the In-carnation of the Word and expounds, whether explicitly or by implication, how in her most intimate being the Church depends on this coming toward her of her heavenly Spouse. He mentions in passing the virginal conception, birth, and infancy of Christ, but has more to say about the Incarnation as the *total* mystery that includes within itself all the other mysteries of the life of Jesus, the means chosen by God to effect our salvation.

Like Saint Paul, Origen considers that the Incarnation happened "when time had fully come" (Gal 4:4). His dis-tinctive understanding of this fullness of time is that it was *when the Fiancée was sufficiently prepared.* Enough people in Is-rael had enough of the right attitudes—one thinks, of course, of Our Lady, Saint Joseph, Simeon, and Anna, the first dis-ciples—for the Incarnation not (so to speak) to misfire.

This fullness of time we are still living, and its law, as it were, still holds good. The companions of the Bride have the capacity to draw the Bridegroom to them. To do this, the soul of each person in the Church must have its own beauty—Origen stresses the share the free creature has in its own sanctification. And yet the main initiative is with the Lord, who consents to let himself be thus "seduced" (in the erotic language of the Song).

Every soul that has been educated in the moral sciences and then introduced to the sciences of nature—thanks to the instruction these disciplines contain [he means, every soul that has taken to heart the lessons of Proverbs and Ecclesiastes] attracts the Word of God to herself by the purity of her morals, by her knowledge and by the honesty of her conduct—and the Word willingly lets himself be attracted, for with all his heart he comes towards souls thus formed and graciously and generously consents to be attracted by them.[30]

Origen also transposes this to the level of the entire contemporary Church. That Church advances toward the goal, inviting Christ to come ever more fully to seal his communion with her to the degree that the voice of the Church is unanimous in confessing one faith and to the degree also that this faith is transformed into an increasingly luminous and fervent understanding of its own Object. What is this Object? It is the living Word of God found in the flesh of Jesus Christ. Such knowledge, inseparable, so Origen stresses, from love, constitutes the act whereby the union of Bride and Groom is achieved. The consummation of the union, which will also be the Church's perfecting, coincides with Christ's full epiphany, his Parousia or plenary presence. At that point, the image of God in us will reach full term and so become true likeness.

As Origen explains, since God is love, and the Son who is God from God is love, Father and Son ask that there should be in us something of the same character as there is in them. So it is, "by virtue of the as it were kinship and affinity the presence in us of love gives that we enter into communion with the God who is love in the manner of him who, already united to him, cried out, 'Who will separate us from the

---

[30] Ibid., 102–3.

love of God that is in Christ Jesus our Lord' (Rom 8:39)."[31]
That is why the Church, Christ's Spouse, "desires him to
sit down in the shade of the apple tree, so as to share in the
life which comes from his shadow".[32] That is an allusion
to Song 2:3:

> As an apple tree among the trees of the wood,
>   so is my Beloved among the sons.
> Under the shadow of him whom I was desiring, I sat down,
>   and his fruit was sweet to my throat.

For Origen the phrase "the shadow of Christ" corresponds
to the actual situation of the Church, for she is in possession of truth and life (Christ) but unable to enjoy it fully
(shadow). The phrase "Christ's shadow" may also mean his
humanity. But it would be an awful mistake to suppose that
the passing of the shadow-side of the Church's faith in the
full light of the age to come will deprive the humanity of
Christ of its role. On the contrary, that humanity has abiding meaning for the Bride. The Word will come again in
the same human flesh that he took from Mary, to bring to
its climax his union with the Bride who has imitated him
in his mysteries by discipleship and the sacramental life. In
the bodies of her members—in her own flesh, then—she
has acquired the purity of the lily, just like his.

Without the humanity of Christ, there is no condescen-
dence, no kenosis, no self-emptying of the Word. And without the kenosis of the Word there is no manifestation of the
Bridegroom's merciful love. When the Bride says, "My kinsman is between my breasts as a drop of myrrh enclosed in
a sachet" (Song 1:13), what does this signify but the saving
abasement of the Word in the Incarnation, on the Cross?

---

[31] Ibid., 70.
[32] Ibid., 182.

14

A THOMIST FINALE:
THOMAS AQUINAS
ON THE TORAH

Saint Thomas' treatise on the Torah, the Old Law, is the longest of any in the *Summa theologiae*. But by and large it is only fairly recently that its importance for the shape of that work has been given its due. Likewise, it is only in the last few decades that people have come to terms with Thomas' excellence as a biblical theologian. One notable harbinger of this development was the English Dominican David Joseph Bourke who was responsible for the relevant volume—number 29—of the Blackfriars Cambridge bilingual edition of Thomas' *Summa*. Published in 1969, with assistance from a diocesan priest, Arthur Littledale, the copious notes and excellent introduction did Thomas on the Torah justice after long neglect. Bourke points out that Thomas' treatise is an exercise in anti-Marcionism—a heresy that in Thomas' time was long condemned, and even longer condemned by the 1960s. The Catholic Church had —could have—no Schleiermacher, Harnack, or Bultmann, with their radically revisionist views surveyed in chapter 4 of the present book. And yet, as Bourke writes: "Many of the prejudices voiced by Catholics and others of the present day who lack a genuinely biblical tradition are still astonishingly reminiscent of Marcion's views."[1] In Germanic or

---

[1] D. Bourke, "Introduction", in D. Bourke and A. Littledale, eds., *Saint*

Anglo-Saxon countries, some of that may of course be due to the influence of liberal Protestant Neo-Marcionism. But more important than the origin of the disease is its cure. And this Thomas proposes to furnish.

The Continuing Validity of the Old Testament

For Thomas, not only was the Old Law, within its limits, good—as it had to be if it was going to prepare people for the coming of Christ—more than this, it remains valid for the Church in two respects. First, it contains the universally binding principles of the natural law, now confirmed by revelation—precisely through inclusion in Old Testament teaching. Secondly, insofar as the Elder Testament also comprises special precepts applicable to the Jews alone and designed for their sanctification as the people of the Promise, even this has an abiding value for the Church. How so? Because, while the binding force of these special precepts *as law* has been abrogated by the new dispensation of Christ, those same precepts *inasmuch as they foreshadow Christ*, can still deepen our understanding of him. And in this sense they remain pertinent to the salvation of Christians too.

As may be patent from my use of the word "foreshadowing", Thomas remained faithful to the typological principles stated by Hilary and the other ancient writers on whose work we have touched, or, in the cases of Augustine, Gregory, and Origen, studied for its own sake. However, Thomas does something that is *not* to be found in patristic exegesis of the Old Testament. He takes the typological idea of God

---

Thomas Aquinas: Summa theologiae, vol. 29, *The Old Law* [1a2ae. 98–105] (London, 1969), p. xiv.

providing religious education for his people throughout the course of Israel's history and fits it into the framework of a perspective on causality derived from Aristotle. Aristotle and the Platonist tradition are about equal contributors to Saint Thomas' philosophical culture, but here it is Aristotle who prevails—prevails as the source of an approach that can throw rational light, Thomas thinks, on the biblical and patristic data that are his real authority.

Saint Thomas' starting point is the Bible's revelation that man's ultimate good is the vision of God in heaven: that is the message, after all, of Scripture's closing book, Revelation. In Aristotelian terms, that vision is, then, the supreme "final cause" at work in all God's dealings with mankind. And of course the supreme Agent, acting efficiently to enable man to come to this desirable perfection, is God himself. What Scripture also shows, for Thomas, is that at the first God works through subordinate agents, preparing man by these agents for an eventual reception of the grace of the Holy Spirit who will "justify" man. In justification, the Holy Spirit will obliterate original sin and replace it with charity. It is through justifying grace and the life of charity following from it that heaven lies open.

In this overall context of the biblical revelation as a whole, the Old Law can be defined by Thomas as such a subordinate cause of man's salvation. Its entire tendency is to remove whatever dispositions in man are opposed to the reception of grace.[2] At the same time, it binds the Jews, to whom it is chiefly directed, into a single community, united in worship of the one true God and in expectation of the promise made to their forefather, Abraham.[3] Saint Paul declared in Romans, "Christ is the end of the Law" (10:4). Consonant

---

[2] St. Thomas, *Summa theologiae*, 1a2ae, q. 98, art. 1, corpus.

[3] Ibid., q. 98, art. 4, corpus and ad i.

with the patristic interpretation of Scripture, Thomas understands this to mean that Christ is the *goal* of the Law, taking "goal" there in the strong Aristotelian sense—once more—a final cause. Christ, the Messiah of God, is what the Law is ultimately *for*.

To Thomas' mind, the Old Law is more "perfect" than the natural law in regard to its origin, God himself; in regard to its subject matter, man's salvation; in regard to the goal to which it is directed, Christ; and in regard, lastly, to the agents through whom it is promulgated, the holy angels. Unlike the natural law, it does not concern just the minimum decencies of human living but the new plan of God, starting with the call of Abraham, to bring men into supernatural communion with himself.

Moral, Ceremonial, Judicial

The Torah—in regard to which the Jews considered the rest of their Scriptures either a development, with the prophets, or an appendage, with "The Writings", contains, as we saw in our opening overview of the Books of Moses, much legal instruction on a wide range of issues from universal morality to liturgical law and case law for highly specific situations. Thomas took from the early medieval commentators who had preceded him a helpfully straightforward division of the precepts of the Old Law into three sorts: *moralia, ceremonialia,* and *judicialia*.[4] *Moralia* are the Ten Commandments, the "Decalogue", found in both Exodus and Deuteronomy. *Ceremonialia* are the cultic prescriptions found throughout the Torah, but primarily in Leviticus, the "Book of the Service of the Sanctuary". These precepts render concrete and

[4] Ibid., q. 99, arts. 2, 3, 4.

specific the general command to worship God found in the *moralia*. For Thomas, *judicialia* are above all Israel's earliest criminal code, the "Book of the Covenant", which occupies three chapters of Exodus, from 20:22 to 23:33, and covers various kinds of application of the *moralia*, other moral precepts of the Law than those respecting divine worship.

In the Christian dispensation, only the *moralia* have permanent and definitive applicability, and the rest are reduced to *figuralia*, "figural" or—as we have learned to say—"typical" realities. My word "reduced" is perhaps unfortunate, since for Thomas the "superabundance" of divine truth makes "representation by sensible figures" vital for us.[5] In its own period, the cultus of the Old Law was ordained for two purposes: "literally", for the worship of God, "figuratively", for the prefiguring of Christ.[6] And even now, in the Christian dispensation, the figures of the Old Law retain their value since they are *still* prefiguring—no longer the Messiah in his first advent, but the glory of the age to come, which will follow on the Parousia of his Second Coming.[7]

It is important to note that what the *figuralia* can teach us— since they concern supernatural salvation, by far the greatest good with which we have to do in life—actually exceeds in scope what the *moralia* present to us, since they center on utterly basic justice, whether toward God or toward our neighbor.[8] True, if we withhold from God and our neighbor what is most basically due them, we debar ourselves from receiving salvation. And yet obedience to the Decalogue cannot of itself win salvation for us, since our salvation does

[5] Ibid., q. 102, art. 2, ad ii.

[6] Ibid., q. 102, art. 3, corpus. In this text Thomas points out their affinity with the prophetic corpus in this twofold reference to present and future.

[7] Ibid., q. 101, art. 2, corpus.

[8] Ibid.

not turn on the natural moral order *taken by itself alone.* The Old Law presupposes the natural law. It summarizes it. It restates its general principles. But it also goes beyond the natural law as a revealed and supernatural aid to the work of grace. The Torah defines the duties of the Israelite not just as any man but, more than that, as a *member of the people of the coming Messiah.* According to Thomas, those duties consist first and foremost in the right worship of God, a worship based on faith and love—for Thomas the two supernatural principles most fundamentally presupposed in the Law of Israel.

This worship has as its most basic constituents three of the *moralia,* for the first three commandments cover fidelity, reverence, and service.[9] But these quite basic constituents are expressed for Israel in actions prescribed by the *ceremonialia,* which go far beyond anything available in natural religion and help worshippers who, lacking the light of the beatific vision, cannot see the God they worship. The cultic activity laid down in the ceremonial precepts provides them with figures foreshadowing the dispensation of the New Law—Christ and his Church, and, more remotely, the beatific vision itself, in heaven. They foreshadow these in a manner appropriate to a relatively uncultivated people (the ancient Hebrews), who were capable of only implicit knowledge of what was to come. Thomas stresses that if this people were to be withdrawn effectively from idolatry, the ceremonial precepts had to be ample enough to provide them with an adequate outlet for religious instinct—hence the ritual complexity of the cultic Torah. That complexity was also pertinent, as the following citation shows, to their being the *messianic* people.

[9] Ibid., q. 100, art. 6, corpus.

> For those prone to evil. . ., since there were many forms of idolatry, many ways had to be devised to counter them. . . . As to those with a propensity to good . . . they too had need of a variety of ceremonial precepts; both because their minds would thereby be turned to God in many different ways and more continuously, and because the mystery of Christ thus prefigured was to bring all kinds of benefits to the world, and many aspects of him had to be brought to man's attention by a variety of ceremonial observances.[10]

For Thomas, these ceremonial precepts were formulated by the wise—in fact, by the wisest—men in the Israelite community, Moses and Aaron, working under God's guidance.

Those wise men also gave shape to the *judicialia*, the judicial precepts, and if we ask why, the answer will deal with the remaining foundation of Israel's life, once we have spoken of love of God, and that is love of neighbor.[11] Once again, the duties of an Israelite toward his neighbor are not just a matter of giving the neighbor what is due him by nature—for the very good reason that the nation to whom the Torah was directed was not a nation in a merely natural sense. As the people of election, the people of the promise, Israel was a divine community, destined for a closer union with its Founder, God, than any natural community could be. And so it is that the love of God, which, along with faith in God, is the primary presupposed principle of the Old Law, also extends to a distinctive kind of love of neighbor who is to be loved as God loves him.

The most fundamental constituents of such love of neighbor are set forth in the remaining *moralia*, the other seven commandments. Like the first three commandments, these remain, however, general directives needing application to

[10] Ibid., q. 101, art. 3, corpus.
[11] Ibid., q. 100, art. 6, corpus and ad i.

the concrete conditions of Israel's covenant nationhood, and it is the function of the *judicialia*, the judicial precepts to make sure that they get it. While the *judicialia*, like the *ceremonialia*, have a figurative as well as a literal meaning, they differ from the ceremonial precepts in that the figurative meaning is quite secondary. A theme of the judicial precepts such as holy war may look ahead to the spiritual warfare practiced by Christians in the Church, but *judicialia* do not furnish figurative meanings anywhere near as rich as those found in the precepts governing Israel's worship. Thomas gives many thought-provoking rationales, whether by shrewd guesswork or poetic intuition, for the practices and institutions of ancient Israel, especially in what concerns her liturgy.

Torah and Salvation

Here we must be content with a brief conclusion on the ultimate upshot of his highly theological exegesis. First, the gift of God to Israel in the Torah could not cure the evil effects of original sin in such a way as to render the people of the Old Covenant radically and totally just before God. But, secondly, it could and did signify to that people, notably in their worship, the radical and total justice of the Messiah, a justice that in the future was to be imparted to them. And so thirdly, and this is, I think, the high point of Thomas' evaluation of the entire Old Testament, the gifts of God to Israel disposed men to submit themselves to Christ in order one day to be radically and totally just before God. That is how, for Thomas, Jesus was able to find a ready cooperation when he told the twelve apostles that in the regeneration, with his paschal mystery, "you will sit on thrones judging the twelve tribes of Israel" (Mt 19:28), so that, justified and sanctified by his grace, they could be the founders of his Church and her permanent foundation even to the New Jerusalem. For, so we are told, the "wall of that city has twelve foundations and on them are the twelve names of the twelve apostles of the Lamb" (Rev 21:4). As the American Thomist scholar Matthew Levering has written: "In recognizing that Israel prefigures Christ, one does not therefore dismiss Israel as a reality in itself. Rather, as Aquinas explains, each aspect of Israel's history takes on importance in a way that no other ancient people's does."[12] In Israel, the Wisdom of God *began to be incarnate.*

[12] M. Levering, *Christ's Fulfillment of Torah and Temple: Salvation according to Thomas Aquinas* (Notre Dame, Ind., 2002), p. 27.

CONCLUSION

Hans Urs von Balthasar remarks, strikingly, "There is no greater unity in the world, according to God's plan, than that between the Old and the New Covenant, except the unity of Jesus Christ himself who embraces the unity of the covenants in his own unity."[1] That is the tragedy of Israel, in a Christian perspective. Von Balthasar speaks of her as doubly isolated. Thanks to her election, she is cut off by her uniqueness from those interrelations of nations and ethnicities that can be "wholly expressed in philosophical and universal terms". But at the same time, by a failure of response to electing grace she is cut off from her sister "people", Christians. She is separated from them by her "refusal to allow the prophetic principle its transcendent culmination in a fulfillment given by God alone", as well as—what follows from this—the "refusal to look for the solidarity of love in the one Jewish-Christian salvation".[2] This isolation adversely affects the Church. It is the "first and fundamental schism". Robbing the Church of the kind of unity Providence intended, it ruptures the unity of the Covenants. The failure of Israel to respond to the New Covenant is, for von Balthasar, reflected in the failure of the Church to recognize herself fully in the Old.

It does not suffice us as Catholic Christians, thinks von Balthasar, to have the text of the Old Testament. Equipped merely with the text, we might content ourselves with being

---

[1] Von Balthasar, *Martin Buber and Christianity*, p. 109.
[2] Ibid., p. 77.

philologists, antiquarians, or historical-literary critics. What the Church needs is more than texts. What she needs is the heart of Israel. The Church "does not want its praise of God to derive simply and solely from the written word, but from the mind and heart of the Jews at prayer, from those who first formed the words, so that it can embrace them in its living tradition."[3]

I hope that the reflections on the Church's appeal to the Old Testament contained in this modest book will further appreciation of the Scriptures of Israel, which are indeed "lovely, like Jerusalem".

---

[3] Ibid., p. 78.

SELECT BIBLIOGRAPHY

Here are some elements of bibliography which include the principal books and articles cited but go beyond them to suggest further reading.

I. An Overview of the Old Testament

Baker, D. W., and W. T. Arnold, eds. *The Face of Old Testament Studies: A Survey of Contemporary Approaches*. Grand Rapids, Mich., 1999.

Childs, B. S. *Introduction to the Old Testament as Scripture*. Philadelphia, 1979.

Coppens, J. *L'Histoire critique de l'Ancient Testament: Ses origines; Ses orientations nouvelles; Ses perspectives d'avenir*, 3rd ed. Bruges, 1942.

Harrison, R. K. *Introduction to the Old Testament*. Peabody, Mass., 2004 [1969].

Kline, M. G. *The Structure of Biblical Authority*. 2nd ed. Grand Rapids, Mich., 1975.

Von Rad, G. *Wisdom in Israel*. Nashville, Tenn., and London, 1972.

II. The Pattern of Revelation

Bruce, F. F., ed. *Promise and Fulfilment*. Edinburgh, 1963.

Hebert, A. G. *The Authority of the Old Testament*. London, 1947.

―――. *The Throne of David: A Study of the Fulfilment of the Old Testament in Jesus Christ and His Church*. London, 1941.

Von Balthasar, H. U. *The Glory of the Lord: A Theological Aesthetics. Vol. 6, Theology: The Old Covenant*. San Francisco: Ignatius Press, 1990.

―――. *Martin Buber and Christianity: A Dialogue between Israel and the Church*. London, 1960.

Von Rad, G. "Grundprobleme einer biblischen Theologie des Alten Testaments", *Theologische Literatur Zeitschrift* 68 (1943): 225–34.

―――. *Old Testament Theology*, Vol. 2. Edinburgh and London, 1965.

Watson, F. "Erasing the Text: Readings in Neo-Marcionism". In *Text and Truth: Redefining Biblical Theology*, pp. 127–76. Edinburgh, 1997.

―――. "Old Testament Theology as a Christian Theological Enterprise", in *Text and Truth*, pp. 179–224.

―――. *Text and Truth: Redefining Biblical Theology*. Edinburgh, 1997.

III. Two Important Presuppositions

Eichrodt, W. *Theology of the Old Testament*. Vol. 1. London, 1961.

Johnson, A. R. *The One and the Many in the Israelite Conception of God*. London, 1942.

Knight, G. A. F. *A Christian Theology of the Old Testament.* 2nd ed. London, 1964.

Watson, F. "Creation in the Beginning". In *Text and Truth*, pp. 225-75.

IV. The Typological Interpretation of the Old Testament

Bouyer, Cong. Orat., L. "Liturgie et exégèse spirituelle". *Maison-Dieu* 7 (1946): pp. 27-40.

Coppens, J. *Les harmonies des deux Testaments: Essai sur les divers sens des Ecritures et sur l'unité de la Révélation.* Paris-Tournai, 1947.

Daniélou, J. *The Bible and the Liturgy.* London and Notre Dame, Ind., 1960.

————. *From Shadows to Reality: Studies in the Biblical Typology of the Fathers.* London, 1960.

Daube, D. *The Exodus Pattern in the Bible.* London, 1963.

Farmer, W. R., ed. *The International Bible Commentary: A Catholic and Ecumenical Commentary for the Twenty-First Century.* Collegeville, Minn., 1998.

Goppelt, L. *Typos: Die typologische Deutung des Alten Testaments im Neuen.* Gütersloh, 1939 [Darmstadt, 1969].

Levoratti, A. J. "How to Interpret the Bible". In Farmer, *International Bible Commentary*, pp. 9-35.

V. Fathers and Doctors Interpret

Balás, D. L., and D. J. Bingham. "Patristic Exegesis of the Books of the Bible". In Farmer, *International Bible Commentary*, pp. 64–115.

Bardy, G. "Commentaires patristiques de la Bible". *Supplément à la Dictionnaire de la Bible* 2 (1931): pp. 73–103.

———. "Interprétation chez les Pères". *Supplément à la Dictionnaire de la Bible* 4 (1949): pp. 569–91.

Bourke, D., and A. Littledale, eds. *St. Thomas Aquinas: Summa theologiae.* Vol. 29. *The Old Law* [1a2ae. 98–105]. London, 1969.

Chênevert, J., S.J., *L'Eglise dans le Commentaire d'Origène sur le Cantique des Cantiques.* Paris-Montreal, 1969.

De Margerie, S.J., B. *An Introduction to the History of Exegesis.* 3 vols. Petersham, Mass., 1990–1994.

Fiedrowicz, M. "General Introduction". In Rotelle, *Works of Saint Augustine*, I/13. Hyde Park, N.Y., 2002, 13–22.

Gregory the Great, Saint. *Morals on the Book of Job*, 3 vols. Oxford, 1844.

La Bonnardière, A.-M., ed. *Saint Augustin et la Bible.* Paris, 1986.

Lawson, R. P. *Origen: The Song of Songs; Commentary and Homilies.* Westminster, Md., and London, 1957.

Levering, M. *Christ's Fulfillment of Torah and Temple: Salvation according to Thomas Aquinas.* Notre Dame, Ind., 2002.

Norris, Jr., R. A. *The Song of Songs: Interpreted by Early Christian and Medieval Commentators*. Grand Rapids, Mich., 2003.

Simonetti, M. *Biblical Interpretation in the Early Church: An Historical Introduction to Patristic Exegesis*. Edinburgh, 1994.

Pontet, M. *L'Exégèse de saint Augustin prédicateur*. Paris, 1947.

Rotelle, O.S.A., J., ed. *The Works of Saint Augustine*. I/13. *On Genesis*. Hyde Park, N.Y., 2002.

Schreiner, S. E. " 'Where Shall Wisdom be Found?' Gregory's Interpretation of Job". *American Benedictine Review* 39, no. 3 (1988): pp. 321–42.